WHAT OTHERS ARE SAYING ABOUT
YOUR ROAD TO A BETTER LIFE:

"It is difficult to express my love, respect and appreciation for the entire Roberts family. Their influence on me and my family cannot be overstated. I first heard the call of God on my life when I was 11 while watching Oral Roberts on television. In later years, Carolyn and I were honored to personally know Oral and Evelyn Roberts as friends and mentors, and we were never the same. That relationship then brought Richard and Lindsay into our lives, and they have become our dear and valued friends.

In watching Richard minister and flow in his anointing, it is obvious that he carries the same healing anointing that was on his father. He has laid hold of that miracle mantle and is fulfilling the call to take healing and miracles to a hurting world.

His new book, ***Your Road to a Better Life***, reveals the depth of his compassion for people and his commitment to reach far beyond where he can physically go. He has outlined—in black and white—the heart of God to heal and the keys to laying hold of God's healing power in your life.

The words that came to my mind as I read were: comprehensive—understandable—compelling—and TRUTH. He leaves no question unanswered concerning the will of God for your total well-being, and I love the keys he shares that lead you from where you are today to where you (and God) want you to be -- HEALED and WHOLE!"

> Dr. Jerry Savelle
> *President & CEO*
> *Jerry Savelle Ministries International*

*"**Your Road to a Better Life** by Richard Roberts is the most exciting book I've read in a very long time. You will laugh especially at the cat and the bowl. I remember Richard's dad, Oral Roberts, telling that story 50 years ago. It broke me up then, and it did it again yesterday. You'll cry, and you'll get excited. But best of all, you will finish this book healed in your body, renewed and refreshed in your mind and filled with faith and strength in your innermost being. You will be well established on your road to a better life financially. Don't miss this opportunity. I'm glad I didn't."*

    KENNETH COPELAND
    Founder of Kenneth Copeland Ministries and Eagle Mountain International Church

"Richard's book is a roadmap for your life. We all want God's best, and **Your Road to a Better Life** will give you principles along with life lessons on how to experience the miraculous, blessed, abundant, better life that God wants His people to have. I enjoyed every moment with it, and I believe you will also."

    DR. MARILYN HICKEY
    President/Founder
    Marilyn Hickey Ministries

*"**Your Road to a Better Life** truly is the roadmap for abundance and wholeness—nothing missing, nothing broken. I was amazed at how anointed this book by Richard Roberts is…a Must-Read! I love how it stands on the Word of God, and is so practical and relatable. Richard says, "If you're like me, you are striving for a

better life." Through the biblical principles to the amazing testimonies, stories, and "God-Given Keys," it's a step-by-step guide through growing in faith and understanding how to receive the better life God has for you. There is so much faith in this book, I believe miracles will manifest in your life. I believe the same double portion on Richard Roberts' life will come upon yours as well by the supernatural wisdom found here. This book truly will lead you on *Your Road to a Better Life.*"

>   PASTOR PAULA WHITE-CAIN
>   *Senior Pastor, New Destiny Christian Center*

"In his book, *Your Road to a Better Life*, Richard Roberts has compiled principles and truths from his own personal experience with the power of God from decades of fruitful ministry, much of it at the side of his father, Oral Roberts. What he shares with you is not theory or speculation—he has experienced the benefits that have come from applying these principles in his own life, and I am confident they will work for you as well. These truths are so clear that they can easily be applied to any circumstance you may be facing. They are so powerful that they cannot help but change your situation. They are so timeless that they will work at any stage of your life. Allow Richard Roberts to walk with you on your road, and experience the richness and abundance that God intends for you."

>   DR. ROD PARSLEY
>   *Pastor and Founder, World Harvest Church*
>   *Columbus, Ohio*

"Richard Roberts' book, ***Your Road to a Better Life,*** defines sympathy as "wishing one could help" as opposed to compassion being the "urge to reach into a person's life and pull out the sickness, the disease, the problem"…in the authority of JESUS' Name.

This book is the manifestation of Richard Roberts' urge to do just that…coming from a heart of love. The book could well be titled, *Your Road to Your Best Life.*"

    JAMES BROWN
    Network Broadcaster/Studio Host

"I have known Richard Roberts for over 30 years. Richard is so qualified to write this book ***Your Road to a Better Life*** — not because he is the son of one of the world's greatest apostles and evangelists to have ever walked — but because of his own walk — because of his own experience. Being close to such a ministry as the Oral Roberts Ministries, one would think that Richard would automatically have revelation and knowledge. But that is not necessarily true all the time. But in this case, Richard watched his father live what he preached, and then Richard developed his own voice, his own walk and his own anointing.

Richard is full of wisdom in this book… full of God in this book… and I highly recommend this book for everyone to read… to hear the insight and wisdom that this man has to offer. And not just to the body of Christ, but to anyone who is seeking to know Him.

Great book—great read. You'll love it!"

    DON COLBERT, MD
    New York Times Best Selling Author

"If you're searching for a book that will challenge you and inspire you, read **Your Road to a Better Life**. Richard's words are inspiring as you discover his ability to communicate with insight and wisdom.

This book is a reminder we all need the tools to impact the world one life at a time. Do not settle for anything less than God's best. Believe God is preparing you for greater things!"

>   Dee Simmons
>   *Chairman and Founder*
>   *Ultimate Living International, Inc.*

"What a powerful prophetic word to change your life! This is especially true in this day where there are so many things trying to get us in fear, steal our peace, our joy, and affect our lives in a negative way. My good friend, Dr. Richard Roberts, shares anointed revelation, concepts, and instructions throughout his new book, **Your Road to a Better Life**!

What an amazing blueprint to aid you in these difficult and challenging times. Dr. Roberts has years of wisdom, experience, and anointing that you can glean from. Be healed, encouraged, and discover how to live victoriously as you have your peace restored and learn to live your life to its fullness in God's blessings. I encourage you to allow the pages of this book to transform you and put you on the *road to a better life!*"

>   Hank Kunneman
>   *Senior Pastor, Lord of Hosts Church, Omaha, NE*
>   *Founder/President, One Voice Ministries*

"Having witnessed the Roberts' Ministries since 1968 and seeing the prayer of faith go up, we have believed in the miracle power of prayer. Upon the graduation of Dr. Oral Roberts to heaven, we believe his spirit went to heaven, but the anointing was left on earth. In Richard's book, **Your Road to a Better Life**, he is imparting to you the multiple generations of the healing power of God. As you read, we pray that you build your faith to expect a miracle in your life!"

HARRY AND CHERYL SALEM
Salem Family Ministries

"Richard Roberts has written a marvelous must-read. **Your Road to a Better Life** will change your life."

MIKE EVANS
#1 New York Times Bestseller

"We all want a better life, and in this book Richard Roberts shows you how! Through the Word of God and his own life experiences, he teaches you how to receive God's best. In every area of life, Richard helps walk you through your path to abundance and victory!"

KATE MCVEIGH
Kate McVeigh Ministries

YOUR ROAD TO A ✓Better Life

RICHARD ROBERTS

Unless otherwise indicated, scripture quotations are taken from the New King James Version®. Copyright © 1982 by Thomas Nelson. Used by permission. All rights reserved.

Copyright © 2017
by Richard Roberts
Tulsa, OK

Published by Oral Roberts Evangelistic Association
P.O. Box 2187
Tulsa, OK 74102
SKU 2542

All rights reserved.
Printed in the United States of America
ISBN 978-0-9990524-2-6

TABLE OF CONTENTS

FOREWORD

WEEK ONE

Sunday:	Devil, Take Your Hands Off Me! I Am God's Property!...	21
Monday:	God Cares About Me	29
Tuesday:	Jesus Lives at My House	33
Wednesday:	God Wants Me to Prosper and Be in Health	37
Thursday:	Jesus Is at the Point of My Need.............................	40
Friday:	I Will Be a Person of Integrity in Life by Paying My Bills	43
Saturday:	Something Good Is Going to Happen to Me	46

WEEK TWO

Sunday:	God's Way Will Be My Way	49
Monday:	God Is My Source	53
Tuesday:	I Will Plant My Seed and God Will Move the Mountain	56
Wednesday:	God Is the Multiplier of My Seed Sown..................	61
Thursday:	It Is More Productive to Give than to Receive........	64
Friday:	I Will Have a Seed-Faith Project.............................	66
Saturday:	I Will Plant Seed "Away from Myself" and Learn to Rely on My Source	71

WEEK THREE

Sunday:	God Is My Source of Total Supply, Even When They Say It Will Never Happen	77
Monday:	I Will Not Limit God	80

Tuesday:	I Am Not a Loser…I Am a Winner	85
Wednesday:	I Really Know God Will Help Me	86
Thursday:	Jesus Is a "Right Now" Jesus…Right at the Point of My Need	88
Friday:	When I Have Done All I Can Do, Then I Must Leave it in God's Hands	93
Saturday:	God Will Work for Me Through My Need	98

WEEK FOUR

Sunday:	I Will Sow for a Desired Result	103
Monday:	God Loves My Cheerful Giving	108
Tuesday:	I Will Give God My Best…Then Ask Him For His Best	110
Wednesday:	You Must Put Something in if You Want to Get Something Out	113
Thursday:	When One Door Closes, God Will Always Open Another One	115
Friday:	I Must Give God Something to Work With	118
Saturday:	I Can Expect Great Miracles and a Better Life with a Little Measure of Faith	121

WEEK FIVE

Sunday:	The Greatest Thing You Could Ever Learn is How to Expect a Miracle	125
Monday:	My Miracle Will Settle the Issue	128
Tuesday:	God Has a Time and a Way for Me	132
Wednesday:	God's Due Season Will Not be Too Early or Too Late for My Needs	135
Thursday:	God's Storehouse Will Never Fail	137
Friday:	My Faith Is Something I Do	140

Saturday:	My Miracle Basket Is about to Touch the Ground	143

WEEK SIX

Sunday:	I Know God, and I Am in Him… And He Is in Me	147
Monday:	I Will Use My Inner Resources of Prayer and Faith	151
Tuesday:	God Loves Me, and He Will Never Give Up On Me	156
Wednesday:	I Can Walk with Jesus Every Day	159
Thursday:	Jesus Has Walked This Road Before Me… All I Need To Do Is Follow Him	162
Friday:	One of the Greatest Seeds I'll Ever Plant Is Forgiveness	165
Saturday:	I am Obeying God and Expecting Him to Bless Me	169

WEEK SEVEN

Sunday:	I Believe in Miracles… TODAY	175
Monday:	I Will Not Take "NO" for An Answer	178
Tuesday:	God's Works Mean a Miracle to Me	181
Wednesday:	I Can Claim My Family to Be God's Property Now, for There Is No Distance in Prayer	184
Thursday:	When I Pray for Someone Else's Healing, I Have an Opportunity for God to Heal Me	186
Friday:	When Nothing Less Than a Miracle Will Do	188
Saturday:	God Is My Healer	190

WEEK EIGHT

Sunday:	When I Act, My Faith Begins to Work	195

Monday:	Jesus is Unlimited, and There Is No Distance in Prayer	201
Tuesday:	I Can Have a Point of Contact with God	203
Wednesday:	I Am Focusing My Faith on Jesus	206
Thursday:	I Will Touch and Agree for My Need to Be Met	208
Friday:	I Will Plant Seeds of Faith, Hope, and Love Every Day	211
Saturday:	Seed I Have Planted Is Ready to Be Harvested Back in the Form of Miracles to Me	214

WEEK NINE

Sunday:	I Talk to God, and He Talks to Me	217
Monday:	God Is…in Heaven	220
Tuesday:	I Will Honor the Name of the Lord	222
Wednesday:	God's Kingdom and Will on Earth and in Heaven Is Important to Me	224
Thursday:	God Will Meet My Daily Needs	225
Friday:	Forgiving Is the Great Stress Reliever	227
Saturday:	God Is Leading Me, Delivering Me, and Setting Me in His Kingdom by His Power and Glory	229

WEEK TEN

Sunday:	God is Concerned About My Daily Needs	233
Monday:	I Will Pray and Tell God Exactly How I Feel	236
Tuesday:	God Loves It When I Pray Because His Business Is Me	238
Wednesday:	I'll Do the Praying and Leave the Miracles Up to God	240
Thursday:	God Is My Healer	242
Friday:	God Is Superior in Quality… Excessive in Quantity	244

| Saturday: | I Will Release My Faith for Healing .... 246 |

WEEK ELEVEN

Sunday:	I Can Communicate Directly with God… Because He Helps Me 251
Monday:	I Can Pray with My Spirit and Not Just My Intellect 253
Tuesday:	The Holy Spirit Now Lives in Me 256
Wednesday:	The Holy Spirit Lives Deep Down Inside Every Believer 258
Thursday:	If You Trust the Holy Spirit, He Will Never Let You Down 261
Friday:	The Prayer Language of the Spirit Puts Me Together 265
Saturday:	Praying in the Spirit Is Part of Our Spiritual Armor 267

WEEK TWELVE

Sunday:	I Will Be a Lifter-Upper 273
Monday:	God Is Alive, and Continuously Active in My Life 276
Tuesday:	God Knows the Feeling You Are Experiencing Right Now 278
Wednesday:	God Is a God of the Miraculous 282
Thursday:	Seven Proclamations for Me to Make Every Day of My Life 284
Friday:	We've Got to Have Miracles 286
Saturday:	Lord, Help Me to Be Successful 289

WEEK THIRTEEN

| Sunday: | No Weapon Formed Against Me Will Prosper…if I Keep My Spirit Right .... 293 |

Monday:	Truth Will Always Outlast a Lie	296
Tuesday:	I Will Walk in Forgiveness	298
Wednesday:	Don't Let Hatred Get Hold of You, and Don't Strike Back	300
Thursday:	Quitting Is Not an Answer	304
Friday:	There Is Much Power in Prayer	307
Saturday:	Take the Seven-Way Test	309

FINAL WORD

ABOUT THE AUTHOR

FOREWORD

Your Road to a Better Life

I believe in miracles.

I believe in miracles so much that I want everyone to believe in them and to have a Better Life.

Every day, I receive prayer requests from people all over the world. They share with me their problems and pain, their hopes and hurts. They share what they are going through, and they don't leave much out.

I hold those prayer requests in my hands and pray every day. Every day, I tell the devil to take his hands off of the lives of my partners and friends. Then I write them back and bring them a powerful word from the Bible to lift them up and let them know I am standing with them, in faith believing for every need they have to be met by God's mighty power.

Having grown up as Oral Roberts' son, I had the opportunity to learn the great biblical principles and spiritual keys that God revealed to my father. I was right by his side as God gave him the key phrases that helped to shape and form the course of our ministry:

God is a good God…

Release your faith…

Get a point of contact…

God is your Source…

Plant your seed…

Expect a miracle…

My father was an apostle of the healing ministry and was raised up by God with a powerful message of God's delivering power to touch the lives of people everywhere. As his son, I received a personal impartation from his life and ministry. Among the many things he taught me is the fact that God works generationally through families. Just like God worked through Abraham, then Isaac, then Jacob, then Joseph, and on and on, He would work through our family, and more specifically through me.

My father actually prophesied that when he went home to be with the Lord, a double portion of the Lord's Spirit, which rested on my father, would come upon me as his son, so that I could carry on God's healing stream of prayer through this earth.

I was with my dad in his hospital room, when two angels appeared. I blinked my eyes to see if I was imagining things or instead, seeing what I thought I was seeing. I watched as the angels reached into my dad's body and lifted up his spirit and began carrying it up to God in Heaven. As I looked and watched, I saw a mantel fall off. I reached out my hand just like Elisha did when Elijah's mantel fell (2 Kings 2:9–14), and I picked it up and said, "That's mine." And a stronger anointing than I have ever known came upon my life.

This new anointing has been growing every day, and I give God all the praise and honor for the miracles, answered prayers, and changed lives that are happening because of it.

Today, because of all the great instructions I received as I was growing up, plus what I learned standing by my father's side for more than 40 years, I am writing this book. It is my desire to show you the many keys I have learned and used so many times in my life through prayer—keys that have brought God's miracles into my life when I needed them, and had to have them, keys that showed me *the road to a Better Life*.

That's why I have gone through my notes, journals, and sermons, to share with you my experiences of God's miracle power at work. I am breaking these experiences into weeks…then each

FOREWORD

week into days…91 days…3 whole months. I am writing this so that you will be able to read it and live it. It is broken down into 3 months so you will be able to repeat the reading four times a year.

I believe that as you do, a burning fire for God will come forth in you… to expect, expect, expect the miracles you need from God!

Now as you begin to read, let your expectations soar to God. Believe that He is the Source of your total supply. Cast off any negative thing that would try to hold you back. Then with your whole being, open up to the goodness and power of God as never before. Allow me to help you. Cooperate with me and with God by simply reading day by day, and expecting to grow in faith. Let me be His servant to you.

As you read and start seeing that what I am saying is real and alive to you, I encourage you to be a partner together with me to find God's best for your life… to be on top, not on bottom… to be the head, and not the tail, as the Bible says in Deuteronomy 28:13… to succeed and not fail.

Start with the first week. Take the first day, and read it… Devour it. Then take the first 7 days, just like I wrote it. At the end of the week say, "God, what are You saying to me now? Show me how to apply this to my life." Then expect Him to do it. Pray, and look for God's miracle touch… and don't forget to act on the key phrases in this book as you build your faith for miracles.

These are things that I want you to say to yourself. Say them until they become a part of your life as they are to mine.

These keys are really giant truths to open doors, and release your faith, and fill you with God's good things… to bring you miracles until you can shout for joy, remembering the joy of the Lord is your strength.

Right now in my spirit, I am visualizing you picking up this book… holding it in your hands…

Reading…

Stopping...

Reading...

Smiling...

Crying...

Meditating...

Believing...

Receiving...

And finally,

Know that you know that you know that God is the greatest power you have, and He desires to be right in the middle of your life.

Your friend and partner,

Richard Roberts

P.S. I urge you to keep this book with your Bible and compare what it says with what the Bible says. I am praying for you to feel God's presence, receive His guidance, and get on HIS ROAD TO A BETTER LIFE.

WEEK 1

[SUNDAY]

KEY: *"Devil, Take Your Hands off Me, in Jesus' Name. I Am God's Property!"*

The truth about you, God, and the devil

Why do we as human beings often find ourselves carrying around extra worry and anxiety because something has gone wrong and something is falling apart that is precious?

I ask you, "Why?"

You say, "Richard Roberts, are you out of your mind? Haven't you ever had things go wrong and fall apart in your life? Haven't you had times when things got really bad…bills piling up…debts you seemingly can't pay…sickness strikes, accidents happen, trouble comes, and it looks like you're going under?"

Have I? Yes, I have, many times. Sometimes the devil strikes at me and my family so hard that it is difficult to raise my head up, and it is even harder to pray. But I know Jesus; I know who my Source is. Jesus is my personal Lord and Savior and my Baptizer in the Holy Spirit. And He is the ONE who will supply all of my needs with many miracles. I know Him.

In spite of the struggle, the weariness and the feeling of sometimes being forgotten, I have learned the greatest secret in the world is to expect miracles.

Now, let me talk to you plainly about you, the devil, and Jesus Christ. Let me show you that:

You are God's property.

First: Believe the truth about the devil and his purpose towards you, and the truth about Jesus Christ and His purpose towards you.

The truth is spoken by Jesus Himself in John 10:10, *"The thief* (the devil) *does not come except to steal, and to kill, and to destroy. I* (Jesus) *have come that they* (you) *may have life, and that they* (you) *may have it more abundantly."*

There is a devil, and you must understand that he exists. Jesus called him a thief, and says he comes to steal from you, to kill you, and to destroy you.

Believe that. Don't shrug it off. Don't just fall back and say, "I don't understand it." In the natural, you may not ever truly understand it. But remember, Jesus did not tell you to try to understand it… He told you to *believe it.*

Then Jesus tells you to believe Him… Believe Him when He says that the reason He came was to give you life… and give it to you …MORE ABUNDANTLY.

Look, you can draw a line right down the middle. Put the devil with all his badness on one side and Jesus with all His goodness on the other, and with you in the middle:

THE DEVIL   YOU   JESUS

On one side of your life is the devil; on the other side is God. But don't ever forget:

The devil is a bad devil.

God is a good God.

There is no goodness in the devil and no badness in God.

The devil is totally bad.

God is totally good.

The devil hates you, but God loves you. God is greater than the devil, and He can command the devil to take his hands off you.

So, if you have been blaming God for all the bad things, it is time to stop and instead start putting the blame where it belongs …on the devil.

Listen to this…

The devil comes to steal from you: your faith, your love, your hopes, your desire to trust in God, your earning power, your right relationships with your family and others, your health and well-being, and your expectations for miracles. You name anything that is good in life, and the devil will try to steal it.

The devil is trying to kill you…to destroy everything good about you… and to stop anything good from coming to you. He is trying to get you down in your spirit…down in your mind with depression…and down in your body with weakness and disease.

He is trying to ruin you…to keep you from advancing…from receiving the money you need…from prospering and being in health physically, mentally and spiritually. Make no mistake about it—that is what the Bible says.

Since we know all of this is true, what can we do? *Resist the devil, and he will flee from you* (James 4:7).

Resist the devil!

This means stand up to him; don't give an inch. Take charge of him, in Jesus' name.

Now, let's focus on the second half of John 10:10. Jesus is telling you the reason for His coming to this earth—dying on the Cross… rising from the dead… ascending back to heaven, and sending the blessed Comforter, the Holy Spirit, Who is Jesus' other self, the unlimited form of His presence and power. It is to give you life… *fully and continually.*

Believe that.

Don't ignore it.

Think on it.

Know it.

Say this great living truth.

Jesus came...

Jesus came to give me life...

Jesus came to give me life more abundantly...

Me!

Me!

Remember, Jesus and the devil don't mix. Their purposes don't mix. Their works don't mix. Believe and know this, so you can doubt what the devil tries to tell you, and trust in God.

SECOND: Believe that you are God's property... not the devil's.

Say it out loud... "I don't belong to the devil. I am GOD'S PROPERTY."

Say, "I will resist the devil's efforts to steal the good things in life from me... to kill me with his oppression of sickness, poverty, fear, anxiety, a down spirit, and a negative attitude."

Say, "I will resist the devil's efforts to destroy the things God has done for me to believe... the things that help me to believe in Him and keep trusting Him for miracles."

Say, "I believe Jesus Christ. I believe He has come to fill me with His life, His love, His faith, His hope, His spirit, and His power."

Say, "I believe Jesus has come to bless me, to heal me, to prosper me, to guide me, to open up my inner person, to teach me to love and give...to plant seeds of faith because...

"I am God's property!"

Say these words over and over. Say them out loud until they get deep down into your spirit and become a part of you.

You see, when you know you are God's property, it puts you in a take-charge position, even when you are hurting. And when you don't seem to know where to turn or where to go, *you can really know that there is a God and He loves you because you are His property.*

Now, just to make sure that this truth gets inside of you, read the words of the Apostle Paul in 1 Corinthians 6:19–20: *"Or do you not know that your body is the temple of the Holy Spirit who is in you, whom you have from God, and you are not your own? For you were bought at a price; therefore glorify God in your body and in your spirit, which are God's."*

Do you see now that God wants you to believe that you don't belong to the devil? You are God's property… You are GOD'S PROPERTY.

Do you see that the Holy Spirit is in you, and you don't belong to yourself but to Him? Do you see that Christ actually died for you and therefore, in your body and spirit, which are God's, you are to submit to Him?

I pray that you do, and that you see and believe that you are unique and irreplaceable. There is no one else like you. You are God-created, God-bought, God-filled, and God-owned.

Although the devil may tempt you to believe that your battle is with God, it is not now, nor has it ever been.

God is always mindful of you. He loves you and is concerned about you. He wants you to prosper, and He wants to give you physical and spiritual health and wholeness.

Remember, God has given you weapons to fight against your adversary, the devil (1 Peter 5:8). Your weapons are not carnal, or of the flesh; they are spiritual (2 Corinthians 10:4). Here are more weapons God has given you:

> The power of the measure of faith (Romans 12:3)
>
> The power to love and the power to hope
> (1 Corinthians 13:13)
>
> The power not to fear, but to believe
> (2 Timothy 1:7)

He has given you the knowledge that you are not the devil's property, but God's (1Corinthians 6:19).

But don't ever forget, even though you have these weapons…the devil is devious and will not fight fair. He will not come to you and say, "Good morning, this is the devil. I have come to tempt you today, to trick you, and to deceive you. I am your adversary, and I am out to do you in." No!

His strategy is deceitfulness, cunning, craftiness, subtlety… He hits below the belt. Believe me, he is out to destroy you. And on your own, you are no match for him. But let me tell you something very important. You are mighty through God to the pulling down of the devil's strongholds (2 Corinthians 10:4).

Remember, God is the Source of your total supply. He is mightier than the devil.

GREATER IS HE (GOD) THAT IS IN YOU THAN HE (THE DEVIL) THAT IS IN THE WORLD (1 JOHN 4:4).

King David said the battle is the Lord's. Therefore, you must learn these great truths …and make them a part of your being…until you know they are absolutely true.

I know it!

And I want you to know it for yourself.

THIRD: Don't let outward appearances deceive you.

In other words, don't let the devil trick you into believing something is good when it is really bad, or bad when it is really good. As the Apostle Paul said, we are not ignorant of his devices (2 Corinthians 2:11).

For example, a shot of heroin will make you feel good for a few hours. And some would say, "If it makes me feel good, why shouldn't I continue it?" But you see, the devil is a liar and a deceiver. The truth is, a person *will* feel good for a few hours, or for a few times, but later, the drug will begin to take its toll and leave a person feeling wretched... and wrecked for years, or maybe life, until ultimately, it leaves them destroyed.

I have had people tell me they thought they could handle the heroin and other drugs, until they discovered the drugs handled them. I have prayed prayers of deliverance for many who were hooked on drugs. I have shown them that they had to come to a point of turning to God and telling the devil, "Take your hands off me. I am God's property!"

I also pray for sick people every day. In fact, we receive thousands of phone calls daily through the Abundant Life Prayer Group. And sickness and disease are frightening...especially cancer.

Let me remind you that sickness does not come from God. It is sent directly from satan himself. It is the devil who is trying to steal your health. And if he can't get your whole body, he will try to take part of your body... an arm, or a leg, or an important organ.

If the devil can't take all of your earnings away, he will try to take part. If he can't take your job, he will try to lay you off for awhile. If he can't get all your money, he will try to kill the economy or make inflation take it.

You see, the devil will come at you from all sides. And if you try to face him alone, you cannot possibly win.

So...your only chance is to remember that you don't belong to yourself or to the devil. You belong to God.

You are God's property.

Believe me, the devil knows who you belong to... He believes and trembles (James 2:19).

And the moment he finds out that you know you belong to God, half of your battle is won. And when you say, "Devil, take your hands off God's property...*Me*"... you have begun to drive the devil out of your life, and away from you, and to get yourself under God's great protection.

How this will work throughout your life

In your day-by-day life, the little things that seem so ordinary are really the groundwork for bigger things. So, remember that things like these will arise, and you can attack them with your faith.

- The devil putting in your mind the thought of an unkind word about yourself, which he tempts you to say to yourself, or to a loved one, or to someone else...
- Starting to develop a bad attitude at your work which may cause a demotion or a layoff, or even the loss of your job or position...
- Doing little things which lead to the beginning of a breakdown in your health—not taking care of yourself...
- Letting tension and fear buildup...
- Being angry too long and too often...
- Not planting your seeds of faith in the form of your giving of love, kindness, time, talent, money...
- Forgetting about miracles, and God's great concern to give you those miracles.

On the other hand, these are the little things you can do toward God:

- Be positive in your attitude, believing for the best to happen...
- See the good things in yourself, your loved ones, and others...
- Keep a good attitude, which can lead to a promotion...or being kept on in bad times... or even a new and better job or position...
- Keep yourself on a more even keel and in balance not permitting the devil to steal your peace of soul and mind...
- Refuse the suggestion to get angry and try to hurt someone.

In short, your daily goal is to go from planting bad seeds, which are multiplied back into bad things...to planting good seeds, however small, every day…good seeds, which are multiplied back into good things.

It's a decision.

Start believing Jesus, rather than the devil. Believe that each good seed you plant will be multiplied and sent back to you in God's own way and time, and in exactly the way you need it most.

Right now, I want you to know and feel down in the depths of your soul the loving care God has placed in my heart for you. I want you to feel it… my belief and faith that God wants the devil to take his hands off of God's property…you…and your loved ones!

I remind you and will keep reminding you to tell the devil:

"I am God's property—take your hands off me!"

YOUR GOD-GIVEN PRAYER KEY FOR TODAY:

Pray this prayer: *Father God, I know that I am Your property. I do not belong to the devil. So therefore, I say to the devil right now in the name of Jesus, God's only Son, "I rebuke you and command you to take your hands off me, and all of my loved ones, and everything that is mine." Amen.*

[Monday]

KEY: *God Cares About Me.*

Growing up as Oral Roberts' son was both good and bad at the same time. On the good side, I loved my dad with all my heart and loved to be with him. I liked the things he liked. We both loved basketball and golf. We loved horses and cattle… and we loved to fish together.

On the bad side, he was gone a lot because he had to travel. He was called by God as an evangelist, and that meant being away from home for long periods of time, sometimes two, or three, or even four weeks at a time, and sometimes trips overseas were even longer.

Once, he took a trip to Asia and Australia and was gone for six weeks. It was bad enough that he left, but he took my mother with him.

It was just after my birthday, and they had given me a little Boy Scout hatchet. It had a very sharp blade, so in defiance, I used it to cut off the wooden knob on the top of my bed post… But they left anyway.

School was tough on me… and not just because I was more interested in recess and playing ball than in reading, writing and arithmetic. But it was because I got the brunt of all the jokes and criticism from the other kids because of whose son I was. Sometimes, they would come up behind me and cover my eyes and touch me and say, "Be healed!" And then they would laugh. And sometimes the teacher would laugh too.

As the years passed, it drove me inside myself. By the time I was a teenager, a deep unrest had grown inside me. I didn't feel like God really cared about me. I didn't want to be Oral Roberts' son anymore. I wanted to be me. I wanted my own will and plan. I rejected God, even though deep in my heart, I felt that God would use me someday.

Now as I said, I loved my dad. I knew that he was real, and so was his ministry. I had been in those tent crusades. I had seen great miracles as he laid his hands on people in prayer. Many times, I had walked the prayer lines with him. I had seen blind eyes opened and deaf ears healed. I had seen cripples walk. I had seen cancers fall off of people's bodies.

But at about age thirteen, I discovered I had a singing talent, and offers began to come my way. Soon, I had learned to play the guitar, and by the time I was sixteen, I was singing in clubs and

WEEK 1: MONDAY

singing lead in a local rock band. I was traveling all across the state, singing on the weekends. By eighteen, I had left home to go to college, now singing in clubs in Kansas City and doing Summer Stock Theater with well-known stars like Shirley Jones, Gordon MacRae, Charles Nelson Reilly… and many others.

It was the late 1960s, and everything in the world was being offered to a single boy like me… and I was ready to try it all.

Naturally, my dad wanted me to use my talent for God through his ministry, but I just told him to get the hell out of my life! He replied, "Son, that is what I am trying to do…to get the hell out of your life." I laugh now, but as I look back on it, what he said made perfect sense. I was living like hell…involved in everything I could get my hands on. I had totally rejected God and a call that, somehow, I knew was on my life. And he wanted all that "hell" in my life to be gone, so that I could use my talent in the ministry and stand by his side.

I got an offer to sing and play in the lounges of the Sahara Hotel in Las Vegas. I thought, "This is it; this is my big break." And from there, I would be a headliner. I wouldn't have to put up with the stress of being the son of an evangelist who was known around the world. And I could put out of my mind all of the criticism and hate that my father and family had taken from the media… Like the cruel and vicious lies printed by LIFE and LOOK magazines and newspapers all over the world, and even our hometown. I hated it, and I hated the so called "Christian publications" that struck so hard at my dad and his ministry.

How could God allow it? Didn't He care? "Well, I guess not," I thought. So I would get as far away as I could. The bars and lounges in Las Vegas, promised to me by a talent agent, looked pretty good. Maybe someday, I thought, I would come home a big star, and I would get praised instead of being ridiculed.

*But a funny thing happened on the way to Las Vegas…*I got sick. And after several visits to the doctor, I was hospitalized at the University of Kansas Medical Center, and they scheduled me for colon surgery. Me? Surgery? Not me! I was young and talented and *healthy*. Surgery? How could I be facing surgery?

I will never forget the night before the scheduled operation. I was in a ward with four other young men. I lay in that hospital bed praying. Praying? Yes, I said praying. It is amazing who you call on when you get into trouble.

"God, if You will heal me and cancel this surgery," I prayed, "I will serve You." Wow! That was a dangerous prayer. But I meant it! Maybe He did care about me after all.

As I lay there praying, I was aware of a strange Presence...a warmth filling me up on the inside. Something was different, and I knew it.

The next morning, the surgeon examined me and found the problem was gone and cancelled the surgery. No surgery! Wow!

The papers were signed and I was released from the hospital. God did care...and He cared about me!

Suddenly, I knew it and I believed it. He cared for a boy like me...a boy who had run away from home... a boy who was now ready for a life-change because of a life-changing experience.

And... if God could care for me... and if He could take me and make something of my life... and if He is no respecter of persons like the Bible says in Acts 10:34, then *get ready for this...*

God cares about you too!

>I know
>>that I know
>>>that I know
>>>>that He cares for me!

I was not just Oral Roberts' son running to Las Vegas for a career. I was somebody special to God, and He had a plan for my life.

What to do, what to do? Well, it took a little while. In my flesh, I still fought it for almost a year. But the day came when I drove home and got on my knees in my parents' bedroom and prayed a prayer of repentance. I asked Jesus Christ to come into my heart. I repented of all my sins and received the Lord into my life. When I got up, I had been forever changed and would never be the same again.

Now, just as I got this truth deep down inside of me, I want you to get it deep down inside of you.

God cares about you!

It doesn't matter where you are, or what road you're on. It doesn't matter what you've done or not done, or what you've felt or said or not felt or said. What matters right now is that in spite of it all…

God cares about you!

Say it out loud, "God cares about me." Say it again, "God cares about me." Now, say it like you mean it…

"God cares about me!"

Believe it, say it, know it. Even if you feel low, say it over and over until it becomes a part of you.

YOUR GOD-GIVEN KEY FOR TODAY:

God really does care about me.

[Tuesday]

KEY: *Jesus Lives at My House.*

It has been said that the thing or things that we adore…or the person or persons we choose to adore…often help us to determine what and who we become, and who we finally are. If this is true, then we must ask ourselves, "What or who is it that I adore?"

Oftentimes, children will try to emulate or imitate their parents or others in the family. I remember a minister friend telling me the story of his son, Peter. Peter had bright red hair, which was about as bright in color as his father's was when he was the same age. The only problem was, by the time my friend was around thirty years old, he lost most of his hair, except for a little patch right in the front.

One day, he came into Peter's bedroom, only to find him with scissors in his hand, cutting off his beautiful locks of red hair. Most of it was gone now, lying on the floor in a pile. All that remained was a short growth of hair, *right in the front.*

My friend quickly grabbed the scissors from Peter and said to him, "Son, what in the world are you doing? Why would you cut off that beautiful red hair?" Peter looked up at his father and said, "Dad, I just wanted to look like you."

My dad told me the story of when he lay bedfast with tuberculosis for five long months. He was only seventeen, and there were no miracle drugs in those days. He was dying, and nothing short of a miracle could save his life. (I will get to the rest of this unbelievable powerful healing testimony later on in this book.)

Because my dad was flat on his back in bed, he became a captive audience for his parents' prayers and conversations, since their bedroom was right next to his.

He told me that Mama and Papa Roberts, my grandparents, had a habit of awakening before dawn each morning and lying in bed for fifteen to twenty minutes, talking to Jesus and to each other about Jesus. And they talked to Him in such a personal way that my father actually believed that Jesus was in the room with them.

They talked to Jesus as if He were a member of the family. It was authentic…conversational… It was loving and real.

Sometimes, they carried on what must have seemed like a running conversation about Jesus, or with Him, all day long.

When I was a boy, the same thing happened in my family. My parents, Oral and Evelyn, talked to Jesus like they knew Him personally. It was in the tone of their voices…the look in their eyes. It was in their mannerisms and the feelings they showed…especially in my mother when she would sing to Jesus as she worked around the house.

Just as in the case of my grandparents, my parents made me feel like Jesus lived at our house. I discovered that I could talk to Him, just like they did. And even though I drifted away from the Lord during my teenage years, when I came back to Him (as I told you about earlier), I picked right back up in the conversation with Him and prayers to Him.

When our children were little, Lindsay and I always talked about Jesus in front of them. We never tried to make our prayers private. We talked to the Lord in everything we did…in the morning, at meal time, when we joined hands in prayer at bedtime, when we anointed them, and each other, with oil.

We always tried to make it personal. We did not want them to be afraid of God…as many people are.

Many have the idea that God is someone up in Heaven with a stick, waiting for them to make a mistake so He can whip them, and then say, "I knew you were no good. I knew I couldn't count on you!"

But that's not a picture of the God I know, for He is a personal, loving God. He cares about you… He feels your hurts and pains. He knows all about you…when you're up and when you're down… when you're weak and when you're strong. And He loves you.

You may ask, "What was that you just said, Richard?"

Let me say it again. *He loves you. He loves you.*

Who is He? He is the God who scooped out the beds for the oceans and piled high the mountains, Who dug deep the gorges and traced the rivers with His fingernails. He is the One who flung the stars from His hands and hung this world on nothing...I am talking about God almighty.

God loves you!

He loves you!

Let that resonate inside of you.

Knowing that God loves me has helped me to know who I am and what I am called to do. The knowledge of it causes a stillness to run deep through my character. I listen to Jesus...His voice. I awaken early in the morning before dawn and seek His face...and pray.

I talk to Him like He is in the room...because you know what? He is. And I carry Him in my heart wherever I go...the secular realm, as well as the spiritual realm.

Remember, Jesus said in Hebrews 13:5, *I will never leave you or forsake you.* And since He is omnipresent, or able to be everywhere at the same time because He is the Lord, then He DOES actually live at my house.

But that is not all the story...If you love Him, then He is living in your house too.

You may ask, "At my house?"

Yes...at your house.

YOUR GOD-GIVEN PRAYER KEY FOR TODAY:

Jesus lives at my house.

Pray this prayer: *"Jesus, thank You for living at my house. Because I know You are here, I will let Your presence fill me up on the inside... I will let Your presence influence everything I do and say."*

"I won't get angry."

"I will be kind to people."

"I will be aware of other people's problems and needs."

"I will be considerate and not judgmental."

"Help me to let my life be a constant reflection of You."

"In Your name I pray."

"Amen."

Now, say it again… "Jesus lives at my house."

If you keep saying it until it becomes a part of you, I believe that the truth of it will cause you never to be the same again.

Now, one more time, say it:

"Jesus lives at my house."

My address is _____
_____
(Please fill in your address.)

[Wednesday]

KEY: *God Wants Me to Prosper and Be in Health*

The greatest discovery about health, prosperity and spiritual blessing.

During the days my parents pastored in western Oklahoma, they came across a great discovery. It happened one morning as my dad was on his way out the front door to catch the bus. You see, not only was he pastoring a small, seventy-member church, but he was going to college to get a degree. Plus, he and my mother had two children: my sister, Rebecca, and my brother, Ronnie.

It was my father's custom to read a scripture or two from the Bible before he left for class. This particular morning, he was running late. As he left the house, he remembered he had not read a scripture. So he ran back inside and quickly opened his Bible. It fell open to 3 John 2.

Beloved, I pray that you may prosper in all things and be in health, just as your soul prospers.

He was astonished at what he had just read. He called to my mother, "Evelyn, look at this!" And he read it out loud.

She said, "Oral, is that in the Bible?"

"Yes, Evelyn, it is. I just read it to you."

They were so overtaken by this scripture that they both sat down and began to praise God. My dad didn't make it to school that day.

You see, that verse became a revelation to them. The old way of thinking was that God was a judgmental God and was waiting in Heaven for His children to make a mistake so He could punish them, saying, "I knew you were no good and I couldn't count on you."

But these words from 3 John 2 rang out in their hearts…GOD IS A GOOD GOD, AND HE WANTS US TO PROSPER IN EVERY AREA OF OUR LIVES.

Now, my parents were tithers, but they had never been taught to expect something back from God. In other words, they gave to God as if it was a debt they owed, instead of as a seed they sowed. They were paying God instead of planting seed. They didn't understand that when God sent His only Son, Jesus, to this earth to be crucified on the Cross and raised from the dead, it was to pay man's debt, once and for all, and to provide salvation and healing.

They didn't understand that God, in His great love for mankind, paid the debt in full, through Jesus. And from that day forward, people do not give to God because we owe God, but instead, we tithe and give offerings to God, because we love God… and also, so that God can take the seed-planting, and use it for His glory, and then multiply it back in the way it's needed most.

Now, as I grew up, this Bible principle was taught in our home. And I remember how my parents showed me that anything I gave to God was a seed sowed...my love, my time, my prayers, my compassion for others...anything I did for good was a seed. And as a sower, I had a Bible right to receive a harvest.

I learned that it is God's highest and greatest wish that I prosper in every area of my life, and that God is for me and not against me. He wants me to do well and have success in my life. He does not want me to just get by, but to thrive, so that I will not only prosper, but teach others how to prosper. In short, He wants me to have a Better Life.

This principle was driven home to me by my mother, when one day she said to me, "Richard, we are going to plant some vegetable seeds out behind the house." So, she showed me how to prepare the ground, dig little rows, and begin planting little seeds in the ground. Then she saw that I didn't really understand, so she reached into the apron she was wearing and pulled out a seed packet. On the front was a picture of juicy, red tomatoes.

I said to her, "Is that what it is going to look like?"

"Yes," she said. "Not today, or tomorrow, or next week. But the day will come when you and I will pick dozens and dozens of tomatoes."

That day, I got a glimpse of "the harvest." I saw it. And each day, as I went out and looked for the tomatoes, I watched the growing process. It took some time, but just like she said, the day came when those beautiful, red tomatoes were ready to be picked from the vines... And did they ever taste good!

You see, the principle of sowing seed, then time, followed by a harvest, had gotten into my spirit... And I never forgot it. It is strong in me today. Every time I sow a seed of my faith...whether it be money, or time, or a prayer, or a good word to someone, or whatever... it is a good seed sown unto the Lord, and He, God, will multiply it back in ways I need it most. The Bible guarantees it in Luke 6:38.

Now, what am I really trying to say to you? It is really so simple that it is easily missed…so don't miss this.

God wants you to prosper in every area of your life and be in health, even as your soul prospers.

God's highest wish is that you prosper in your finances, in your health, in your soul…and in every other area of your life. So…say this out loud to yourself: *"God wants me to prosper in every area of my life."*

Say it again: *"God wants me to prosper in every area of my life."*

Say it until it explodes in your mind and throughout your entire life. And as you do, begin to expect, expect, expect things to change for you.

YOUR GOD-GIVEN KEY FOR TODAY:

God wants me to prosper in every area of my life.

[Thursday]

KEY: *Jesus Is at the Point of My Need.*

Discovering this key issue gave me a balance I never had before.

Jesus is oriented towards people. After all, we were made in His image (Genesis 1:26).

Yes, God loves all the human family, but it is much more personal when you understand that GOD LOVES *YOU*. Knowing this causes His love to crystallize in you and fills you with His love, and becomes infinitely more precious and desirable. Really, it means *God is in the midst of life…your life.*

He is always in the midst of your life, and you are very important to Him. You are more important to Him than your home, or your car, or your clothing, or anything else you possess.

This is a key issue that keeps me in balance in my life—knowing that God is in the midst of my life, and He values it above everything else.

Do you remember what happened in the life of our Savior when He was traveling with His disciples through a cornfield on the Sabbath day? His disciples were hungry. Having nothing to eat, they took the ears of corn and rubbed them in their hands so they could get the kernels (Luke 6:1). The religious leaders of that day said, "You have broken the Sabbath. Rubbing the ears of the corn constitutes work! You are not to do any work on the Sabbath; therefore, you have broken the Sabbath."

Jesus replied in Luke 14:5, *"Which one of you, if you found his ox in the ditch on the Sabbath, would not go out and get him?"* Then Jesus made this statement: *"The Sabbath was made for man, not man for the Sabbath"* (Mark 2:27).

No greater statement was ever made by our Lord in connection with His concern and care about you and me as individuals. The great Sabbath day, with all of its rules and regulations, which dated back to the days of Moses, is not greater than man. The hunger of these individuals was more important to Jesus Christ than strict religious observance of the Law of Moses. In contrast, the Pharisees had made the observance of the law more important than life itself.

Jesus pointed out that people are more important than any special religious day. He said that every day is made for human beings (Mark 2:27). Whatever accrues to our benefit is important, even though it might happen on a so-called holy day. In the Lord's view…

Every day is a holy day.

Every day is a day in which to enjoy life.

Every day is a day to worship God.

Every day is a day in which you are the center of His love, and He is the center of yours.

He is concerned about the details of your existence, even numbering the hairs on your head (Matthew 10:30).

Jesus Christ is a person. That means He cares about you... He is always in the midst of your life...He is at the point of your need (where you need Him the most).

This is the key issue that will keep you in balance your whole life...And that, my friend, is what a Better Life looks like.

You have needs...and that is a fact. You may have family and loved ones around you; some are in trouble and need help. You may have financial needs. Whatever it is you are facing, the key issue is:

Jesus is at the point of your need... right where you need Him the most.

Now, say it out loud.

"Jesus is at the point of my need."

Don't stop saying it. Today and every day, repeat it to yourself. Say it over and over again until it becomes a part of your life.

YOUR GOD-GIVEN KEY FOR TODAY:

Jesus is at the point of my need...right where I need Him the most.

Now, write it several times in the spaces below...

_____
_____
_____
_____
_____

[Friday]

KEY: *I Will Be a Person of Honesty and Integrity in Life by Paying My Bills.*

As I grew up, my parents taught me about integrity; it seemed very important to them. They said, "Integrity it what you do when nobody is watching."

Keeping your word was always emphasized in our home. My mother taught me that if you tell the truth, you will never have to remember what you said. I remember once, I had been given an old secondhand typewriter to use for school work. I had gone to a summer business school and learned how to type when I was fourteen.

I loved that old typewriter. I could type almost 60 words a minute on it!

One day, I was invited to go out with some of my friends, and I needed some extra spending money. I said to myself, "I'll just sell this old typewriter. No one will know it. It won't be missed." So I took it to a secondhand store, and sold it, and pocketed the money.

The months passed, and no one ever mentioned that old typewriter to me again. I thought I was in the clear.

Then one day, a woman came to stay in our home for a few days. She was a minister and was a friend of my parents. My mother came in and asked for the typewriter. She said the Lord was leading her to give it to this woman as a seed.

Well, I stammered a moment, trying to think what to say, to figure out how to get out of what I had gotten myself into. Suddenly, I realized the significance of what I had done. I had sacrificed my integrity over some money and the sale of an old typewriter. I swallowed hard and told my mother I had sold it.

"Then, where is the money you got for it?" she said.

My head dropped as I told her I had used the money so I could have fun with my friends.

She looked at me... And brother, did I know that look! It was a look of total disappointment in me. Again, the significance of what I had done hit me. I felt so ashamed already. But the look she gave me just about did me in.

I began crying and started to apologize. My mother heard me out and then said to me, "All of my life, I had been taught that part of your integrity is to tell the truth, no matter how hard it is."

Then she said, "If you needed some extra money, you should have come to me and your father and told us the whole story. The answer might have been yes and the answer might have been no, but at least everything would have been out in the open."

I apologized over and over again. My mother said, "I forgive you, but have you asked the Lord to forgive you?" I hadn't thought about that.

We both got down on our knees, and I repented before the Lord, and I told Him I was sorry, that I had done wrong, and I would never sacrifice my integrity like that again.

Afterwards, I felt so much better. However, there is a second chapter to the story. My mother said I would have to work off all the money I made by selling the typewriter. Well, I supposed that it was only fair. The typewriter was gone, and so was the money... and I needed to pay it back. She laid out a number of jobs that I could do. It took me several weeks of working after school, but I paid it all off.

The lesson I learned about integrity has served me all of my life, and I poured it into our children... Always tell the truth, and be honest with money. Now, that is integrity.

Through the years, I have had opportunities to be a part of people's financial schemes, some promising millions of dollars. But to be a part of their plan (which may have been only to get money from me or our ministry) would have meant sacrificing my integrity, and that is something I just won't do.

Even today, I still look back on the typewriter incident and remember the lesson I learned. My parents also taught me to sow my tithes and offerings and to pay my bills. "Remember the Lord first," they taught me. That is the best way to be able to pay your bills. And whenever I face a financial problem, the first thing I always do is to make sure my tithes and offerings are up to date.

When I became president of Oral Roberts University in 1993, one of the first things I discovered was that our Finance Department had stopped our corporate tithing in order to cover our expenses. That is something that I changed immediately.

In fact, I called the entire staff together and asked them all to repent with me and vow that we would all remember the Lord, and sow our tithes and offerings to Him before the bills were paid. (It was hard to do, because at that time, we were in debt… deep debt. But as we sowed each month, we began getting out of debt.)

Now, don't misunderstand me; it wasn't easy. And as we held seed in one hand and our bills in the other, the devil whispered, "You're going under. You're going under. You're going under." But each time he said it, I remembered, he is a liar, the father of all lies (John 8:44).

Let me say this to you: If there is anything in your life like this between you and the Lord, then I urge you to do what I did…and that is to get down on your knees and repent. Ask God to forgive you. Make a decision today to be a person of honesty and integrity in your life and in paying your bills.

YOUR GOD-GIVEN KEY FOR TODAY:

Say this out loud:

"*I will be a person of honesty and integrity in my life by paying my bills.*"

Now, say it one more time.

"*I will be a person of honesty and integrity in my life by paying my bills.*"

[Saturday]

KEY: *Something Good Is Going to Happen to Me.*

In the late 1960s, my dad would begin our TV program by saying, "Something good is going to happen to you!" It struck a chord in people's hearts and helped them to believe God, instead of believing that nothing good would ever happen to them.

My father called me and Ralph Carmichael, our TV music arranger, and commissioned a new song. "Ralph," he said, "write me a new song that says, 'Something good is going to happen to you.' I want Richard to sing it on the opening of each of our TV programs.'"

A few days later, Ralph had written a great song. It had about four verses and a great chorus. I began to sing that chorus each Sunday morning on our show. People loved it! They called, they wrote letters, and they stopped us on the street to tell us what an encouragement the words to that song were.

And after all these years, the words are just as powerful…*Something good is going to happen to you…happen to you this very day. Something good is going to happen to you…Jesus of Nazareth is passing your way.*

You see, anyone can dwell on his problems until he gets so low that the devil can climb on his shoulders and keep him down. But faith in God changes your perspective. An attitude of expecting something good to happen to you will not only make your day, but also revolutionize your life. Looking to God as your Source brings:

The mountain moving...

problem solving...

need solving...

power of God into your life.

But you know, sometimes we as Christians don't believe that God will ever bring something good into our lives. I heard the story of a man who had a flat tire on an old country road. When he looked in the trunk of his car, he realized he didn't have a jack.

Looking around, he saw a light in a distant farmhouse. He thought, "That farm will probably have a jack I can borrow." So he began walking toward the light.

As he walked, he thought, "Maybe the farmer is already in bed, and maybe he has a jack, and maybe he won't let me borrow it. What if I am stuck out here all night? That farmer might not answer the door when I knock. Maybe he will have a shotgun in his hands because it will be so late."

All the while, his anger was rising. "What if he chases me off of his property?" By the time he got to the door, he was so worked up that when the farmer opened the door, and said, "Hello, may I help you?"... The man said, "Mister, I wouldn't use your jack even if you offered it to me!"

Humorous, perhaps, but sometimes, don't we act as if we think God isn't willing to help us in our time of need? And because of our attitude of doubt and negativity, we rob ourselves of God's gifts.

Our miracle can only begin when we cease being negative and start being positive... when we recognize that part of the problem is inside us. Regardless of how much power God has, miracle power will never fully be effective in our lives until we cooperate with Him...until we fully expect something good to happen to us. But the good news is, when we truly expect God to bless us, we open up opportunities for Him to do so.

Now, say this:

"Something good is going to happen to me."

Unless you come alive and are responsive to the fact that something good really is going to happen, you will miss some of God's best blessings for your life. Good things will happen, and you will miss the full blessing and impact of what you need today.

YOUR GOD-GIVEN KEY FOR TODAY:

Say this out loud:

"Something good is going to happen to me."

Say it over and over again, until it becomes a part of your being.

WEEK 1 RECAP

- **Sunday:** "Devil, Take Your Hands Off Me! I Am God's Property."
- **Monday:** God Cares About Me.
- **Tuesday:** Jesus Lives at My House.
- **Wednesday:** God Wants Me to Prosper and Be in Health.
- **Thursday:** Jesus Is at the Point of My Need.
- **Friday:** I Will Be a Person of Integrity in Life by Paying My Bills.
- **Saturday:** Something Good Is Going to Happen to Me!

WEEK 2

[Sunday]

KEY: *God's Way Will Be My Way.*

You can learn God's way of doing things. His ways are based on eternal laws…unchangeable laws…laws that are so perfect, they will always work for you.

When I was a boy, I attended many of my father's healing crusades. One such crusade was in the Seattle–Tacoma, Washington area in the Pacific Northwest, which is one of the most beautiful areas of the country.

One day, we were driving through a well-watered valley. It was harvest time and the farmers were bringing it all in.

My dad began to talk to us about seed time and harvest, and to tell us children how seeing it all reminded him of many scriptures in the Bible. Scriptures like these:

While the earth remains, seed time and harvest…shall not cease.
—Genesis 8:22

Whatever a man sows, that he will also reap. —Galatians 6:7

Now may He who supplies seed to the sower, and bread for food, supply and multiply the seed you have sown and increase the fruits of your righteousness. —2 Corinthians 9:10

If you have faith as a mustard seed, you will say to this mountain, 'Move from here to there,' and it will move; and nothing will be impossible for you. —Matthew 17:20

It is more blessed (productive) *to give than to receive.* —Acts 20:35

For God loves a cheerful giver. —2 Corinthians 9:7

> *Surely blessing I will bless you, and multiplying I will multiply you.*
> —Hebrews 6:14
>
> *Give, and it will be given to you: good measure, pressed down, shaken together, and running over will be put into your bosom. For with the same measure that you use, it will be measured back to you.*
> —Luke 6:38
>
> *And my God shall supply all your need according to His riches in glory by Christ Jesus.* —Philippians 4:19
>
> *Beloved, I pray that you may prosper in all things and be in health, just as your soul prospers.* —3 John 2

These, and other scriptures, just kept pouring out of my dad. And the more they poured out of him, the more they began to pour into me. At that young age, I didn't realize the day would come when I would be living those scriptures.

But those farmers (along with God's Word) showed me the biblical principles of seed time and harvest in very practical terms...in terms that I could understand.

Today, as those and many other scriptures pour out from my spirit, they are a pattern...a way of life.

Just as I began to see it back then, I see it clearly now. I see God's way of doing things...Yes, God has His own special way of doing things.

God's way of doing things is based on eternal laws...laws so exact and perfect... they always work.

If my dad were alive today, he would call it a "Blessing-Pact Covenant with God"... a pact made with God to learn His ways of doing things and to do them...then asking Him to pour out His blessings, as we expect miracles from expected and unexpected sources.

Now, as I grew up, church in general did not put much emphasis on God helping people with their finances or their physical and emotional needs. Yes, there was a spiritual emphasis,

WEEK 2: SUNDAY

and that was good. But too often, the needs people faced were not addressed. But in our home, we children were taught that God cared about every area of our lives... spiritually, physically, emotionally—and financially too. We were taught to give tithes and offerings to God as a seed, not as a debt or an obligation. We learned to give willingly out of our heart, not as if we were forced to give.

My parents taught me that man cannot pay God, but he can plant a seed to God.

Now, planting or sowing seed was one thing, but expecting a miracle...well to some, that seemed like blasphemy.

My father caught heavy criticism for this kind of teaching. We children also caught the backlash at school from other children and teachers as well. Even though the criticism came, these principles of sowing to God and reaping His harvest back into our lives got deep down in my spirit.

Yes, it was revolutionary in those days...but it was the Bible.

I could have a "blessing-pact covenant" with a God who loved me and would meet all my needs. I could sow of my love, my time, my money and my prayers. In fact, I could make all that I did as a seed...and as I did it in faith I could believe God would use it for His glory and then multiply it back to me in the way I needed it most.

God became the Source of everything in my life. I realized that the devil only comes to me to steal, to kill, and to destroy. But God comes to me with abundant, eternal, everlasting life (John 10:10).

Thank God, these and other spiritual truths have continued flooding up in me for all these years, and the "three keys of seed-faith" my father taught me have helped sustain my life and total being.

Yes, there are three keys... *three master keys*... and I will share them with you later on in this book.

Without these three keys operating in my life, I might never have known just how great and forever-good God really is. He, and only He, is the Source of my total supply.

GOD HIMSELF…the One Who knows who I am, where I live, and what I am going through…is my Source of total supply. Knowing this has been a tremendous blessing in my life and has given me an attitude of miraculous living, instead of negative living.

Now, this is the same attitude and lifestyle God has for you. The Bible says so and confirms it over and over again. And as you learn God's way of doing things, you begin to believe for…and expect… miracles every day of your life. God will become your Source, and you will include Him in everything you do…every decision you make…and every step you take.

When you learn God's way of doing things, and do things His way, you discover who your Source is. You find your greatest supply by giving to Him and then expecting many miracles from your seed-faith lifestyle.

So…say it to yourself until you know it by heart:

"I will learn God's way of doing things and do them His way, and then, I will ask Him to bless me and expect Him to do it."

YOUR GOD-GIVEN KEY FOR TODAY:

God's way will be my way.

[Monday]

KEY: *God Is My Source.*

One of the greatest discoveries I have made in my life is that God is the Source of my total supply, and that in Him I live, and move, and have my being (Acts 17:28). This is why I put my trust in Him.

The Blessing-Pact Covenant with God is one of the most powerful ideas in the history of Christianity. Yet, as I grew up under my father, I watched as people opposed it, especially some of the religious leaders. They actually told my father he wasn't preaching the gospel.

But he was preaching the gospel…the full gospel of Jesus Christ, Who came so that we might have life and have it more abundantly. More importantly, the message was working in his life and in the lives of many others. People were getting their needs met in miraculous ways. Testimonies were coming in, and people were seeing the results of making God Almighty the Source of their lives.

As I look back on those days of criticism now, I wonder if those religious leaders who were so cruel and seemingly uncaring about people's needs felt that in making God the Source of life, they were somehow losing control over people. Perhaps that was really the basis for their contention.

I remember my father saying to one critical leader, "The only church people I know who are getting their needs met and experiencing miracles in their lives are those who believe God is "in the now." And every one of them is practicing some form of a Blessing-Pact with God. Maybe not in the exact terminology I use, but certainly the principles are the same. Besides knowing they are going to heaven, they are experiencing the kingdom of heaven here on earth in their lifetime."

Wow! Those were rough words, but as it is often said, "In life, the first one through the wall always gets bloody."

Even today, there are still those who oppose the idea that God is a good and loving God. They seem to prefer a God who is judgmental and just waiting for you and me to make a mistake so He can punish us. But I tell you, that is a lie from the very pit of hell! So, don't believe a word of it.

The truth is, if God is not in the PRESENT of our lives, then He has never been, nor will He ever be. If He can't supply your needs on earth, then He won't be able to supply them in heaven either.

Yes, it is true that there are specific needs that God will only meet in the Resurrection. But I also believe and know the Resurrection starts in this life.

Philippians 4:19 says, *And my God shall supply all your need according to His riches in glory by Christ Jesus.*

Read this scripture over and over until it becomes a part of you.

God will supply…not the bank, not your job, not your family. Those people and things are instruments that God can work through to bring opportunities to you, but it is God Almighty who is your Source. It is His power, His love for us, His wisdom to guide us that opens up opportunities, blessings and miracles in our lives.

This is the **First Miracle Key** of Seed-Faith:

God is my Source of total supply.

This means He will supply all of my needs. How? He will do it His way… not my way…not depending on whether the economy is up or down… not depending upon old unbiblical methods, but rather methods that are directly from the Lord Himself.

And when you adopt this kind of attitude, God becomes very big to you, bigger than all your needs. He cannot, *and will not,* fail. It gives you a new confidence and a new strength, knowing that by obeying Him and doing what He says, He will keep His part of the bargain.

WEEK 2: MONDAY

Now, here is something very important my dad also taught me. You're not married to methods, or bound by them, but to God's own eternal principles.

Perhaps you have exhausted doing everything your way—it hasn't worked, and it is not working now. Well, all hope is not lost. You can start fresh in accordance with God's way of doing things, and enter into a new relationship with Him and His eternal supply.

You say, "You mean I have to change?" Yes, that is exactly what I mean, for God is not going to change. He is God. He has a set way of doing things… and we, as human beings, have to get on His agenda, His plan, and His timetable. (See Isaiah 55:8–9.)

It boils down to trust. So, don't be afraid to change, for it's a change for the right reason. It is using new methods, biblical methods, but not changing biblical principles.

Just look at people in the Bible who changed methods and got results. Look at the little boy who gave his lunch to Jesus in John chapter 6, and consider the widow who gave her last two coins. (See Mark chapter 12.) And look at the woman who gave a portion of her last meal to Elijah, the prophet. (See 1 Kings chapter 17.) Through their willingness to change methods, they all got their needs met. And in changing, and in doing things God's way, He will become first in your life. Literally, He becomes the Source of your total supply—so much so that when you give to Him your best, then with all boldness, you can ask Him for… and expect… His best in return.

Now, that's a blessing-pact covenant with God!

When you make Him the Source of your life, you get into a position for Him to bless you so that He can meet all your needs, according to His riches in glory by Christ Jesus (Philippians 4:19).

Knowing this has meant everything to me. God as my Source is:

- My Lord and Savior
- My hope and whole life

- My protection and guide
- My all in all

This means you start with God…you stay with God…and you end with God. In every situation you face in life, God is your Source.

Now, say this out loud…

> There is only one Source…God.
>
> He is the Source of my total supply.
>
> Say it again…
>
> He is the Source of my total supply.

Now, say it one more time, and this time…*really believe it!*

YOUR GOD-GIVEN KEY FOR TODAY:

God is my Source.

God is my Source.

God is my Source.

[Tuesday]

KEY: *I Will Plant My Seed, and God Will Move the Mountain.*

You can make your faith as a seed you plant, and cause mountains of need to move in your life.

Jesus said in Matthew 17:20, *"I say to you, if you have faith as a mustard seed, you will say to this mountain, 'Move from here to there,' and it will move; and nothing will be impossible for you."*

Jesus is telling you to have faith (which is God-given) as a seed... a seed that you can plant.

Notice, He didn't say you need a little *more* faith, so that it can grow until it is big enough to move mountains. No. He is saying something more fundamental to the eternal laws of our Heavenly Father.

You see, from the beginning of the creation of the earth and man, eternal laws of seed-time and harvest were given. Then God sent Jesus, His Son, to show us what the Father Himself is like... to demonstrate His love and His principles... and finally, to give His life on the Cross and rise again to be alive forevermore...and to remind men of this eternal law of sowing and reaping, or of giving and receiving.

The seed of giving is the seed of faith. But the seed has to be planted before we can speak to our mountains of need to be removed. Seed-faith comes first. Then, and only then, do we have a Bible right to speak to our mountain of need.

This may be a totally new concept to you...but hold on...I believe this will be worth something to you.

> Giving is the "seeding" for your miracle.

God promises in His Word that when we give to Him as our Source, He will multiply it back to us with such an increase that it will be bigger, and more powerful, than our mountains of need and problems.

This is:

> POWERFUL
>
> LOGICAL
>
> SCRIPTURAL
>
> WORKABLE
>
> BELIEVABLE

Every farmer understands this truth. He prepares the soil and puts seed in first...before he expects to receive a return (harvest).

Anyone who has ever planted a garden knows that you have to plant seed...and do it first.

Now, read Luke 6:38: *"Give, and it will be given to you: good measure, pressed down, shaken together, and running over will be put into your bosom. For with the same measure that you use, it will be measured back to you."*

This is what I call *"seeding for my miracle"*... the **Second Miracle Key** of Seed-Faith.

Notice that even in the "Golden Rule" in Luke 6:31, we are to do and do first...as you would have men do unto you.

We act first...and then God's blessing comes upon us. It's what we do first that becomes the seed, such as being pure in heart, forgiving first, making peace first, hungering and thirsting for righteousness first, seeking the kingdom of God first, and GIVING FIRST.

In the Old Testament, giving was based on receiving first, and you gave *after* you received. You received... then you gave. That is how they "paid tithes"... by giving one-tenth to God as a debt they owed. (See Malachi 3:8–9.)

Jesus came to pay the debt that man could not fully pay because of sin. He paid it when He went to the Cross for you and me. There, He restored giving to its original purpose.

Remember, in Genesis 8:22, seed time came first... then harvest time followed.

In the time of the prophets of old, this law of giving first was practiced many times, such as what the prophet Elijah did with the hungry widow of Zarephath in 1 Kings 17. But when Israel became a nation, the people were taught God's ownership of them. First, through the dedication of the firstborn son to God, and then every seventh year, all the land was to lay idle... and the fiftieth year was to be a Year of Jubilee, when all the land in Israel which had been sold was to be restored to the original owners. All slaves were freed… and all debts cancelled. It was God's way of teaching them His ownership of them.

But Israel robbed God of the tithe, and of all the other things representing His ownership. It became a burden greater than they could bear. So, in God's mercy and according to His plan, He sowed His Son, Jesus, the Seed of David, to pay the full price of redemption and resurrection (our spiritual seed time and harvest). As a result, no longer was our giving to be a debt owed to God— not something that we would pay—but instead, our giving would become a seed that we could sow.

As a Christian, your giving is not as a debt you owe… but it is instead a seed that you sow.

Jesus Himself fulfilled the old law of tithing by paying the full price on the Cross. The seed that Jesus gave (His life) was multiplied back when God raised Him from the dead.

It takes away the dread of having to pay, of acting from fear and from obligation. So it's not something you owe; it's something you sow. Now, when you sow, you can do it from your whole heart, gladly. The Bible says in 2 Corinthians 9:10 that God loves a cheerful giver.

The Bible also says in Acts 20:35, *"It is more blessed* (productive) *to give than to receive."* That is because only what you give to Him can produce a harvest.

When you face a mountain of need, your seed of faith, planted, can actually move that mountain.

Remember:

Key 1: GOD IS MY SOURCE OF TOTAL SUPPLY.

Key 2: SEEDING FOR YOUR MIRACLE.

You're not under bondage to give to God out of obligation or as a debt owed to Him. But instead, you can become a seed-sower. And as you give, He will multiply it back to you. (See Luke 6:38.) So, you look to Him for the harvest… not to people, banks, properties, or investments. They are just instruments that God may use, but we are to look to Him as our Source.

Now, this is the **Third Miracle Key** of Seed-Faith: *"Therefore I say to you, whatever things you ask when you pray, believe that you receive them, and you will have them"* (Mark 11:24).

When you give... sowing your seed of faith to God, your Source... you are expecting to reap from it. You are to reap the harvest.

Since God is the God of the harvest, He will send the miracle you need as a harvest from the seed you sow (2 Corinthians 9:10). And since He promised to send it, you must expect it. But remember, you are to look to Him, not to people. People are, as I said, instruments. God may use people, but He, God, is your total Source of supply. Sometimes the harvest comes quickly; sometimes it takes a period of time. Why? I don't know. All I know is, if you're planting seed and the harvest has not yet come, don't become weary. The harvest will come in God's timing. He knows the best time.

Galatians 6:9 says, *"And let us not grow weary while doing good, for in due season we shall reap if we do not lose heart."*

When you plant your seed to God, He, as your Source, will set His time and way for you to reap it. That will be your due season. So, don't give up on expecting a miracle... Instead, wait on God for His perfect timing. Your due season will come. Never forget that God cares for you. Expect, expect, expect Him to multiply every seed you sow and to supply all your need.

Now, read these **THREE KEYS** out loud again:

Key 1: MAKE GOD YOUR SOURCE ... PUT HIM FIRST IN YOUR LIFE.

Key 2: GIVE, AND GIVE FIRST... PUT THE SEED OF FAITH IN...THE SEED FOR YOUR MIRACLES.

Key 3: EXPECT A MIRACLE...NOT FROM THOSE YOU HELP OR GIVE TO, BUT FROM GOD... YOUR ETERNAL SOURCE.

Those are the **Three Miracle Keys** to which the Heavenly Father will respond, the keys which open up opportunities for Him to meet your needs, according to His riches in glory by Christ Jesus.

Now, pray this powerful prayer:

Lord, from this hour, I will make a seed-faith covenant with You. I will endeavor with all my heart to practice the Three Miracle Keys and teach them to all those who will allow me to, and I will begin by counting my next gift to God as a seed I sow. In Jesus' name, Amen.

You plant the seed and expect God to move the mountains.

You don't have to beg God…Just sow your seed to Him. Do it joyfully, and believe Him to do the rest.

YOUR GOD GIVEN KEY FOR TODAY:

I will plant my seed and expect God to move my mountains.

[Wednesday]

KEY: *God Is the Multiplier of My Seed Sown.*

I hear from individuals and families every day. They call the Abundant Life Prayer Group, or they write, or contact me on Facebook, or email their prayer request(s). I have made it a matter of urgency for many years to pray over every prayer request…and to do it every day. And what a blessing it is to do it! I believe in prayer with all of my heart, and I also believe that God wants to answer prayers and give us a Better Life in Christ.

I also receive many testimonies of the miracles people are receiving in their lives and families as a result...some who are at life's lowest ebb. The stories of how God has raised them up from near poverty to prosperity are truly amazing.

Angela, from Pennsylvania, told me that she had been in serious debt for four to five years, but through our prayers and her seed-sowing, all the debt has been paid off. Now, friend... that is the beginning of a Better Life!

Alexandra, from New York, said that she attended my service in New York City some years ago and was delivered from a serious drug habit. That was the beginning of her better life. She turned her life completely over to God, even though she didn't have a job or a place to live.

She told me that she began sowing her seeds to God and expecting miracles. Then recently, when I was again in New York City for a Healing Service, Alexandra met me at the door. She said that since I had last talked to her, she had received a great job. It was only part-time at first, but it paid a full-time salary. Now, that is marvelous! Then two other companies hired her, and she is now making over $100,000 a year on part-time hours! She also got a new apartment. Talk about a Better Life!

Alexandra found that something good and big has happened... It's that Better Life that God has for her. She also told me that she is sowing her seed to the Lord on a regular basis now.

Darlene, from Virginia, related that since she began sowing her seed to the Lord through the Oral Roberts Ministries, she has been blessed so outstandingly, she hardly has words to tell her story! Just in the last year, she has had things happen that she had hoped for, but never dreamed would happen.

She got promoted on her job to a position that takes most people several tries and years of job training. But her promotion came with two months of documented job training. She told me she was promoted quickly, making $10,000 more than her last position.

And there was built-in overtime pay, almost double her straight time rate of pay!

But that is not all... A family member offered her a little over twelve acres of land. All she had to do was pay a $267 tax bill and a $26 deed registration, in order to gain full control of a piece of land her grandmother owned. Now, Darlene owns over 20 acres of land that her great-grandfather bought in 1911. She said she always dreamed of it, but never thought it was possible.

Well, when you sow into the work of the Lord and begin to expect Him to multiply it back, dreams really can begin to come true. It happened for Darlene. Not only was it a harvest, but it was God's Better Life coming to her.

The Bible says, God shows no partiality (Acts 10:34). If He will do it for Darlene, He will do it for you. But you have to sow seed toward the miracles you need. Every farmer knows that the only way to get a harvest is to sow a seed. That is the *only* way.

It is just like that with the Lord too. There really is no other way, and believe me, it is the best way to achieve the Better Life you desire.

Now say this:

1. God is the multiplier of my seed sown.
2. I will let these testimonies help me to realize that if miracles happened for other people, they can happen for me.
3. I will keep faith in my Source, who is God.
4. I will allow Him to show me where to sow my seed(s).
5. I will expect Him to meet my every need and give me a Better Life.

YOUR GOD-GIVEN KEY FOR TODAY:

Say it over and over and over:

"God is the multiplier of my seed sown and the provider of a better life."

[Thursday]

KEY: *It Is More Productive to Give than to Receive.*

What did Jesus mean when He said in Acts 20:35, *"It is more blessed to give than to receive?"* In one way, it seems contrary to real life, doesn't it? How can it be better to give than to receive? Aren't you happier when you receive something than when you give something? I am sure many people are…but that is not what the Bible says.

> More blessed to give
>
> means
>
> more productive to give…

Jesus was actually saying that it is more productive to give than to receive, because only what you give to God can be multiplied back to you.

In other words… The greater the sacrifice, the greater the blessing.

When I was a boy, my mother showed me how to plant a garden of vegetables in our backyard. At first I didn't understand. But after she and I harvested the first tomatoes and radishes and onions and other vegetables, I was excited about planting seed again for another harvest.

Little did I realize at that early age, the Lord was teaching me that is it more PRODUCTIVE to give than to receive.

Now, don't think the scripture in Acts 20 is a complete put-down on receiving. Actually, the opposite is true. I still get excited when I give because I know that it will be multiplied back to me bigger than it would be if I didn't sow at all.

My dad used to tell me the true story of a farmer named Art who occasionally attended a little church he once pastored. One night, the church was collecting a special offering to buy a new building, and that farmer saw how joyful my father was when he made his pledge and gift for the new project. Even though it touched the man's heart, he gave nothing.

At 2 am, there was a knock on the door of the home my parents were living in. It was Art.

"Oral," he said, "I saw how joyful you were when you gave tonight, and it got to me. I realized I have not been planting any seed to God. My farm is down. My crops are down, and I have lost a lot of money over the past several years. I am unhappy; my whole family is unhappy."

"Tonight, you reminded me that there is true joy in giving to God. I saw it on your face. I want that same joy. Tonight, the Lord reminded me that it is ...*more blessed to give than to receive* ...so, I brought my offering to you. Here it is. Take it and be blessed." Then he left.

My dad and mother looked at each other and then counted the money. It was exactly seven times what my father had given in the offering that night. My dad told me that the man started coming back to church every Sunday. His farming business began to turn around. His family was restored, and he began to prosper again.

I tell you, it is more blessed ("productive") to give than to receive.

Why? Because... Jesus said so.

As I look back and remember my dad telling me this story, it also reminds me of the many seeds that my wife, Lindsay, and I have sown, and how happy we are at seed-time. Why is that, you say? It is because we know that harvest time is coming.

Now, read this:

It is more productive to give than to receive. For what you receive is not multiplied... only what you give is multiplied.

It is an eternal truth ...and it works.

Just ask yourself, "Is my seed-planting up to date, or have I left it out of the equation?" And if you look at yourself in the mirror of life and ask those questions honestly, the Lord will give you the answer. And then...well...

You will know what to do.

YOUR GOD-GIVEN KEY FOR TODAY:

I am happy when I give, because it is more productive to give than to receive.

[Friday]

KEY: *I Will Have a Seed-Faith Project.*

Would you like to know how your "pockets full of need" can instead be full of blessings from God and running over?

Well, in order to answer that question, I need to take you to the fifth chapter of Luke and tell you a story. Everyone loves a good story...especially one that has a good ending. And this one really does!

Now as I tell it, I want you to put yourself in it. Think of yourself and how this passage of scripture relates to you and what you are going through. For it deals with "pockets full of needs" and how they can be full and running over.

The story begins with Jesus preaching to a large crowd off the shore of the Sea of Galilee. Right in the middle of His message, He stops and sees the pockets full of needs of a single individual. (See Luke 5.)

Jesus saw Simon (later called Peter), a fisherman washing and mending his nets there by the seashore.

Listen to that… Jesus sees us and the condition we are in.

When Jesus saw Peter, He also noticed His empty boat. So, He said to Him, "Lend me your boat."

Why would Jesus ask for the boat? Was it only so that He could stand in it a ways off shore so that the crowd could both see and hear Him? (Water has a natural way of amplifying a person's voice so that it can be heard from a distance.)

Well, surely Jesus was concerned about the crowd, but He was also concerned about the fisherman and his empty boat.

Notice the boat was empty, not full.

Jesus knew that the man and his fishing partners had fished all night and had caught nothing.

So he offered Peter a project. Peter agreed to loan Jesus his boat… Jesus preached from it… and no doubt, did many miracles there.

You know, there is nobody in the world like Jesus to ask for something out of your need and then send it back full and better than you gave it to Him.

"Push Me out a little from the shore," Jesus said.

As Jesus stood in the boat, Peter and the others pushed Him out a little from the shore. Afterwards, Jesus looked at Peter and said, "Now, take your boat back out into the deep waters and let down your net again."

Naturally, Peter didn't understand. After all, they had fished all night and had caught nothing. Now they were washing their nets and putting them away.

I believe there was just something different about Jesus. Maybe it was His manner, or the way He carried Himself, or how He talked. But nevertheless, Peter said, "I will go back out fishing again."

But this time, Jesus was in the boat with him. Peter's discouragement was melting away. There was a light in his eye. I believe he was expecting something to happen…something like he had never experienced before. He was expecting a miracle.

And when he got out into the deep waters of the Sea of Galilee, he and the other fishermen threw the net over. Immediately, they felt something hit the net.

Unlike the previous try, this was big…perhaps bigger than any haul of fish he had ever caught before…a whole school of fish! In fact, there were so many fish that as he began to pull the net into the boat, the boat began to sink. It was a…

Net-Breaking, Boat-Sinking Load!

Suddenly, Peter realized that by listening to Jesus and obeying His word, he had caught "a boat-load of miracles." He fell on his knees and said, "Depart from me, for I am a sinful man."

But Jesus simply said, "Peter, just get up and follow Me, and I'll make you a fisher of men." Or, in other words, "I'll give you a Better Life."

Later, Peter became the number one man among the twelve Apostles that Jesus chose. He not only learned how to plant a seed and receive a mighty harvest, but he was the one who best understood who Jesus was, and told Him so, saying, *"You are the Christ, the Son of the living God"* (Matthew 16:16–18).

Talk about a Better Life! The best was yet to come for Peter. Through that miracle, his needs were met and his faith was inspired.

Remember, Jesus had said to Peter, "Launch out into the deep and let down your nets for a catch." Let's examine what He meant by "the deep."

Most fishermen at that time fished along the shoreline, because the Sea of Galilee was 200 feet below sea level and subject to violent storms without much notice. Their little boats weren't strong enough to withstand those sudden storms and could capsize or even be broken apart by the winds and waves. Thus, they fished close to the shore.

The problem was, only the small fish were near the shore. The big fish were out in the deep water.

Many people today want a better life, but they are not willing to go the full distance with God in order to receive their miracle. They are too happy playing it safe, so they don't launch out to do all that the Lord has spoken to them.

Jesus was talking to Peter about more than just the deep waters and big fish. He was talking about a Better Life…a life full of miracles. Peter caught a vision of it and obeyed, and wow, what a life-changer it was for him!

Everyone has a certain depth that God wants them to launch out into. Your depth may be different than mine, and my depth may be different from yours. But whatever it is that the Lord has shown you, that is just the right depth… and that depth is where the miracles are. That is the beginning of the Better Life God has for you and me.

Just as Jesus offered Peter the project of loaning Him his boat, the Lord has a project for you—something you can do for His sake and for you to be involved in and to be a part of. It may be in your church or some mission's project He will speak to you about. It may be partnering with the Oral Roberts Ministries or another ministry. But I am telling you, Jesus is calling out to all of us and saying…launch out into the deep and let down your net for a catch.

That is something for you to sow into, not only for you to get your own needs met, but for you to begin to experience the Better Life that I believe God has for you.

You say, "Well, Richard, how do I know my depth? How do I know what God wants me to sow into?"

Those are good questions. Here is where you pray and ask the Holy Spirit to speak to you. And believe me, He will, if you ask Him to. You may hear His audible voice, or He may just fill your head with thoughts that just won't go away, or a deep impression in your heart that makes you feel very peaceful. It will be something that is consistent with the New Testament, but it will probably stretch your faith or pull you out of your comfort zone.

Believe me, if you ask, He will respond. I always just keep praying and asking until He does. I suggest you do the same.

Now, say this:

"I will get involved in a project from the Lord."

Here is what I want you to do:

1. Get yourself a seed-faith project.
2. When you decide what it is to be, focus your thinking on the result you want to see... Get a faith image and begin to imagine it coming to pass.
3. Don't start too big! Find your "depth"... You'll feel it when it's right.
4. Work at your seed-faith project. Keep notes. When you have received the desired results, start another project.

I believe that you will be thrilled as you see this key working. It is the start of God's Better Life for you. Pretty soon, it will become natural.

WEEK 2: SATURDAY

Now write down what you decide upon for your first seed-faith project.

YOUR GOD-GIVEN KEY FOR TODAY:

I will get a seed-faith project.

[Saturday]

KEY: *I Will Plant Seed "Away from Myself" and Learn to Rely on My Source.*

After I gave my heart to Christ in the fall of 1968, I immediately joined my dad's ministry. He and I became almost inseparable. We did practically everything together. As time passed, I learned more and more about the calling God had placed on *my* life.

My dad became more than just my father… He became my spiritual mentor. Where he went, I went. What he did, I did. What he said, I said.

One day he said to me, "Son, follow me, as I follow Christ." Then he explained what the Apostle Paul meant, when in the Bible, he said those same words. Dad said, "Richard, as long as you can look over my shoulder and see Jesus, then follow me." I understood what he meant. I wasn't just following my dad; I was following after the Lord.

Of course, I was involved in every part of our ministry…television, radio, magazines, letters, building projects…just about everything.

My dad was the kind of man who worked all the time, seven days a week, especially from about 10 AM to 3 PM. Those were his most productive hours.

Often on Saturday morning around 9:30, I would get a phone call from him. "Can you come over for a while?" he would say.

"Sure," I would always respond. Those were great mentoring sessions. Over discussions, we would touch on a lot of subjects on those Saturdays.

One Saturday morning, we were setting on my father's couch in the little den where he loved to study and write his books, when the phone rang.

It was his friend, Charlie. Charlie was a car dealer who had befriended my dad some years earlier. He had always done well with his car dealership.

But this morning, something was wrong. "Oral?" Charlie said.

"Yes, Charlie? What's wrong?"

"I have had a bad downturn in my business. It has been getting worse for months. Oral, it looks like I could lose the dealership and my business. Cars are just not selling like they used to. It's dried up, Oral. What am I going to do? Everything I have is tied up in my business. What am I going to do? My wife...my children...my grandchildren...what are they going to do? This business was supposed to be the future for my family after I retire." Again he said, "Oral, what am I going to do?"

I sat nearby, close enough to my dad to be able to hear most of the conversation.

My dad smiled at me. Then he asked his friend, "Charlie, have you been sowing any seed to the Lord?"

"You mean offerings?" Charlie replied. "Oral, how can I give anything to God? Didn't you just hear what I told you? I am nearly broke. The dealership is almost bankrupt. It looks like I am going to lose everything. What do you mean, 'Have I given anything to God?' I don't have anything to give to Him."

"Well, Charlie, that may be part of the problem. You are a Christian, aren't you?"

"Oral, you know I am. I go to church every Sunday with my wife."

"Charlie, have you been sowing to God? Have you been giving away from yourself?" (My dad used that expression, "giving away from yourself," to express sowing seed to God and others.)

"Oral, he said, "I just told you. I don't have anything to give to God." Then his voice dropped and he said, "I haven't given anything to the Lord in a long time."

"Charlie, you have got to begin to give to the Lord again. That is your answer."

"Well, Oral, I have a rainy-day account. There's not much in it now, but I will give it all. Who should I give it to?"

"Charlie," my dad said, "you sow it where you feel God is leading you."

"Well, can I sow it into your ministry?"

"Yes, Charlie, if that is what you feel in your heart," my dad replied.

Charlie immediately wrote out a check and brought it over. My dad and I prayed over it and put it to work in our ministry.

Several weeks passed, and on another Saturday morning I got a call from my dad. "Richard, can you come over for a few hours?"

"Sure, dad," I said. I will be there in a little while."

When I got to his house, and as we immediately began talking about the events of the week and our plans for the next week, the phone rang. It was Charlie. But this time, there was no panic in his voice. I leaned over to listen while my dad held the phone a little away from his ear so I could hear.

"Oral?"

"Yes, Charlie?"

"I've got great news! Remember a couple weeks ago, when I began sowing to God and away from myself?"

"Yes, Charlie. I remember."

"Funny thing happened a few days later, Oral."

"What's that, Charlie?"

"Out of the blue, for no apparent reason, cars started selling. Oral, people are all over my lot buying cars. I am not going to go under! I am not going to lose my dealership!"

Wow! After Charlie hung up, my dad and I just looked at each other and smiled.

Maybe you have faced a situation in the past that is similar to what Charlie faced…or maybe you are facing that kind of loss or setback right now. Well, there is something you CAN DO … and you can start today. You can begin to sow to the Lord and "give away from yourself."

Here are two reasons to begin doing it:

1. God is the Source of your total supply.
2. When you give away from yourself, you are actually giving directly to God…and He is at the point of your need—right where you need Him the most.

Now, if you will begin to do this and to do it on a regular basis, then I believe God will multiply the seed back to you, just like He did for my dad's friend, Charlie.

Intellectually, it may be hard to understand, so you will have to listen to your spirit, deep down inside of you. I am talking about your inner-self, way down inside of you where your spirit lives… where the Holy Spirit is in residence in you… For He can make it really clear to your heart and mind.

I can still hear Charlie's voice on the phone… "Oral, I have had a miracle; I am not going to close my business."

That's what I am believing for you… a miracle for whatever you may be facing.

Remember, above all, you've got to begin to sow.

God is with you.

God is working to meet your need as you plant your seed.

God is individualizing you.

God is individualizing your needs.

God is individualizing His supply for your needs.

Giving to God away from yourself, away from your need, is the best way I know to receive a miracle answer from God… and that's a Better Life!

YOUR GOD-GIVEN KEY FOR TODAY:

Say it again:

"I will sow unto the Lord away from myself, and learn to rely on Him as my source for a better life."

WEEK 2 RECAP

- **Sunday:** God's Way Will Be My Way.
- **Monday:** God Is My Source.
- **Tuesday:** I Will Plant My Seed and God Will Move the Mountain.
- **Wednesday:** God Is the Multiplier of My Seed Sown.
- **Thursday:** It Is More Productive to Give than to Receive.
- **Friday:** I Will Have a Seed-Faith Project.
- **Saturday:** I Will Plant Seed "Away from Myself" and Learn to Rely on My Source.

WEEK 3

[Sunday]

KEY: *God Is My Source of Total Supply, Even When They Say It Will Never Happen.*

Have you ever faced a situation when you had a need and like a super charger on your faith, suddenly you could believe God for something like never before?

I have had experiences like this many times. And in those times, I have had people do their best to rain on my parade and tell me that what I was believing for would never happen.

Now, it is easy to get down on people, especially when the negativity is so strong and they just want to get into an argument with you over what you are believing for. I remember the time when our ministry desperately needed to sell a piece of property. We were facing a real need, and the sale of the property would solve the problem. It would allow me to pay off the loan to the bank completely.

I knew the Lord was going to help me with the sale. I just knew it. Then while I was praying, the Lord spoke to my heart and told me the exact amount the property would sell for.

Now, the problem was, that price was much higher than the appraisal value of both the land and the building, yet I knew God had spoken that large number in my heart. It made no sense in the natural.

I said to the Lord, "I want what You want, and if You say that is the price, then I will believe Your word, and I won't take a penny less."

Several weeks passed, and then I got a call from an interested buyer. Their group came out and toured the property. Then they made a firm offer. Now it was a good offer, right in line with the appraisal, but I said, "No, your offer is too low."

When my banker heard what I had done, he came out to my office. "This is a good offer," he said. "You really need to pay off the loan to the bank. I am advising you to sell now at this price."

Again, I said, "No." Then I told him that God had given me a higher number and that I wouldn't sell for less than that.

He laughed at me. He told me it was crazy. He thought the offer was a good one and that I would not ever get a higher one. He left my office disgusted at me...not understanding anything I had said to him. Actually, he came very near to calling *me* crazy.

A month passed, and I got another offer. It was a much better, considerably higher offer than before.

Once again, my banker came out to see me. "You have made your point," he said. "The offer is good. It is very good. It is much higher than I thought possible. And you should take it today."

"But I have a problem," I replied. "The Lord told me to wait for an even higher amount, and I am not to sell until I get it."

This time, my banker got angry with me. He spoke in very sharp words and told me I was making a huge mistake. He also said the bank fully expected me to reconsider and take this offer now. I just said, "No, I won't sell until the offer is what God spoke in my heart." The meeting didn't end up very friendly.

A few more weeks passed...then a month, then another few weeks passed.

Then, I got a phone call with a third offer. It was for exactly the amount the Lord had spoken in my heart...way above what the world and the appraisal said the property was worth.

I remember the tears that filled my eyes as I began to thank the Lord for doing exactly what He said He would do. I accepted the offer.

Soon, word of the pending sale reached the banker. He came over to my office again, but this time he had a very contrite look on his face. He didn't say anything at first. Finally, he said, "Mr. Roberts, I have come here today with my hat in my hand. I am just amazed. I have never seen anything like this in my life." Then he said, "I just didn't believe…"

Before he could finish his statement, I interrupted him and said, "Yes sir, you are correct. YOU DIDN'T BELIEVE. BUT I DID. I believed God, and He did exactly what He said He would do."

The banker sat there with a strange look on his face, and I just smiled.

The contract was signed; the sale closed. We paid off the bank, and that banker got a crash course in FAITH 101.

Now, perhaps you need a crash course in FAITH 101, or maybe you just need a refresher course. Perhaps you're facing a situation right now where you feel a deep impression in your heart that God wants you to do a certain thing, but you feel that it won't be understood… that some might question you or even think you are out of your mind.

Believe me, I know how you feel. In fact, I believe all Christians face this feeling at times. The disciples must have thought Peter was pretty strange when he asked Jesus to let him walk on water. But when Peter stepped out of the boat, the laughing stopped.

And in your situation, yes, some people may laugh a while. They may tell you that you have missed it…that you didn't really hear a word from God.

But listen to me. You know the voice of the Lord, don't you? And since you do, if He has spoken something into your heart, don't let anyone talk you out of it.

> Hold on to that word.

Let me say it again:

> Hold on to that word.

Don't let it go, just keep believing. It took awhile for God's word to be fulfilled and for my property to sell. But it was well worth the wait. God had the last word. He showed Himself alive and full of power in my circumstance, speaking and keeping what He spoke.

Now, listening to and obeying the voice of God is what I am talking about…and it's part of the Better Life that I want you to have, in Him.

Let me say it again: God is the Source of your total supply… Not your bank, not your job, not your ministry, not your family, not your government…GOD IS YOUR SOURCE.

Let this thought get deep down in your spirit. God, as your Source of total supply, can become a constant in your life… a lifestyle that you can depend on… God's faithfulness to His Word. You don't have to constantly make a hurried prayer when you find yourself in crisis. You can expect Him to be at work in your life every day. Go ahead… Dare to take God at His Word… *And my God shall supply all your need according to His riches in glory by Christ Jesus* (Philippians 4:19). In doing this, you'll never forget this principle or neglect to apply it.

Your God Given Key for Today:

God is your Source… and He will never let you down.

[Monday]

KEY: *I Will Not Limit God.*

My mother, Evelyn (Lutman) Roberts, was of German origin. My dad's family, the Roberts, were a mixture of Welsh (Roberts is a Welsh name), and Native American Indian—Cherokee and Choctaw.

My dad and mother met at a summer camp meeting in eastern Oklahoma where they were both playing instruments in the camp-meeting orchestra. My dad said to her, "Is my hair combed?"

"Yes it is," my mother replied. She went back to her room that night and wrote in her diary, "Tonight, I met the man I will marry."

At that time, my dad was living in Oklahoma and had been healed from tuberculosis just a few years earlier. My mother was living in south Texas and was teaching school.

My dad grew up in Pontotoc County, around Ada, in southeast Oklahoma in an area that was known as Little Dixie.

Some of my dad's family farmed, including his dad, my grandfather, Papa Roberts, who also pastored a church there. Others in the family discovered oil on their land and received royalties from it.

One of my uncles, my Great Uncle Willis, was a peach farmer. He grew the most delicious Elberta peaches.

Every year, it seemed like he would win the blue ribbon for the best peaches at the county fair. Then something happened that changed everything. My granddad and my dad told me the story of Uncle Willis' peaches over and over again as I was growing up, and I'll never forget the faith lesson in it.

One year, Uncle Willis' peaches were not as good. The next year, they were even worse. They looked all shriveled up and dried out.

Something bad was happening to the prize peaches, and he did not know how to fix it. No storm ruined the crop. Insects had not done it. He said, "I did it."

You see, as long as the fruit came in each year, Uncle Willis was satisfied to leave the trees alone. The trees bore the fruit, and he thought his source of supply was the fruit. The peaches fed the family. He sold thousands of bushels and used the money to live. The fruit from the orchard became everything to him. It was his business. He depended upon it.

Now, everything had turned bad. After having done everything he knew to do, he called on the county agriculture inspector.

The inspector took one look at that peach orchard and knew exactly what the problem was. He said, "Mr. Roberts, you have made a critical error. You paid attention to the fruit, instead of the trees. You are going to have to take out these trees and plant a new orchard." Then he added, "Sir, if you will take care of the trees, the trees will take care of the fruit."

What a statement…*If you will take care of the trees, the trees will take care of the fruit*. And so, my great uncle dug up those old trees and started over, having learned the lesson of a lifetime.

As I have grown older, that story means more and more to me.

My point in telling you this story is to reiterate that:

GOD IS YOUR SOURCE. And if you will take care of God by doing what He has said to you, then He will take care of you and give you a Better Life. Yes, you deserve a better life, but you will never get it just because you deserve it. You get it by obeying God…by doing what His Word says…and by looking to Him as the Source of your total supply. Everything has a source. Nothing comes from nothing.

Some years ago, I conducted a healing crusade in Kampala, Uganda, in Eastern Africa. I had been invited to speak by then President Yoweri Museveni, who really paved the way for the crusade. He paid for my hotel and eventually gave us the stadium for the services. He also assigned security guards to me and gave me one of his own vehicles to ride in.

Years before, the President and his close friend, Baliki Kyria, were imprisoned by the ruthless and violent dictator, Idi Amin. When they were finally released from prison, they wanted to make a difference and help rebuild their nation after all the atrocities that had been committed there.

It was decided that Museveni would run for President of Uganda, and if he won, Mr. Kyria would be his number one advisor.

WEEK 3: MONDAY

They were both strong Christians. As it happened, Museveni won the election and became the leader of the nation.

When I went there, the President, whom I had met the year before in Washington, D.C., assigned Mr. Kyria to be with me and make smooth the way of the crusade.

Kyria himself was an ordained minister. He had loved my dad, and so he loved me. He never missed a service and marveled at all the healings, and the thousands who prayed to receive Christ as Savior and Lord, as I ministered during that week.

On the morning of the last day there, Mr. Kyria said to me, "Would you like to see the source of the Nile River?"

Being a student of geography, I knew that the mighty Nile River's headwaters were in East Africa and that the river, unlike most rivers, flowed from South to North. I said I would love to see it.

We got in the presidential limousine and drove about twenty-five miles outside of town. Suddenly, there it was in front of us... the beginning of a mighty river. It looked so small, yet my experiences in life told me that most big things start out small. Such was the case with the Nile.

Then Mr. Kyria asked me a question. "Brother Roberts, what do you suppose would happen if the source of this river, Lake Victoria, stopped feeding water into the beginning of the river?" Even before I could reply, he answered his own question. He said, "I will tell you what would happen... Millions of people along this river, in nations one after another, would be affected. No doubt many would even die, because this river is the source of life, from here in Uganda all the way up through central and northern Africa, right up to the Mediterranean Sea."

As I took in his words, I stood there in awe, imagining how small it was where I stood, and how mighty it would become, as it flowed to the north.

And you see, it is just like that with God. Everything has its own source... a foundation or starting place.

God is the Source of your total supply.

Not man—not things—not institutions.

God is

your

Source.

Without God in your life...without His concern for you...without His power to meet your needs...without His personal presence with you and in you, you are not a whole human being. Something is missing. There is a void... a gap that nothing else can fill.

Without God as your Source, life is reduced to darkness, emptiness, failure, futility, fear, panic, loss of faith to believe, and perhaps, even loss of the will to live.

With God as your Source, you can do all things through Christ who strengthens you (Philippians 4:13). You can do all things, and nothing shall be impossible unto you (Mark 9:23).

So, what's the bottom line? People may let you down... Things may turn sour. It may look like you will never get out of the hole you are in. But God is still God. And as you put your trust in Him, believing and acting on His Word—as you sow your seeds of faith—He is faithful to watch over and perform what He has promised. And that is the beginning of a Better Life.

YOUR GOD-GIVEN KEY FOR TODAY:

People may let you down... circumstances may change and let you down... but God is your Source, and He will never let you down.

[Tuesday]

KEY: *I Am Not a Loser…I Am a Winner.*

There are two ways you can look at yourself. You can see yourself as a loser, or you can see yourself as a winner.

It doesn't matter what somebody else says or what the circumstances say. You are a winner because God says you are. He made you in His image. He sent His only begotten Son for your salvation, because He loves you.

When the devil looks at you, he sees the image of God, and it just infuriates him to no end. He wants your position, because he lost his when he and one-third of the angels were tossed out of heaven.

Believe me, it's not you who is the target of his wrath, it's God in you. The Bible says that the devil will ultimately be thrown into the bottomless pit, while believers will go to heaven to live with the Lord for all eternity. (See Revelation chapter 20.)

That's Not a Losing Position.

So, stop saying negative things about yourself; stop putting yourself down.

Say instead:

I am the righteousness of Christ Jesus (2 Corinthians 5:21).

I was made only a little lower than the angels (Hebrews 2:7).

I can do all things through Christ who strengthens me (Philippians 4:13).

Greater is He that is in me than he that is in the world (1 John 4:4).

Don't ask, "Why has this happened to me?" Instead, ask, "Am I doing all that God has told me to do? Am I giving as a seed that I plant? Have I made God my Source? Am I expecting miracles?"

Don't dwell on negativity.

Dwell on the positive.

Whatever things are true, whatever things are noble, whatever things are just, whatever things are pure, whatever things are lovely, whatever things are of good report, if there is any virtue and if there is anything praiseworthy—meditate on these things (Philippians 4:8). Set your mind and your heart on the Better Life God has for you.

Yes, He has a better life planned for you, and it is a good plan. (See Jeremiah 29:11.)

YOUR GOD-GIVEN KEY FOR TODAY:

I am a winner…and God is causing me to triumph in all things.

[Wednesday]

KEY: *I Really Know God Will Help Me.*

In John 10:10, Jesus said, "I've come that you might have life." Now, that's the real "Better Life" that I am talking about.

This concept is much different from what the world usually considers to be coming from God. For instance, in many contracts, a phrase like… "Not responsible for acts of God, such as earthquakes, floods, lightning strikes, hail, tornadoes, hurricanes, etc." is routinely used.

Not so with Jesus. "I have come," He declares, "so you might have life, and so you might have it more abundantly."

WEEK 3: WEDNESDAY

When His own disciples wanted to incite a riot and have a certain city burned to the ground, Jesus replied, *"For the Son of Man did not come to destroy men's lives but to save them"* (Luke 9:56).

The Bible says, *"Every good gift and every perfect gift is from above, and comes down from the Father of lights, with whom there is no variation or shadow of turning"* (James 1:17).

And to us as His children, He says in 3 John 2, *"Beloved, I pray that you may prosper in all things and be in health, just as your soul prospers."*

The father of the Prodigal Son said to the elder brother (who was angry because the father had received the wayward brother back, and gave him new clothes, a ring, and a feast with his friends), "Son, all that I have is yours."

But the elder brother didn't really know his own father's nature. He had to be reminded that all his father possessed was his, anytime he asked for it. (See Luke 15:31.)

Jesus demonstrated the principles of a Better Life to everyone He came into contact with. He thought in terms of their needs being met, their sicknesses being healed, things they had been denied being restored to them, torments they had brought on themselves being relieved, and the curse of sin over them being removed.

He came in the form of an answer to their needs. In other words, He met people at the point of their need. He looked on a need differently than we often do. Many today encounter a need and automatically become negative. Often, they say, "Why? Why has this happened to me? What have I done to deserve it?" But Jesus looked on a need in the most positive way. To Him…

A need exists to be met.

To Jesus, a need in your life is not something to discourage you and make you negative. It is, instead, a legitimate claim you have upon His limitless resources to be met IN FULL. And you can claim that supply according to Philippians 4:19, which says, *"And my God shall supply all your need according to His riches in glory by Christ Jesus."*

In other words, the moment your need faces you, God"s "shall supply promise" begins to go into effect.

This is something you really need to know deep down in your spirit and something you can get positive about. No need you face, or ever will face, should intimidate or bully you.

If Jesus is first in your life and you are giving to Him, then you are connected to Him. You're plugged in… and you have the right to a Better Life… a life that is abundant.

God will answer.

You should be expecting Him to answer. What a difference this will make in your attitude.

Say this scripture over and over again to yourself until you feel it deep down inside:

And my God shall supply all your (MY) *need according to His riches in glory by Christ Jesus* (Philippians 4:19).

All! All! All!

YOUR GOD-GIVEN KEY FOR TODAY:

I really, truly, deep-down-in-my-heart, believe that God wants to help me and give me a better life.

[Thursday]

KEY: *Jesus Is a "Right Now" Jesus… Right at the Point of My Need.*

As I read the Bible and study the life and ministry of Jesus, I have seen how He:

WEEK 3: THURSDAY

- Cared for people—having compassion on them and healing them.
- Came in the likeness of man and in the likeness of God — Son of God, Son of man.
- Came to show us what God is like… that He's for us and not against us.
- Came to deliver and heal people… to set them free and give them an abundant life… *a Better Life.*

I saw that He's the same yesterday, today, and forever, and what He did in Bible days, He's still doing in our day.

In fact, He is right in the middle of this generation and He wants to be the Source of your total supply.

He sat where we sit. He feels what we feel. He is at the point of need in each human being.

Well, if all I just said is really true, and I believe it is, then why aren't we more like Jesus? Why aren't we Christians bringing healing to a sick and suffering world? Why aren't we more concerned about the total man… his mind, body, and soul… all of his needs, as well as his future in eternity?

Why aren't we witnesses of what Jesus has done and will do… what He's waiting to do in the lives of others? Good questions, aren't they?

As I studied the life, teachings, and ministry of Jesus, I saw that everyone is sick in some way, and I saw the sickness was really disharmony.

If something is wrong in the soul, to that extent, the person is sick.

If something is wrong in the mind, then to that extent, the person is sick.

If something is wrong in the body, to that extent, the person is sick.

If something is wrong in a family member, a person is often thrown out of rhythm and balance, and to that extent, the person is sick.

If something is wrong financially, to that extent, the person is sick. If something is wrong in any way in any part of our existence, to that extent, we are sick.

The good news is, Jesus is in the world to touch people at the point of their need.

And it's the reason that even at a young age, I knew I would someday be in the healing ministry. Even during my teenage years when I rebelled against my parents and ran away from God, still I knew that someday I would pray for the sick and see great miracles.

After I gave my life to Christ at age nineteen, and while enjoying being a part of my dad's ministry, I got as close to healing as I could... working with my dad, laying hands on people and praying for them, and studying the scriptures.

Then in 1977, a specific word of prophecy was given over me... a word that changed my life forever. That word confirmed the future ministry I knew I'd be doing and what I was called to do. But I still had to prepare.

It wasn't until 1980 that Lindsay and I felt the time was right, and we began to actively seek the Holy Spirit for a healing ministry.

Together, we got hold of Mark 11:24, where the Bible says, *"Whatever things you ask when you pray, believe that you receive them, and you will have them."* Our desire was for an active healing ministry, with real miracles and healings... not something we just talked about, but actually saw happening on a daily basis... literally.

I knew I couldn't get away from it.

It burned in me like a fire.

It blew through me like a wind.

It pounded me like a hammer.

It roared in my head day and night.

I couldn't get away from it.

WEEK 3: THURSDAY

Lindsay and I continued to pray and seek God. Then one day, I was preaching, and I heard myself say, "Lord, heal that man's big toe." I didn't know what prompted me to say it, but I said it... And it shocked me!

Lindsay said to me after the service was over, "Richard, that's the beginning of the healing ministry you've dreamed of."

I said, "A toe?"

"Yes," she said, "And don't despise a small beginning."

I knew what she meant.

Just a month or two later, miracles began to break out in every service where I preached. There was an operation of the word of knowledge and the laying on of hands (1 Corinthians 12), just like the Bible says. And those same miracles are still happening every day in my ministry. I'm talking about people being healed of cancer, heart disease, blood pressure and blood sugar problems, loss of hearing, cataracts, arthritis, you name it. I've seen AIDS completely healed and had it confirmed by doctors. I've witnessed toes growing back after they have been amputated. I've seen people, once crippled, restored, walking, even running.

I've seen just about every kind of healing you can imagine.

At this writing, in just the last 20 years or so, the Oral Roberts Ministries has had over 150,000 healing testimonies reported, and that doesn't count the miracles that have happened to people who have not told us about them.

I tell you, Jesus hasn't changed. He's the same yesterday, today, and forever. And if He ever healed in Bible days, then He's still healing today.

Listen, with all the great doctors and all the modern hospitals and clinics ... with all the discoveries of new medicines for treating diseases...it seems that people are sicker than ever.

So, if ever there was a time for the healing ministry... it is now.

I constantly feel the Lord's anointing to pray over people for their healing. In fact, I feel led to pray over *You* right now. Just lay your hand on yourself as I pray:

Father, I come to You, not in my name or in my strength, but in the name of Jesus, Your Son, and in His power. In that Name, I now take authority over sickness and every disease. I say to the devil, "You stop it. That's enough. I rebuke you. Take your hands off of God's property!"

My dear friend, I pray for God to touch and heal you now in every area of your life... and I'm not coming out of this prayer of agreement until the miracle comes. In Jesus' mighty name, I pray. Amen.

Wow! I really felt the power of that prayer, and I encourage you to be expecting miracles in your life.

Believe me, the power of God is real today. You have faith. You were born with it. God gave it to you (Romans 12:3). Now release it to Him, believing, and I join you by adding my faith to yours.

Now, that's the call of God upon my life and ministry. I am so honored to be in the healing ministry. More than anything, I want you well. I want you to have a Better Life in Christ.

Remember, God is at the point of your need right where you need Him the most.

God is in the now, or He's never been.

God is here, or He's nowhere.

God loves you, or He doesn't love anyone.

God is concerned about your existence, or He's never been concerned about the existence of anyone.

YOUR GOD-GIVEN KEY FOR TODAY:

Jesus is a "right now Jesus"... always at the point of your need and where you need Him the most.

Say this out loud: *"Jesus is right at the point of my need."*

[Friday]

KEY: *When I Have Done All I Can Do, Then I Must Leave It in God's Hands.*

Nowhere is there a greater need for the healing of relationships today than in homes. You can probably count on your fingers the members of families in our country who haven't faced problems between parents and children, both young and grown ... and minister's families are no exception. The day I said to my dad, "Get off my back" was a terrible day... yet the beginning of a great relationship between us.

You may say, "What do you mean by terrible, but also great?"

Well, it's a long story. You see, growing up as Oral Roberts' son was both great... and difficult.

Now, don't misunderstand... I loved my dad. When I was young, we were almost inseparable. We did nearly everything together.

But having him as my dad was rough on me... especially at school. I was the butt end of all of the Oral Roberts jokes and criticisms. Also, all that I went through took its toll on me.

By the time I was fourteen, I was singing a great deal in school choirs, plays, and musical productions.

When I reached high school, I was playing the guitar and singing lead in a rock-and-roll band and traveling around our city and state, playing concerts and dances. I was invited to attend the number one music camp in the world, the famed Interlochen National Music Camp in Northern Michigan. Only the cream of the crop of young musicians and singers were selected to get in. I got in because I auditioned for the founder, Joseph Maddy.

Naturally, my dad wanted me to use my singing talent for the Lord in his ministry, but I wasn't really interested in that, because I wanted to make my own mark singing. I realized, while I was at Interlochen, that I could make a living doing it.

College time came, and I went away to a state university outside of Oklahoma because I wanted to pursue my singing career. Soon, I was performing in clubs in Kansas City and singing every chance I got... and making good money doing it.

I worked for the summer at the Kansas City Starlight Theater, where I performed every night for nearly three months. Then, I was offered a contract at the Sahara Hotel in Las Vegas, to sing in their lounges, and I was really considering it.

I hadn't been home for months, so I decided to take a break and visit the family. Almost immediately, my dad wanted me to play golf with him. I had been a junior champion at a young age, and loved to play. Golf was something my dad and I had in common.

Driving to the golf course was like old times... No pressure... No questions... Just a son and a father out for a relaxing afternoon... That is, until the sixth hole, when my dad started talking to me about my relationship (or in this case non-relationship) with the Lord, and the talent I had for singing.

Suddenly, a deep anger and resentment rose up and came flying out of my mouth. "Get off my back, Dad, and get the hell out of my life!" I shouted.

We both just stood there on the green for a moment. Then he said to me, "Son, that's what I'm trying to do... get the hell out of your life." It sounds funny now, but it sure wasn't funny then.

Our golf game ended abruptly right there. I said, "Let's go home."

But when we got in the car, my dad surprised me. He looked me straight in the eye and said, "Richard, I'll never mention God or singing to you again unless you ask me to."

I said, "That's fine."

There it was. That was my passport to freedom. My dad would actually leave me alone and not pressure me to be a Christian and to sing for his ministry. I could go my way now... Or could I?

My dad had done everything he could in the natural. Now, he was turning me over to God and giving me into His hands. And my friend, when you've done all you can do, that's when you surrender it (whatever it is) to God, and leave it in His hands.

When my dad turned me over to God and took his hands off the situation, he set something spiritual into motion in my life. Almost immediately, the Lord Himself started dealing with me. I began dreaming that I was in the ministry. Then I got sick and was hospitalized at the University of Kansas Medical Center. After diagnostic tests, I was scheduled for surgery the next morning.

That night, I lay in the hospital ward with several other young men. Right there, I made a vow. "God," I said, "if you will heal me and cancel this surgery, I'll commit my life and my talent to You."

I don't really know how to describe what I felt, except to say there was a rush of energy that went through my body. I knew I had been touched and healed by God.

The next morning, after the doctors re-examined me, they canceled the surgery and released me from the hospital. But I quickly forgot my vow.

Another year went by, and during that year, for some strange reason, I felt led to change schools and come home to attend Oral Roberts University. That was something I said I would never, ever do. But I did. My dad's plan of letting me go and turning me over to God was working.

Suddenly, I was hanging out with a different crowd than before. They were young people who really loved God and cared for me. They were very genuine and seemed to know that there was a special call of God on my life, even though I had not accepted it.

That January, I went on a concert tour with a university group. I both sang and played in the band. While performing in Chicago, I got sick again. I lost my voice and was burning up with fever. When I got back home, I could hardly stand up, because I was so ill.

I managed to drive to my parents' home. My mother took one look at me, and immediately put me to bed. To bed... in my old bed. It had been a long time since I had been in that old bed... It felt like home, and it was.

My mother told me that my dad was out of town preaching, but he would be back home the next day and would lay his hands on me and pray.

Well, to me, that meant healing... And then I could go back to *my* plan.

While waiting for him to come home, I was a captive audience for my mother. She told me that I would never be fulfilled without a personal relationship with God.

When my dad arrived home, he came into my bedroom. As he began to lay hands on me in prayer he said, "Son, I had no idea."

I said to him, "What do you mean, Dad?"

He said, "I had no idea the call of God to a healing ministry was on your life." Then he began to prophesy.

He said, "I see you standing before presidents, prime ministers, kings and queens. I see you before huge crowds, preaching and praying for the sick and having great healings. I see you on television. I see you having twice the number of miracles that I have had."

WOW! WOW! WOW!

The tears flowed from my eyes as he prayed for me. I was immediately healed. The fever left. My voice came back. I rolled out of bed, got on my knees, and gave my heart to the Lord.

Wow! What a day that was. My dad had taken his hands off me and had given me to God. And God had turned my life around. Dad and I hugged each other. I asked him if I could be a part of his ministry.

He said, "Yes, you can." And I stood by his side for more than 40 years in ministry, all because he let go, *and let God.*

It hasn't always been easy. Sometimes, it's been very rough. Oftentimes, the road has been bumpy. But God set my feet on a path to a Better Life than I knew was possible, and I would not trade it for anything.

God is my Source of total supply. I'm His and He's mine ... both now and forever... through thick and through thin.

Perhaps you're facing a similar relationship problem. Why don't you consider trying my dad's method of turning loose and giving that person to God?

It worked in my family, and I'm praying that it will work in yours. Remember now what my dad did with me... He turned me loose and gave me over to God... *and* God did the rest.

YOUR GOD-GIVEN KEY FOR TODAY:

When you've done all you can do in the natural... Turn it over to God and expect a miracle.

Now, that's the beginning of a Better Life.

[Saturday]

KEY: *God Will Work for Me Through My Need.*

Sometimes, there's a feeling that can come into a person's heart when he feels he has it made. And no matter what happens, he thinks he's okay.

He feels so secure in himself that he thinks he can take it easy and just glide along with life.

In Luke 12:16–21, Jesus told a story about a man like this. (I'm not going to print it all out here. Please read the story for yourself.)

Now, here's a man who felt no sense of need. As a matter of fact, he thought that he controlled his own life. He really believed that he would gather and hold on to the things of this world, and with them, satisfy the deepest longing of his soul.

It was in his heart so much that he carried that thought right into death and judgment…and God did indeed judge him. The Lord said to him, *"Fool! This night your soul will be required of you; then whose will those things be which you have provided"* (Luke 12:20)? In other words, the man had spent all his energy on temporary things, rather than what is eternal. He rested his life on things that, in the end, could not save him. Jesus said, *"So is he who lays up treasure for himself, and is not rich toward God"* (Luke 12:21).

Then Jesus spoke a word directly to you and to me for today, in Luke 12:27 and 28: *"Consider the lilies, how they grow: they neither toil nor spin; and yet I say to you, even Solomon in all his glory was not arrayed like one of these. If then God so clothes the grass, which today is in the field and tomorrow is thrown into the oven, how much more will He clothe you, O you of little faith?"*

Some time ago, there was a certain man who applied for employment in our ministry. Believe me, he was well-qualified, and more than that, we needed what he was gifted to do. But when it came down to decision time, he declined our offer.

No, it wasn't over salary or hours or working conditions. It boiled down to the man's faith. You see, he wanted a long-range plan for his career, and working in our ministry would have required him to depend more upon God for his future security. He was more interested and concerned with his own plan and his future employment than bringing something to the table for the good of our ministry or in serving God.

When he turned our offer down, I was secretly glad. I want people with me who, like the disciples, surrounded Jesus as a team, and were willing to take a risk of faith and believe God for their future.

Now, that's not to say that we don't make plans and then work on our plans. No…not at all. I believe in planning, but I plan on depending upon God more than I do plans.

I'm sure the Apostle Paul made plans, but his circumstances were constantly changing. He could make a plan and travel to a certain city to establish a church or visit one he had already established, and end up being beaten and jailed for preaching the message of Christ and His saving, healing, delivering power.

Look at Jesus' disciples. Peter said to Jesus one day, "We have left all and followed You. Therefore what shall we have" (Matthew 19:27)?

Believe me, the most dangerous time in our lives is when we don't use our faith… when we're not trusting God that no matter what, He will see us through.

You see, I know that I have no promise of tomorrow. That's why I live as Jesus said, "One day at a time." That's why I'm ready to meet Him in the twinkling of an eye, but working as if He's not coming for a thousand years.

I've often faced difficult circumstances in this ministry. I watched what my dad went through. Then, I experienced all of that—and more, myself. So many times, I have felt like I had been left high and dry ... almost like being up a creek without a paddle.

Sometimes I've cried out, "God, where are you? Don't you know what I'm going through?"

But then, I hear His still, small voice say to me, "Son, I have heard your prayer. Trust Me that I am working all things together for your good."

I'll tell you plainly... It's a wild ride when you don't know what's coming next. But faith is what you hold onto until you receive what you're praying for to manifest in your life.

Remember, God put you on this earth to till it and to plant faith seeds for Him to use and then multiply back to you to meet your needs. God did not put you here to have everything provided so you could make those things a false god and put your trust in them.

No. God put you here to trust in Him... hour-by-hour and day-by-day.

If you lack ability, that can be a great source of motivation for you to turn to God and call upon Him to help you. (See Proverbs 16:3.)

If you don't have enough money, God's principles of seed time and harvest—sowing and reaping—can be a great source of security to you if you will turn to God and say, "God, I don't have enough money. I'm working as hard as I know how, but I need your help." (See Luke 6:38 and Malachi 3:10.)

Honestly, I don't ever remember God telling me to do something in this ministry when all the money to do it was available. No I usually find myself starting out with nothing and believing God to supply all my needs. Over the years, this approach has become a way of life to me.

Do I like it? No, not always. Would I like to have more of a sense of security? Of course, I would. I'd love to know where all the money is coming from so that I could plan accordingly and not

WEEK 3: SATURDAY

have a moment's stress and worry. Sure! I'd love to start at the top rather than starting everything at point zero.

I want… I want… I want… and on and on and on.

But God's way of living develops strength, and you advance through the stage of having just enough faith to start, to higher levels of faith. The key is to let Him increase your strength, as you use it day-by-day to trust Him.

Really, you get to your goal by reaching down deep inside and pulling up those extra resources of faith, trust, and inner strength out of your spirit…when you hurt and reach and strive and sow that extra seed. It's when you get down to the pain level and begin believing God like never before that you begin to see miracles.

This is the way to a Better Life. And by your faith… your sowing and your obedience to God… I believe you will reach it too.

If I've learned anything, anything at all in this ministry, it is to TRUST in God and make Him the Source of my total supply. Anything else will ultimately fail you.

You must learn to trust in God … your One True Source. Learn to press your way through.

To reach your goal of a Better Life in Christ:

> Pull up from your inner resources.
>
> Plant your seeds of faith…
>
> and keep on planting.

Now, ask yourself this question: Am I depending on things, or am I trusting in God, my Source?

Write your answer in the lines below:

_____
_____
_____

_____
_____
_____

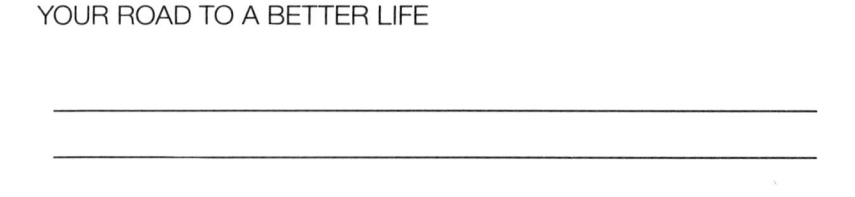

YOUR GOD-GIVEN KEY FOR TODAY:

Say this:

"God will work for me through my need."

WEEK 3 RECAP

- **Sunday:** God Is My Source of Total Supply, Even When They Say It Will Never Happen.
- **Monday:** I Will Not Limit God.
- **Tuesday:** I Am Not a Loser…I Am a Winner.
- **Wednesday:** I Really Know God Will Help Me.
- **Thursday:** Jesus Is a "Right Now" Jesus… Right at the Point of My Need.
- **Friday:** When I Have Done All I Can Do, Then I Must Leave It in God's Hands.
- **Saturday:** God Will Work for Me Through My Need.

WEEK 4

[SUNDAY]

KEY: *I Will Sow for a Desired Result.*

If you're like me, you don't want to read too many news headlines... the murders, the hijackings, the terrorism, the strife, bitterness, hatred... and all the other news that is tearing at the fabric and values of this country.

In many ways, it's a dark hour, yet the light of God has not been snuffed out. But remember that the darkest hour is just before the dawning of a new day.

Let's look back in time for a moment. It was a dark hour in human history... the time when God sowed His best in order to receive a desired result.

For God so loved the world that He gave His only begotten Son, that whoever believes in Him should not perish but have everlasting life
(John 3:16).

For God so loved that He gave. His love became a gift, and giving is what love is. You can't say you have love if you are not giving. Neither can I. Love has to become an act. Really, love isn't love at all until it's given away.

God so loved that He gave... And He gave His what?

HIS ONLY SON.

God gave His best. Listen. GOD GAVE "OFF THE TOP." He gave His best... not off the bottom, but off the top. Let me explain...

When I was a boy, we lived on a farm about 30 minutes outside of town. We had some cattle, a few horses, some chickens, and a couple of milk cows. We also grew a few crops, and there was a three-acre lake that I loved to fish in.

One of the things I loved the most was when they let me milk the cows. I would sit on a stool and do the milking by hand. It was so much fun!

Afterwards, my mother would take the containers of raw milk and put them in the barn's refrigerator. The next morning, we would go down to get it, but I always noticed a change. The cream had risen to the top.

"That's the best part, Son," my mother would say. "The cream is the best, and it always rises to the top."

God didn't send an angel to save us from our sin. He could easily have spared an angel or two, but no, He "spared not." He gave His only Son. He gave off the top. He gave His best, and He did it both for people who would love Him and for others who would never love Him.

And He did it for a purpose... or what I call a desired result.

Now, let's look at John 3:16 one more time:

For God so loved the world that He gave His only begotten Son, that whoever believes in Him should not perish but have everlasting life.

This is God's desired result: God gave so you should not be without life (desired result)... so you shouldn't be without your needs being supplied (desired result), so you would have life—eternal life, abundant life, and everlasting life (desired result).

God so loved; therefore, I must love. Richard Roberts must "so love" that he gives; and he gives off the top. He must give his best.

My dad, Oral Roberts, also grew up on a farm. He learned about sowing his best from his dad, my grandfather, Ellis Roberts. Papa (that's what we called my granddad) was a farmer. Among the crops he grew was corn... and nothing tastes better than fresh Oklahoma corn, which usually is at the height of its season around late June or early July.

WEEK 4: SUNDAY

In those days, they used wagons pulled by mules or horses, and when my dad and his brother Vaden, my uncle, would bring a wagon load of corn back to the barn, Papa would watch as they pitched the corn into the barn.

"Be very careful, boys," he would say. "Take the big ears, the choice ears, and put them in a special pile over here. That's our seed corn. That's what we will plant for next year, so we'll get an even better crop." Then he would say, "Boys, we never eat our seed corn."

Top quality seed corn, when planted, always produces a good harvest, and that's what every farmer wants.

That story is one I heard many times as I was growing up.

It reminds me of God.

He gave His best and He gave first.

He gave of the cream.

He gave off the top and not off of the bottom.

And He gave for a desired result…to get you and me back!

This principle of planting good seed is something that many Christians have never grasped. But those who have understood it have come into a whole new dimension of faith in God's Word, and I believe it will serve them well, as they are the ones who are going to go through this present "darkest hour" and come out on top.

When you *know that you know* that you've given off the top (or given the best of the cream), and your best is exactly what God is going to use to multiply a harvest back to you, then you can get excited about it. You're literally giving for a desired result. You're focusing your giving, and you know God will give back to you. And when you expect miracles, you receive them!

The last few verses of Mark 12 tell about Jesus Christ being in the temple watching the people as they gave. Those who were rich were contributing, as well as those who were not so rich.

The last person Christ saw was a widow who had only a couple of coins to give. The woman got Jesus' attention. He said to His disciples, "She has given more than all the others put together, including those who are rich."

Now, that's obviously a mathematical impossibility. The rich people had given a lot of money out of their surplus. The widow, however, had given only a couple of coins, which seemed like such a small gift in comparison.

But Jesus explained that God computes things differently. He said the rich people gave out of their surplus, while the widow had given out of her want... or her need.

Notice, He did not condemn the rich for the giving of their surplus. He just gave praise to the woman because she was giving her best... off the top.

You see, we are to give out of our need... our want... with a purpose in our hearts. We are to give for God's desired results to come into our lives. Surely, the woman faced needs, yet she gave out of her need. We can learn to do the same, in faith, believing for a Better Life.

You may ask, "Does God ever have a need?" Yes, as a matter of fact, He had a big need... to restore mankind back to Himself. That's why He sent His only begotten Son to pay the debt for our salvation and healing.

This is the Second Miracle Key of Seed-Faith, which I talked about in Week 2: seeding for a better life... for miracles. Remember, in Matthew 17:20 Jesus said, *"I say to you, if you have faith as a mustard seed,* (that is a seed that you would plant, and if you'll plant it in faith) *you will say to this mountain* (this need), *'Move from here to there,' and it will move; and nothing will be impossible for you."*

Now, break that down. Here He says, when you have a problem, which the mountain represents, that's what you start thinking about. I know that's what I usually do.

Jesus is saying, "Don't start with the mountain. Don't start with the problem. Start with planting the seed. Then you speak to that problem... because now, you know the seed you gave will be multiplied back to you."

It will come back to you.

The Bible gives three measures of multiplication: 30, 60 AND 100 TIMES (Matthew 13:8).

GIVE.

Say it out loud: Give. I give first, and then I will receive.

It may feel awkward at first, but say it several times until you get used to saying it.

Get used to saying it, because that's exactly what Jesus did in Luke 6:38 when He said, *"Give, and it will be given to you: good measure, pressed down, shaken together, and running over will be put into your bosom. For with the same measure that you use, it will be measured back to you."* That scripture is a part of my everyday life, and I practice it with my love, my time, my money, my prayers, my good words to people... really, I practice it in all I do. I do it as a seed that I sow... and I sow it first and off the top.

I always give as I'm directed by the Lord. I discuss it with my wife, Lindsay, and we pray together until God confirms to us in our hearts exactly what we're to sow. It's amazing. She and I always come up with the same amount.

Jesus said we are to give off the top... And when we do, we will receive back from Him.

You've got to believe it, then do it. Faith without corresponding action is just not worth much (James 2:17). A good intention is only that until it is acted upon.

If you're like me, you are striving for a better life. That's what this book is all about... *your Better Life*. Well, believe me, sowing and sowing off the top is the beginning of that better life.

YOUR ROAD TO A BETTER LIFE

YOUR GOD-GIVEN KEY FOR TODAY:

I will give off the top for a desired result. I will sow my best to God, then ask Him for His best.

[Monday]

KEY: *God Loves My Cheerful Giving.*

Paul makes a statement that is absolutely stunning. It's so different, and yet if you and I could actually put it into practice... and we do sometimes... we would come into a measure of joy, cheer, and blessing that would show us life worth living.

Paul said, *"So let each one give as he purposes in his heart, not grudgingly or of necessity; for God loves a cheerful giver"* (2 Corinthians 9:7). In other words, Paul is saying, "Let every man give in a way that his heart is in it. Not an outward form of giving and not giving because somebody demands it. Or giving grudgingly because someone talks us into it... saying, 'I'll do it, but I don't really want to.'" When we give reluctantly or for the wrong reason, afterwards, we usually feel like, "Well, I gave, but I really wish I hadn't. I shouldn't have let them talk me into it."

Instead, Paul says, "When you give, give because your heart is in it. Give because you have purposed to do it."

In Luke 8, Jesus told a story of the sower, which illustrates what happens when we give. He said,

> *"A sower went out to sow his seed. And as he sowed, some fell by the wayside; and it was trampled down, and the birds of the air devoured it. Some fell on rock; and as soon as it sprang up, it withered away because it lacked moisture. And some fell among thorns, and the thorns sprang up with*

WEEK 4: MONDAY

it and choked it. But others fell on good ground, sprang up, and yielded a crop a hundredfold" (Luke 8:5–8).

The seed the sower used was good seed, but how and where he sowed it determined the amount of his harvest. First, consider the seed sown by the wayside. This was "uncultivated soil." The sower paid attention only to the seed, not to what he was sowing into, and as a result, the seed bore no fruit. Next, the seed carelessly sown on the rocky soil had no depth, nor could it hold moisture. Thus it could bear no fruit. Next, the seed was carelessly sown among thorns and weeds, which already had their growth, and they smothered the seed. Again, no fruit.

Finally, the sower learned his lesson. He sowed only in soil he had carefully prepared and continued to cultivate. There was a hundredfold harvest.

You may ask, "Richard, are you saying that what I give can actually result in nothing?"

Yes, that's exactly what I'm saying. I've seen it happen. It takes more than giving to get a harvest. It takes giving wisely, with God's direction, into soil that actually yields fruit. It takes giving from your heart, in faith.

When you're preparing to give, why not get a mental picture of a sign in your mind, saying:

Handle with care or handle with prayer.

The spirit or attitude in which you give is the most important part of your giving. Now, if your gift is money, remember that money is an inanimate object. Money is just the medium of exchange for goods and services in this world system. It's neither good nor bad. Money simply reflects the one who is using it. In other words, when you give, it reflects you in your total spirit.

Now, there's nothing you can do with the gift once you've given it, but there is everything you can do with your attitude of expectancy.

You must both plant the seed and cultivate the soil.

The seed is what you give, and the act of giving. The soil is your personal relationship with Christ, and your willingness to act on that relationship, in faith. Without this personal relationship, your giving will profit you very little.

I have learned this lesson over these many years, and there's one thing for certain… If you're going to know the joy of receiving, you must first experience the joy of giving. And the good news is… YOU CAN DO IT!

Here's how to check yourself to see if you are giving in joy.

1. Is my life in right relationship with Christ?

    Yes _____

    No _____

2. If you can check "yes," everything will work for your good as you give joyfully (Romans 8:28, 2 Corinthians 9:7).

3. If you have to check "no," skip ahead to week six and read it until you know Jesus Christ in a personal way.

YOUR GOD-GIVEN KEY FOR TODAY:

Say this out loud: *"God loves my cheerful giving."*

[Tuesday]

KEY: *I Will Give God My Best… Then Ask Him for His Best.*

Lindsay and I were once facing a challenging situation. In the natural, it didn't look like the answer was coming. We had done all we knew to do.

Then Lindsay looked at me and said, "Richard, we need to sow a seed… a big seed… maybe the best seed we've ever sown."

Immediately, I felt in my spirit that she was right. I said to her, "What amount is on your heart?"

She said, "Let's pray and ask God to show us the amount He wants us to sow against this need. Then let's tell each other at the same time what amount God impressed on our hearts."

I said, "Okay." We continued to pray and seek the Lord's will. This was a big need, and we had to have an answer. After a while, I said, "Honey, has God given you an amount to sow?"

"Yes," she said, "How about you?" Has He given you what amount we are to sow?"

"Yes," I replied. We both said the number at the same time. It was exactly the same number. We just looked at each other and laughed. We knew we had heard from God.

So, we planted that seed—and it was a big one! It wasn't long until God brought the answer we needed.

I can't tell you how many times she and I have done this. Each time—I mean every time—we always get the same number from the Lord. That's the way He deals with us. That's how we know exactly how to deal with Him.

I have preached this message all over the world, and afterwards, I always challenge people to sow their best seed to God, then ask Him to give His best back to them.

I have received so many testimonies from people who have put this concept into practice…

A woman from Florida shared her testimony… "Last week, I sowed a seed that was equal to ten percent of my weekly paycheck. I asked you to pray for my family and for our finances. The next week, I received a surprise bonus at work. My boss said they were giving it to me because of the good job I was doing with the company.

The bonus was about 15 times what I had sowed. I am so happy! I'm so happy! God is a good God."

A woman from South Carolina told me she had received so many harvests from the Lord that she is no longer a borrower, but has become a lender.

Then a partner from Wyoming said, "We were in the process of selling our home and purchasing a new one. In the middle of the process, the bank called and said we may be denied. I called the Abundant Life® Prayer Group for prayer, and sowed a seed against the need. Then we began to praise God in advance for the answer.

"The bank called back several days later and said that an error had occurred and the financing package was approved. Then God moved again, and our current home sold in two days... and for a large profit."

Another partner from Alabama told me that she had been sowing seeds into our ministry for some time. The seed was aimed at a $39,000 debt. After sowing many seeds, the debt has been completely eliminated.

We get testimonies like these just about every day. They come from all over the world, and we rejoice because it's true... You just can't out-give God. When you give Him your best, and release your faith, you can expect God to use it and give it back to you in the ways you need it most.

YOUR GOD-GIVEN KEY FOR TODAY:

I will give God my very best, then ask Him for his best.

[Wednesday]

KEY: *You Must Put Something in if You Want to Get Something Out.*

Many people today are like the man in this story, a certain antique dealer who tried to pick up antiques for a fraction of their value so he could sell them at a higher price.

One day, while in another small town, he visited a secondhand store. While looking around, he noticed a cat in the middle of the floor drinking milk from a bowl. Suddenly, he recognized that the bowl was no ordinary bowl, and it was worth a lot of money.

He thought to himself, "This store owner doesn't know how much this bowl is worth. Why, I'll buy it for little or nothing, then sell it for much more in my own shop."

So, he walked up to the man behind the counter and said, "My, that's a beautiful cat. I just love cats. Would you sell me that cat?"

"Sure, mister," the man said. "I'll sell anything in this store. Give me a hundred dollars, and the cat is yours." Realizing the value of the bowl, he quickly paid the store owner one hundred dollars.

As he picked up the cat and stroked its fur, he said to the man, "I noticed he's drinking milk from that old bowl. He's used to it. It's not worth much. I believe I'll just take that bowl with me."

"You put that bowl down," the man said. "That's the best cat seller I've ever had."

Now, that's a funny story, but it's also sad. Here are two men, doing their best to get the better of one another. It reminds me of Jacob and Esau in the Bible. Esau wanted the bowl of soup, and his younger brother, Jacob, wanted the older brother's birthright. Both were hungry in different ways. And by acting on their respective hungers, they hurt their relationship for many years. (See Genesis chapters 25-27.)

We all have to watch constantly to keep from falling into this kind of trap. There seems to be something in many of us that wants to get something for nothing. But this is not the way God works. God says the way to receive is to give. In the natural, it seems backwards... But believe me, it's not.

A wise man said it well: "You must put something in if you want to get something out."

Of course, we all want to be a success... a big success. Everyone wants that, but success is not wishing you had what someone else has and envying them for it. Many want success, but are not willing to work for it and pay the price for it.

I once heard a rich man who was turning 80 years old say, "I am an 80-year overnight success." Yes, we all want to get something out, but are we willing to put something in? If you want a Coca Cola from the vending machine, you better put some coins into it.

If you want something out of life, then you better put your heart into it. And if you want something from God, you better begin sowing to Him in sincerity and with a humble spirit.

Do you remember when Jesus went to a wedding in Cana, in John chapter 2? They ran out of wine, which in those days was not a good way to start off a successful marriage.

When Mary, His mother, found out about it, she told Jesus. He knew that in order to get something out, you must put something in. Or another way to say it is, "You better have some seed in the ground, if you're going to look for a harvest."

Jesus said to the servers, "Take the containers and fill them with water." After they did so, He said, "Now, pour them out." And the water had been turned into the best wine.

Notice, they had to put something in first, before they could pour something out. Jesus wanted them to understand that they had to put something in the containers for Him to work with, so that He could perform a miracle.

But if they had not done what Jesus said... if they had not put water in the pots ... there would not have been anything for Jesus to turn the water into.

Are you getting this? Is this principle getting down in your spirit?

If you've been trying to get something for nothing, I suggest you stop it, and begin sowing first, so that you'll have something for God to bless.

YOUR GOD-GIVEN KEY FOR TODAY:

"I have to put something in, if I want to get something out."

Say it again.

Now, say it one more time.

[Thursday]

KEY: *When One Door Closes, God Will Always Open Another One.*

There's a secret in planting seed with a spirit of thankfulness, even in the face of great loss.

Thankfulness... Yes, I said thankfulness. I know, at times, this may be the hardest word for anybody to accept. When people like you and me are going through a difficult situation, it's easy to become disillusioned. But let me show you a verse from 1 Corinthians 15.

Here, the Apostle Paul was surrounded by death, loss, and suffering, but he looked around and found his moorings. Then he made a statement that's absolutely fabulous for you and me in what we have faced or perhaps are facing even now. Here's what he said: *"But thanks be to God, who gives us the victory through our Lord Jesus Christ"* (1 Corinthians 15:57). Even in difficult situations, God has a path to victory for us...a path to a Better Life. Therefore, your labor (your seeds sown in faith) is not in vain in the Lord.

It's hard to look at a paycheck that's been cut in half and say, "Thanks be to God for the victory." It's not easy to thank God and praise Him when sickness strikes you or strikes a family member. Believe me, I know, because I've been there.

My wife, Lindsay, was diagnosed with endometriosis when she was a teenager and told she probably would not be able to have children.

Women who have endometriosis can often get pregnant, but the pregnancy usually ends up in a miscarriage. That's exactly what happened to us... several times. And when you've had a word from God that we would have children sooner than we expected and all you're experiencing is miscarriage after miscarriage, it's really hard to thank God. But we did... every day.

Then a miracle happened on the next pregnancy. Lindsay was able to carry the baby full-term and give birth to a beautiful baby boy. We named him Richard Oral. He looked so perfect, but within hours, he developed a breathing problem. Just 36 hours later, he died in my arms as I stood holding him in the neonatal intensive care unit of the hospital.

"Where's your faith and your victory confession now?" the devil roared at us. "You're in the healing ministry and you can't even get your own son healed." He just laughed at us as we wept.

At the memorial service, through our tears and broken hearts, the Spirit of the Lord rose up in me. I said to Him, "God, no matter what, we're going to serve You."

WEEK 4: THURSDAY

Lindsay, of course, was devastated. She said to me, "Richard, after the miscarriages and the death of our son, don't you ever ask me to get pregnant again." (And who could blame her?) Two weeks later, I was scheduled to go to Nigeria and Swaziland for healing crusades. I didn't want to go. I wanted to cancel it all and stay home with my wife.

Lindsay had not planned on going with me because she had expected to be taking care of a new baby.

My wife surprised me. She said, "Richard, don't cancel the crusades. Go to Africa… In fact, I'm going with you. We've got to plant a seed to God out of our broken hearts. We've got to strike a blow against the devil for our own victory over this terrible loss."

Wow, was I shocked! Suddenly, my faith began to soar again. I knew she was right. We needed to plant seed. We needed to give God something He could use and multiply back to us.

Lindsay went with me. Everywhere we went, we told the people what we had been through, and that we had come to Africa to plant a good seed to help us get well.

At that time, we had no idea that Nigeria had the largest infant mortality rate in the world.

We sowed into many couples who also had children die. There were thousands who gave their hearts to the Lord, and many, many outstanding healing miracles happened.

When the crusade was over, and we were preparing to fly home, Lindsay looked at me and said, "Let's try one more time."

I'm so glad we did, because the next year, our first daughter, Jordan Lindsay was born. Two years later, Catherine Olivia was born. In another two years, Chloe Elizabeth was born.

Now, here's what I want you to learn that will help you:

Don't ever get so down in your losses that you forget to give thanks to God.

Don't forget that God is your Source...

Don't forget, you can plant a new seed...

That seed planted can be the seed to bring in a harvest of healing and miracles back to you.

I believe it.
I know it.
I stake my life on it.
It's working for me... and I believe it will work for you.

YOUR GOD-GIVEN KEY FOR TODAY:

When one door closes, look for God to open another one.

[Friday]

KEY: *I Must Give God Something to Work With.*

How do you tap into God's miracle supply when you face a need? What do you do when the need is so big that there doesn't seem to be a way out?

Some time ago, we received a letter from a couple in a western state. They told us how they had watched our TV programs and heard my dad and me say, "EXPECT A MIRACLE!" They said that it was a new concept to them, even though they were church members and attended regularly.

Hearing "EXPECT A MIRACLE" inspired them... But they were struggling, even though they both had jobs and were working.

They were just beginning to come out of debt when the bottom dropped out.

Have you ever had the bottom drop out on you and your family? I mean like, suddenly, LIFE happened?

First, the wife became seriously ill and had to have surgery. The procedure was successful, but she was told she couldn't work for at least six months… And she hadn't worked long enough at the new job for the health benefits to kick in.

Second, the day she came home from the hospital, her husband lost his job.

There they were.

It was winter. Snow was on the ground, and jobs were hard to find… especially for a man of his age and with a history of poor health.

Well, he searched high and low looking for work, but did not find any. He would spend all day job hunting, only to come home to a crying wife. How were they going to pay their bills? It wasn't long until their savings were gone… and things really looked bleak.

Then they heard us preaching about the **Three Miracle Keys of Seed-Faith.** So, they wrote our ministry to request one of our books.

As they read our book, they realized they weren't giving FIRST so they could RECEIVE back from God. In fact, they had not been EXPECTING God to do anything for them.

They had never read Luke 6:38 before… In fact, they didn't even know it was in the Bible. But as they opened the scriptures, there it was… *"Give, and it will be given to you: good measure, pressed down, shaken together, and running over will be put into your bosom. For with the same measure that you use, it will be measured back to you."*

Well, they were nearly down to their last dollar and with no job opportunities… and seemingly, no one to turn to.

But the wife said to her husband, "Honey, here's all the money we have. Let's sow it as a seed to God and believe that the Bible is true and that He will multiply it back to us and meet our needs."

He thought about it for a moment, then looked at his wife and said, "Yes, let's do it, and EXPECT A MIRACLE!"

As they sowed that seed, something happened inside of them. They suddenly felt positive about things. They realized that God was going to give them a miracle and set them on the road to a Better Life.

And guess what? Within a few days, the husband was offered a new job... a good job... a great job. In fact, the best job he'd ever had!

A short time later, the wife's hospital bill was paid in full in a totally unexpected way. WOW! Talk about two happy people! Their lives were literally turned around, but more than that, they both learned that the road to a Better Life is filled with sowing unto the Lord and expecting miracles.

Yes, everybody faces needs. You do... I do... We all do. But there's a secret we all need to learn. It's the secret of tapping into God's miracle supply by giving Him something to work with.

Jesus teaches us to make our faith as a seed we plant... That is, make your faith something you do... and something you do *first*.

This is seed-faith. This is the message of the gospel. This is the Good News. Here's how you do it:

>You put something of yourself in as a seed...

>No matter how small you feel,

>Or how big your need is,

>Or how difficult your problem is,

>Or how severe the shortages are in your life...

You start giving of your total self, and God's law of the harvest does the rest. It reproduces a miraculous harvest along the road to *a* Better Life.

This is mountain-moving faith, and it never fails… because God is in it.

What a slogan! Mountain-moving faith… make it yours!

YOUR GOD-GIVEN KEY FOR TODAY:

I must give God something to work with.

[Saturday]

KEY: *I Can Expect Great Miracles and a Better Life with a Little Measure of Faith.*

You don't ever have to feel condemned when you hear or read the verse in the Bible where Jesus says, "Oh, you of little faith" (Luke 12:28).

There's a tendency to let these words make you feel bad… as if Jesus is putting you down. But listen to this… HE ISN'T.

He's really complimenting you. He is saying to you, "Little faith is not so bad. You can do great things with your little faith." And if you will learn to use your faith as a seed you plant, as the Bible says in Matthew 17:20, then you can begin to receive great miracles from God on your way to a Better Life.

Jesus mentioned "great faith" only twice. In all the thousands of people He dealt with, only two of them were said to have had great faith. Most of the people had little faith. In fact, not even one of the twelve disciples had great faith. They had little faith. On several occasions, they were the ones to whom Jesus said, "Oh, you of little faith." Yet they were hand-picked to walk beside the Lord while He was here on this earth.

Jesus performed some of His greatest miracles through people who had little faith.

The Apostle Paul said in Romans 12:3, *"God has dealt to each one a measure of faith."* This means...

God has given every human being a part of His own great faith.

Each of us has a little faith. Perhaps you feel like your faith isn't great... or big... or powerful. Maybe you are wondering how the faith you have could possibly help you to receive a Better Life from God. But He is trying to get you to see that the amount of faith you have is not as important as the fact that your faith is given to you by God.

The important thing is not the size of your faith... It is the one who is behind your faith... And that's God Himself.

He's the one you depend on. He is the Source of your total supply. He is the one who returns the harvest to us.

The Apostle Paul says in 2 Corinthians 9:10, *"He (God) who supplies seed to the sower, and bread for food, supply and multiply the seed you have sown and increase the fruits of your righteousness."* So, while the seed of faith we sow is the starting point for a miracle, the most important part of the miracle is God Himself. He is the one who makes the miracle happen...and He is the Source of our faith too.

The real power is not our faith... It is the object of our faith... And that's God.

The Real Power Is God.

However small your faith seems... even if it is only a tiny seed of faith that you put in, something you give, something you do to show your love and concern... the real power, the one you do it unto is God. The power is in God, who multiplies your sowing.

Every day, I receive letters and emails from people all over the world. Many request prayer for situations they're facing. Sickness and disease, financial hardships... you name it. We get just about every kind of prayer request you could possibly imagine.

WEEK 4: SATURDAY

Who am I that so many people could believe in my prayers? Sometimes my faith seems so small. Sometimes I'm using my faith so much, believing for the needs of this ministry to be met, that it feels like my faith is literally worn out when it comes to the needs of others.

Yet, as soon as I receive a prayer request, whether big or small, my faith seems to be built up and literally supercharged so that I can believe for the miracle that particular person needs.

It's really an amazing thing. I call it being… "instant, in and out of season"… whether I feel like it or not, just like 2 Timothy 4:2 tells us to be.

Sometimes when I pray over people's needs, it feels to me like my needs are even greater than theirs. However, I know and believe with all my heart that if I pray for them, God will use that prayer to help them, then multiply it back to me in the way I need it most.

So, I say to you and to myself… HOLD ON TO YOUR LITTLE FAITH… because that faith is in the God of miracles. And nobody or nothing is as strong and reliable as God is. God gives you a measure of faith… a little faith… so you can use this faith to get needs met in your life… so you can make your faith as a seed you plant. God wants you to be in a continuous state of expecting Him to supply your needs and give you a Better Life.

So, when you feel you are just about out of faith, say this, "I will never doubt the power of my little faith. NEVER, NEVER, NEVER! Thank You, God, for even my little faith."

Remember, nothing and nobody is as strong or as reliable as God is, so let me say it one more time.

Never… never… never… doubt the power of your little faith.

YOUR GOD-GIVEN KEY FOR TODAY:

And now you say this:

"I can expect great miracles with a "little" measure of faith."

WEEK 4 RECAP

- **Sunday:** I Will Sow for a Desired Result.
- **Monday:** God Loves My Cheerful Giving.
- **Tuesday:** Will Give God My Best… Then Ask Him for His Best.
- **Wednesday:** You Must Put Something in if You Want To Get Something Out.
- **Thursday:** When One Door Closes, God Will Always Open Another One.
- **Friday:** I Must Give God Something to Work With.
- **Saturday:** I Can Expect Great Miracles and a Better Life with a Little Measure of Faith.

WEEK 5

[Sunday]

KEY: *The Greatest Thing You Could Ever Learn Is How to Expect a Miracle.*

I can expect a new miracle every day.

It was the early days of this ministry. We had traveled to Miami, Florida, for one of my dad's healing crusades. The memories of that time are still precious to me. In those days, after my dad had preached and given an invitation for people to give their hearts to Jesus, people who needed physical healing would begin lining up for the laying on of hands. That's the part I always loved and always looked forward to the most.

I would sit in the front row on the side of the tent, hoping that my dad would call me up to stand by his side while he prayed for people. Oftentimes, he would let me touch them as he did, and I loved it. You never knew when someone who was deaf or blind would be healed… or when a cancer would literally fall off… or someone with crutches would take off running, healed by the power of God.

Believe me, it was a supernatural atmosphere. There was so much faith in action.

During those days, our ministry was under severe criticism and persecution, and if I've learned anything in my life, it's this: The devil hates the healing ministry. At one point, my dad was compelled to stand before a district judge and swear under oath that there was not some kind of electrical device up his sleeve when he touched people. Hard to imagine, isn't it? But it's true. I remember it like it was yesterday.

During the Miami crusade, a group of atheists made threats through the press, the radio, and TV that they would break up the crusade and close my father's ministry down by performing what was called, in those days, a citizen's arrest. Their charge would be that Oral Roberts was practicing medicine without a license by laying his hands on people in prayer.

When he heard about the threats, my father became very concerned. Although he knew that in reality there was no way the charges could hold up in a court of law, still, the news of a citizen's arrest on him would attract national attention, and the media could very easily have been used to mislead the people.

Now, when our family attended a crusade, my parents usually rented two hotel rooms with connecting doors. This was not only for sleeping, but at 3:00 in the afternoon, my dad would close himself off in one of the rooms and shut the door to begin preparing for the evening service. During this time, we children had to be very quiet.

My dad would usually lie across the bed and take a short nap before getting his Bible and studying for the sermon he would preach that night.

Well, this particular day had been very troubling. That group of atheists had announced that this was the night they were coming. My dad was very nervous and worried.

He lay there on the bed for a while and then fell asleep. After a few minutes, he was awakened by a hand on his shoulder. He looked around, but no one was there.

Suddenly, he was aware of the awesome presence of God. Then the Lord spoke these words to him: "Oral Roberts, expect a miracle."

The fear and nervousness left him, and he knew that God was in control and that everything was going to be all right.

And that night, the atheists never showed up. My dad preached a message titled, "Expect a Miracle."

Many lives were touched and changed, and there were many miracles too.

We serve a mighty God who is able to deliver us totally, in every way, and give us the Better Life that we all want.

But there is another part of the story that never got told. It was sort of like the late Paul Harvey's "The Rest of the Story" radio broadcasts.

That afternoon in the hotel room, the Lord said a second thing to my dad… and here it is…

Expect a new miracle every day.

Now, that's the Better Life that God wants you to have… "a new miracle every day."

If it wasn't possible, the Lord would not have said it to him.

Expect a new miracle…

In your body…

In your mind…

In your spirit…

In your finances…

In your emotions.

EXPECT A NEW MIRACLE IN EVERY AREA OF YOUR LIFE.

Now, when you get this idea *expect a new miracle every day* into your life, your whole life can be revolutionized. It can change everything… your circumstances, your hopes and dreams… and the very atmosphere in which you live.

WHY?

Because it is from God… so… say it!

I Expect a Miracle.

Say it.

I Expect a Miracle.

Say:

I Expect a New Miracle Every Day.

Write it on a card and put it in your kitchen by the window or by the sink. Put it on your refrigerator door or on your desk. Put it in your purse or wallet. Put it on your bathroom mirror.

SAY IT OUT LOUD:

I EXPECT A NEW MIRACLE EVERY DAY.

YOUR GOD-GIVEN KEY FOR TODAY:

I can expect a new miracle every day.

[Monday]

KEY: *My Miracle Will Settle the Issue.*

There is a God-implanted image in every human being for miracles. God made you for miracles, and He made miracles for you. Therefore...

The very secret of life is in expecting miracles.

I realize that there are people today who say they don't believe in miracles. Some don't feel a need for miracles, while others say that there's no such thing as a miracle...that your whole life is already set for good or bad, and you just have to live with it the way you are.

Funny how some people change their tune when they desperately need a miracle.

WEEK 5: MONDAY

I remember a man who once said to me, "Richard, I just don't believe in miracles."

I said to him, "You will when you need one."

Then one day, his wife was diagnosed with breast cancer, and the man called and asked for me to pray for a miracle.

Now, I didn't chide him or criticize him or say, "I told you so." No. I just prayed, as he asked.

It's amazing to me that when some people need a miracle, that's when they begin to think about God.

When miracles come, it usually settles an issue. Miracles get the job done, and when they happen, no one can easily explain them away.

Now, let these words resonate in your spirit:

Jesus has miracles... miracles for you!

Some people don't even believe that Jesus existed, much less that, by the power of the Holy Spirit, He can forgive sins and live in a person's heart.

And even though God has given everyone faith to believe, many today choose to believe the wrong thing. It's like the Bible is a blur... its words meaningless.

Many put their faith only in themselves... and sometimes only in others. They literally take their lives in their own hands and do things their own way, not realizing the divine help available, and the miracles that God has for them.

Some try to make their own miracles happen through schemes and scams on other people. Con artists abound. There are those who can get by for a while with these games and lies, but the problem is, soon they have to have a new con or scheme or scam. And it usually has to be better than the last one, if people are going to buy into it.

My dad used to tell the story of an ad in a local newspaper. It read, "This is your last chance to send in your dollar." And before the man was caught, 700 people actually mailed in the dollar to the address in the ad.

The truth is, no man can make his own miracles. Sooner or later, he will run out of steam. Somewhere, somehow, he must come to the end of himself, and realize there's more to life. He must realize he can have a personal relationship with the One who gave His life in the first place.

When I gave my heart to Christ at the age of nineteen, I turned on to miracles. Suddenly, I loved life. I loved people. And that attitude toward miracles has been in me ever since.

The only failures I've had have come because of my own faults and mistakes and shortcomings, or my failure to look to God as the Source of my total supply.

As long as I maintain a commitment of my life to Jesus Christ… as long as I follow the Lord in the *Three Miracle Keys of Seed-Faith*, I'm going to experience His miracle power in my life.

My mother, Evelyn Roberts, believed in, expected, and looked for miracles… every day of her life.

The phone would ring and she would say, "Lord, is this my miracle?" The doorbell would ring and she would say, "Lord, is this my miracle?"

Now, you may ask, "What is a miracle?" Well, a miracle is something happening that cannot be explained away. It's something that makes a profound change in a person's life.

In my life, I've seen many miracles…incredible, wonderful, unaccountable, astonishing, and even mysterious… something beyond the power of nature.

To me, there are many different types of miracles. One is a miracle that might happen to you or me that we've been expecting. There can also be miracles that are unexpected.

There are miracles that are unseen or unknown to anyone but you. In such a miracle, you know that something has happened of an unusual nature, for which there may be no natural explanation.

WEEK 5: MONDAY

The road to a Better Life is paved with miracles. That's the Christian life, and it's how we should live it.

Take, for example, an accident that is averted, and you whisper, "Now that was a miracle. There's no way that car could have missed me." I've been involved in several aircraft emergency landings. Each time, I've declared that it was a miracle. We got on the ground and out of the plane miraculously.

One emergency landing was at Kennedy Airport in New York City. The whole plane could have been engulfed in flames because of the fuel that was pouring out of the left-side wing. But because of a miracle, the other passengers and I escaped without harm or injury. Once again, that was a miracle.

The Apostle Paul stood on the storm-washed deck of that sea-battered ship in the book of Acts (chapter 27). After many days adrift in a storm of near hurricane strength, he said to his fellow passengers, "Boys, we're going to experience a miracle. An angel stood by me tonight and told me we're all going to escape, and not one of us will die." And it happened exactly like the angel said.

When things are going wrong at work, you can pray, and oftentimes, there's such a change that it's a miracle. Tension is lifted. Attitudes are improved. Friendships are formed. Apologies are made. Things get straightened out, and almost instantly, you are aware that everything is all right.

In the home and the family, miracles can change the attitude of sisters and brothers toward one another.

One of the great secrets of life is in expecting miracles where it would seem there's no possible way to get one.

Remember this: Don't ever presume that God is going to do something automatically for you. No. Instead, begin to seed for miracles. Open up your heart and sow seed. Aim those seeds toward the miracle that you desire and really have to have.

Start practicing the *Three Miracle Keys of Seed-Faith* I've been telling you about in this book.

If you have not already started, then start today. Just one word characterizes each one:

Trusting

Seeding

Expecting

Now, when you have this revolutionary thought exploding in your being, you can begin to shout it with everything you have.

YOUR GOD-GIVEN KEY FOR TODAY:

My miracle will settle the issue!

[Tuesday]

KEY: *God Has a Time and a Way for Me.*

A miracle is not something for nothing... You must seed for your miracle. You must give first... before you can expect to receive.

Solomon, the wisest man who ever lived, said, *"Cast your bread upon the waters, for you will find it after many days"* (Ecclesiastes 11:1).

Casting your bread upon the waters is giving. It is putting in the seed of faith first. Giving is sowing in joy. Giving is opening up your inner self and following after Jesus. Giving is truly the road to a Better Life in every area of your life.

Your bread means your existence, your money, your time, your talent, your love, your faith, your life... your very being.

WEEK 5: TUESDAY

And when you give of yourself, always give as unto the Lord. In other words, although your giving may be to some person or group or church or ministry, you're really giving it to God, your Source.

You see, what you sow represents you... your heart, your love, your concern. You may give an offering of money. You may give time and concern. You may pray for someone. You may give friendship or you may give something else. Or, it may be a combination or part of all these byproducts of your heart. Whatever you give, it is an act of your love and faith. It is a good seed sown.

Notice now that the scripture I just quoted from Ecclesiastes says, "upon the waters..." In the Bible, waters often represent "troubled humanity." Read Revelation 13:1 about the sea... the waters... speaking of the mass of troubled humanity, and remember this about casting your bread upon the waters.

First, God says you will find it—the seed you sow—after many days. *You will find it.*

When you cast your bread upon the waters, you may feel like it's gone. You may say, "I put it in, but nobody cares and nobody thanks me." But the Bible says, "You will find it." In other words, God will multiply it and return it back to you.

It may take a few days, a week, a month, or even longer. It may be "many days," but it SHALL RETURN to you. IT SHALL RETURN. This is the promise of God Himself to you.

Second, the wave you cast your bread upon may not be the same wave God returns it on. It may be another wave.

What this means to you is, God will return your giving, and you will receive back from Him.

Now, this is very important, so don't miss it.

God will return your seed in His own way, and in His own time.

I call this God's supply from an unexpected instrument. It could be from someone you didn't expect would help you, or it may come to you in some other way you hadn't thought about.

Many times in my own life, the most important returns from casting my bread upon the waters came in almost totally unexpected ways or times, or from those I least expected it from. But I always knew that it was God, my Source, who was doing it.

That means I must remember to look to Him, and not other ways, or times, or people. Although I'm grateful for the instrument, I give the glory to God.

Today, when you finish reading this... start thinking about someone you know who is in trouble. Start thinking about someone you can give to today.

In other words, ask the Lord to help you decide who you can help, and how.

Now, when you have decided, write their name or names:

_____

_____

_____

Call them, or contact them in some way. Show your love for them. Pray for them. Do for them whatever the Lord directs you to do... and do it in love.

Cast out into the sea of troubled humanity... Do it today. And remember... don't look for the return to come back on the same wave you cast it upon. Instead, look to God, your Source.

YOUR GOD-GIVEN KEY FOR TODAY:

God has a time and a way for me.

[Wednesday]

KEY: *God's Due Season Will Not Be Too Early or Too Late for My Needs.*

Jerry and Carolyn Savelle have been friends of ours for a long time. Jerry's ministry is very powerful, and his preaching, books, CDs, and ministry resources have spoken into our lives many times. We live not too far from one another, and from time to time, we get together for fellowship.

I remember one time when Lindsay and I were watching Jerry on television, and he was preaching on the scripture in Galatians 6:9, which says, *"And let us not grow weary while doing good, for in due season we shall reap if we do not lose heart."* Then he asked a strange question in his message. He said, "What do you call the season between the time that you sow, and the time that you receive your harvest?" He made a dramatic pause.

My wife, Lindsay, reached down and took off her shoe, threw it at the television, and screamed, "You call it hell, Jerry... you call it hell." Then she began to laugh, and I began to laugh. But I knew exactly what she meant. It seems that there is a waiting period between your seed and the harvest... a waiting period that not many of us humans want to hang around for. We want an instantaneous, microwave miracle. But notice that the Bible, in Genesis 8:22, speaks of seed... time... and harvest.

In other words, first comes the seed, then comes a period of time, followed by the harvest. It's always in that order.

Now, I don't know about you, but I've told God how to do it, when to do it, where to do it, and who to do it to. He's never done it my way once.

He's never early, but He's never late either.

Galatians 6:9 says, "In due season we shall reap." In other words, there is a due season in God. There is a due season for you if you plant seed. In due season, you shall reap... In other words, you shall have your harvest. It will come back multiplied... again... and again... and again. That's what the Bible says, and friend, I'll stake my life on it.

Once again, let me remind you that God has His own timetable, and He's saying to us, "When you plant your seed, don't get discouraged. Keep looking to Me for the miracle. Don't whine; don't gripe; don't complain. Don't say that I'm late. Just keep looking to Me as the Author and Finisher of your faith, and believe that I will do what I said I would do."

Just keep believing and expecting a miracle. Just *keep on keeping on* until the miracle comes.

I believe that all of us who are seed-sowers have miracles on the way, even though we have not yet received them. But we have seeded for them, and that means... they've got to come. And that gets me excited!

So, don't get discouraged, or let's say, don't allow yourself to get discouraged. And don't grow weary in your well-doing. Keep seeding and keep expecting miracles. And if you faint not, that is, if you don't give up, you will receive.

In the long run, I think we are all better off for a slow return rather than a fast return. There are exceptions of course, times when you have to have a quick return. You have no choice. But a quick return is easily forgotten, whereas a slow return holds you steady, and you have more time to focus on your Source.

Believe me, my friend, the road to a Better Life is that road upon which you refuse to get weary in your well-doing, believing and knowing that God's due season will come to you.

I know it's hard, but do it... Do it in Jesus' name.

Waiting ... Trusting ... Expecting.

WEEK 5: THURSDAY

YOUR GOD-GIVEN KEY FOR TODAY:

Say it out loud to yourself.

"God's due season will not be too early or too late for me."

[Thursday]

KEY: *God's Storehouse Will Never Fail.*

Did you ever have anything come to you that just seemed to come "out of the blue?" I mean it came in a way you couldn't explain? Well, I believe that what seemed to come out of the blue was really the harvest from the seed you planted sometime before. In other words, your due season arrived. God just gave you the harvest from your seed sowing in a different way than what you were expecting.

As I said earlier, God has His own time schedule and His own way of doing things. He has His own way of sending miracles to you. Do you know that you seldom get anything from God exactly the way you thought God would do it? Yet His way of getting it to you is always a good thing in the end.

Why? "God's ways are not our ways" (Isaiah 55:8). God seldom gives a harvest to me when I want it.

But listen to this. Don't ever stop putting in your seed. Remember to think about the seed and the harvest, and not the need. Instead, focus upon God. Put your faith in Him that in His timing, you will receive from His mighty hand. Yes, I know it's hard to do, but I tell you, do it… and keep on doing it… and DON'T EVER GIVE UP. Keep doing it!

Now, He may not use your methods, and He may use a totally different source than you thought He would. But as I said, in

His timing… Yes, in HIS TIMING, HE WILL BRING THE HARVEST.

I know God is concerned about you because He has put His concern for you in me. And more than anything, I believe He wants you to have a Better Life through Jesus Christ, His Son.

Now, you may not yet understand the principles of seed-faith. You may give a little here and a little there, but you haven't formed a pattern of giving as a seed. That's one thing I try to do… I strive to form a pattern of giving and to make it a forward thrust of my life.

Before I ask for anything from God, I always give something. Time after time, when Lindsay and I have faced a need or asked for something special from God, we have planted a seed. And that seed is usually beyond our regular tithe of 10% on our income to Him, which we regularly give whether we have a specific need or not.

I will admit, however, there have been times when I have forgotten to sow my seed. Sometimes I seem to look at situations only through my natural eyes.

Then after awhile, I realize that I left God out and I have forgotten to sow my seed. But when I repent for forgetting and sow my seed in faith, suddenly, my believing soars, and I begin to visualize God bringing in the harvest.

Now as I said earlier, He does it His way, not my way. But His way always turns out to be better than my way.

I remember once in our ministry when we were facing a financial need. It was big, and we didn't have the money for it. The day the money would be due to make the payment in full (which was required) was approaching fast.

I had done all I could in the natural realm. I mean, I had lost sleep because of worry and was very anxious and nervous. I had walked the floor. I had gotten angry for having to face the problem in the first place. I had almost told God I was mad at Him because He wasn't answering my prayers.

WEEK 5: THURSDAY

But the one thing I had not done was to sow seed against the financial need. It was Lindsay who pointed it out to me. I knew she was right.

So we joined our hands together and prayed. And then we got our checkbook and planted a seed toward the harvest (in this case, the money to satisfy the obligation) that we needed.

The night before the full payment was due, we still didn't have the money. But the next morning, I received word of a FedEx package we had received. It was a special gift for our ministry from a long-time partner who knew nothing about the need, yet felt led to sow their seed into the ministry at exactly that time. The amount more than satisfied the need.

Wow! Now, that was a harvest. True, it didn't come the way I thought it would or from whom I thought it would... *but it came... right on time...* and God did it.

Lindsay and I rejoiced and gave thanks to the Lord for His goodness and mercy. We knew all along how much He cared, but the miracle was just a little shot-in-the-arm reminder.

Please read the following carefully. On every seed I give, there is God's handwriting saying, "I will multiply this seed sown by Richard Roberts." And if I will expect it, God will recognize it and multiply it back to me in the way I need it most.

Now, that's the road to a Better Life in Him. When we say, "a miracle came from out of the blue" — like the FedEx package and check, for instance — we mean somebody, *GOD...* remembered us.

I guess the bottom line is this: God doesn't need what we give Him to keep for Himself... No. Instead, He takes that seed sown and puts it in His storehouse (Malachi 3:10) to multiply it back to us when we face a need.

So visualize, if you can, God's great storehouse. And when you have this faith-image in your mind... Repeat this over and over.

Your God Given Key for Today:

God's storehouse of miracles will never fail me.

[Friday]

KEY: *My Faith Is Something I Do.*

God has provided a way for our needs to be met. But there is something we must do to bring these good things into our lives.

Jesus said in Matthew 7:7–8:

ASK, and it will be given to you.

SEEK, and you will find.

KNOCK, and it will be opened to you.

Notice that Jesus is talking here about things. The Lord is not against you having things. He just doesn't want those things to have you.

Jesus went on, in verse 12, to give us what is called THE GOLDEN RULE:

"Therefore, whatever you want men to do to you, do also to them, for this is the Law and the Prophets."

I believe that it is a law and a promise. The Golden Rule is talked about a lot...but it isn't practiced much. The trouble is, we all want the other person to be nice to us and to practice the Golden Rule first. We say, "If this person would just be nice to me, just look how nice I would be to them."

Being like that is really insisting on doing things your own way... trying to have your own will done... And it just won't work that way.

So many people try to figure out how to get something done, and when it doesn't work out to their satisfaction, they give up. Or they get really frustrated and then blame God for things not working out.

Well, here's a new twist on the Golden Rule. Jesus says, "Whatever you want done to you, you do it, and you do it first." This is the most dependable law in all the universe. The Golden Rule is something you do… and you do it first as a seed.

Jesus was talking about things in Matthew 7 when He gave us this Golden Rule, but many people take the Golden Rule and make it just an ethical code of conduct. Well, in a sense, it is an ethical code of conduct, but Jesus did not stop there. He said something else very important. He was talking about asking and receiving, about knocking on doors and getting doors opened.

We, as humans, knock on many doors to be opened, but sometimes they don't open at all. Jesus said, "Ask, and you will receive." He also said, "If a son asks his parents for bread, they won't give him a stone. If he asks for a fish, they won't give him a snake. And if you know how to give your children such good gifts, how much more will God give good gifts to them … to them who will do first unto others what they want done back to themselves." (See Matthew 7:7–11.)

Call out what your needs are… just exactly like a farmer does. The farmer says, "I need so many thousands of bushels of wheat, so I'm going to go out into the field, and I'm going to sow a certain amount of wheat seed, or I'm going to sow a certain amount of seed corn. I'm going to do what it takes to get the harvest I need."

In other words, why are you waiting for someone else to do for you what you can do? You go do what you can. And what you're going to find is that now you are dealing with God and His eternal law of sowing and reaping. What you're going to discover further is that you are not dealing with things or people at all. You're dealing with eternal principles.

As a matter of fact, you may think you are dealing with things and with people, but you're not. You are actually dealing with God, because surely God is responsible to make His eternal laws work.

The eternal law of sowing and reaping is: if you give, it will be given back, and if you do good to someone, good will come back to you (Luke 6:38).

Now, you cannot expect the person you help to always do good back to you, because that person is not responsible to operate according to God's law. God is the only one who multiplies your giving back to you in the form of meeting your need.

Remember, the Golden Rule is far more than an ethical code of conduct. It is the eternal law of God to meet every need you have on this earth... It is something that you do.

> **In the Golden Rule, Jesus is talking about asking and receiving, knocking on doors, and getting doors opened.**

Sometimes in our lives, some of us wouldn't recognize an open door if we were standing in it. But this is where the "doing" comes in. While you are going about your everyday duties and "doing" and "giving out", God can show you your door and maybe even give you a little push through it.

YOUR GOD-GIVEN KEY FOR TODAY:

My faith is something I do.

[Saturday]

KEY: *My Miracle Basket Is About to Touch the Ground.*

Soon after the resurrection of Christ, thousands of people received Him as Savior and became Christians. Then there came a serious movement against them... persecution, causing many to be put into prison and even put to death.

The ringleader of the persecutors was a man named Saul of Tarsus, who received authority from the religious leaders to persecute Christians in Jerusalem, and as far away as Damascus.

While this cruel and bitter young man was on his way to Damascus, he had a personal confrontation with Jesus Christ, who came to him in a brilliant light, and whose voice called him by name, saying, "Saul, Saul, why are you persecuting Me?"

In this experience, Saul, later known as the Apostle Paul, found Christ to be real and alive in his life (Acts chapter 9).

Later in Damascus, a man named Ananias prayed for him, and Saul was gloriously saved. But it wasn't long until those who had been in league with him to kill Christians turned against him and sought his life as well.

Several men took Paul by night and put him in a basket with a rope, and lowered him over the city walls to escape certain death. Those men who held the rope did not know that the young man would become the greatest apostle ever to live. All they knew was that he had hated them and now he loved them.

Notice, they held the rope at night and risked personal danger to themselves. You know, the nights that you toss in bed... when problems are weighing you down, when you just can't sleep... That's a good time for God to put a rope in your hand so that you can pray for someone.

My parents, Oral and Evelyn Roberts, held the rope for me, even when, as a teenager, I rebelled against God and ran away from the Lord. My mother said to me, "Son, wherever you go, you'll never get away from my prayers." I didn't realize until later the impact those words had on my life. They were like a covering, helping me to know that not only did they love me, but God loved me too.

The day came when I surrendered my life to Christ, and my parents' prayers paid off.

Now, notice that these men not only held the rope, but they didn't turn it loose. Surely they were tempted to let it go and run in fear that they themselves would be persecuted, but they did not turn loose.

You may say, "Richard, I've been holding the rope for this person for such a long time. I just don't believe I can hold on any longer." Let me give you two reasons why you cannot afford to turn loose of the rope.

First, you may be the only one God has holding that particular rope.

Second, your "miracle basket" may be about to touch the ground.

You may be a minister struggling with your church. You're trying to preach the gospel to your congregation, and you may be the only link they have to God concerning going to heaven or hell.

You may be a doctor holding a rope for your patients to get them well and keep them well.

You may be in business, and it's touch-and-go, and you may be feeling like shutting it all down. Yet there are people who are depending upon you as a business person, because without businesses, our country cannot run.

Maybe you're an employer, or maybe you lost your job and you have not been able to find a new one. Or maybe you're in debt, and you just can't seem to get out of it.

Maybe you're ill in your body, and although you've taken the medicines, you're just not getting well.

Maybe you've walked the floor, praying for a child or another family member or perhaps someone else... Perhaps you're facing

WEEK 5: SATURDAY

the fear of something bad happening, or maybe you feel sad and lonely. Maybe you're full of anxiety and depression.

Whatever it is, I tell you today with the full force of my faith:

Don't turn loose of that rope you're holding... your basket may be about to touch the ground.

I mean by that—hold on, expecting the miracle that you've been praying for and believing for. Don't give up... and never, ever quit.

One more thing about these men: They didn't know how great a man they had on the end of their rope. They didn't know that this zealous young man would one day write two-thirds of the New Testament. They didn't know that he would preach the gospel in the streets, in the houses, and in the palaces of the world. They didn't know that he would honeycomb the land with the message of Christ, even lighting the light of the gospel in the household of Caesar himself. They didn't know. They just planted their seeds of faith in this young man's life.

So I say to you, whatever rope God has placed in your hands, hold onto it. You may be the only one holding on.

> Hold on to your rope.
>
> Heaven is bending low.
>
> I believe your miracle is on the way.

Hold on, because your basket may be about to touch the ground. I won't promise you that you won't get an occasional rope burn. But I tell you, there is a balm like no earthly salve, and you'll not only come through on top, but I believe you'll be a better person because of it.

YOUR GOD-GIVEN KEY FOR TODAY:

Remember this and remember it well.

Say it out loud: *"My miracle basket is about to touch the ground."*

WEEK 5 RECAP

- **Sunday:** The Greatest Thing You Could Ever Learn Is How to Expect a Miracle.
- **Monday:** My Miracle Will Settle the Issue.
- **Tuesday:** God Has a Time and a Way for Me.
- **Wednesday:** God's Due Season Will Not Be Too Early or Too Late for My Needs.
- **Thursday:** God's Storehouse Will Never Fail.
- **Friday:** My Faith Is Something I Do.
- **Saturday:** My Miracle Basket Is About to Touch the Ground.

WEEK 6

[Sunday]

KEY: *I Know God, And I Am in Him… And He Is in Me.*

I want you to know that in this world, it is possible for you to know God personally… to know that He's real… to know that He's working in the now of your life and to know that He means something very special to you.

In 1 John 1, verse one and verse three, St. John is saying these immortal words, *"That which was from the beginning, which we have heard, which we have seen with our eyes, which we have looked upon, and our hands have handled, concerning the Word of life… that which we have seen and heard we declare to you."* And then John said in the very next chapter, *"Now by this we know that we know Him…"* (1 John 2:3).

Then, he said, "I know Him" (1 John 2:4).

Then, he added, "We know that we are in Him" (1 John 2:5).

John was one of the twelve disciples. He was alive and walked with Jesus. He talked with Him and heard Him speak. He saw Him with his own eyes. He touched Him. He knew Him personally.

When John wrote his epistles, he was now the oldest of all the disciples. Most of the other disciples had been killed by this time, possibly all of them except for John. He was past 80 years old. Now, in First John, he's looking back. He looks back at the other side of the Cross, back there when he knew Christ personally, and now on this side of the Resurrection, he writes and says, "That which was from the beginning, which we've heard and seen and felt and handled with our hands. Him we declare unto you. We know Him… I know Him… and we know that we are in Him."

You see, it means a great deal for John to look back to Christ and then to look at the end of his own life, which won't be very far away, and to be able to say, "I know… I know… I know Him."

Many years ago, in an eastern university, there was a brilliant, but eccentric, professor of mathematics. One day, he assigned a problem to his students to solve and bring back the answer the next morning. Well, of course, the students spent a lot of time working on the problem. One of them, in particular, spent nearly all night, because he had a feeling this was a very important assignment.

The next morning, the professor said to various students, "Would you go to the board and give us the solution to the problem I assigned you?" They all attempted it, but couldn't solve it. Each time, the professor said, "I'm sorry. That's wrong. Would you please be seated?"

And then he asked another young man, who went to the board and put down the right answer. But the professor still said, "You're wrong. That's not the correct answer. Please sit down."

Finally, the professor called on the young man who had studied throughout the night. The professor said, "Go to the board and give us the solution."

So, the young man wrote down the same solution as the other young man who had been told he was wrong.

The professor said, "That's wrong. Didn't you hear me tell this other student that his solution was wrong? Yet you've written down the same thing!"

The young man said, "Professor, it's not wrong. It's correct."

The professor said, "Are you trying to correct me?"

The student said, "No, sir. I'm not. I respect you very highly, but this is the correct answer."

WEEK 6: SUNDAY

The professor said, "Are you sure?"

He said, "I'm sure."

The professor said, "Are you absolutely sure?"

And the young man said, "I am absolutely sure."

The professor smiled and said, "You're correct. It is the right answer."

There was a wave of protest from the students in the class, but the professor said, "Now, wait a minute. I'll tell you why I did what I did. I know that soon you'll be out in the world, and people will be demanding answers and solutions to problems from you. They will want not only the correct answer, but they will want to know that the person who gives the solution has confidence in his or her answer. This young man has demonstrated to me and to you that he knows for certain this is the solution. He *knows that he knows.*"

You see, you've got to have not only the correct answer, but you must have confidence in your answer.

And that's the spirit that St. John gives us in his great words, "We know… We know because we saw Him."

In the New Testament, we are told of one of the great miracles of Christ—the healing of a man who had been born blind, and one day Christ restored his sight. It was amazing. Some were glad, but many, strangely enough, were angry, because they didn't believe in the Lord. Then they verbally jumped on the man who had been healed of blindness. They tried to argue him out of his healing. Then the theologians got hold of him. They didn't believe in the blind man's healing, and they made it very hard for him.

Finally, the man just stopped them cold with these words, "You ask me all kinds of questions. Well, I'll just tell you one thing: whereas I was once blind, now I can see" (John 9:25).

He not only knew that he saw, but he knew that he was able to see. He knew it, because he had the evidence.

You see, it's not just head-knowing that we need to have. It's heart-knowing.

John says, "We know Him." And then he said, "I know Him." And I tell you with all my heart today, based on the authority of the Bible and the experiences of millions who've gone before us, and millions who are living now, who know it and know Him... You can know Him too. You can know God.

Maybe you've never been told that you can know God personally. If this is so, lean into these truths that I have been telling you about. Lean hard, because it is so.

Here are just some of the ways you can know God:

You can know Him in the might of His healing power.

You can know Him in the joy of salvation.

You can know Him in the solving of your financial problems.

You can know Him by getting closer to your children and grandchildren.

You can know... that you know Him.

You can know Him in these ways and in every area of your life, if you will invite Him into your life and ask for His help. He is more willing to help than you could ever imagine.

The truth is, I know you can do it, because the Spirit of God is already upon our lives, even when we don't know Him. This is why we are all capable of doing good—of loving, giving, being compassionate, or doing anything that is good, because God is a good God, and He pours His Spirit out upon all flesh (See Acts 2:17). But having His Spirit *on* us is different than having His Spirit *in* us. And that's what I'm talking about... I mean, really knowing Him.

Now... get out of all this "head-knowing" and let the Lord get inside you... that's the difference between "head-knowing" and "heart-knowing."

And as you read this book, if you realize that you've never really known Him and you want to, let me pray a prayer of salvation with you. Pray this prayer out loud after me:

Oh God, be merciful to me, a sinner, a backslider. I recognize that I don't know You, and I'm sorry. I ask You to forgive me of every sin. Forgive me and set me free. I renounce the devil and all of his works, and I receive Jesus Christ, God's only Son, as my Lord and Savior. Come into my heart, Lord Jesus. Save me, heal me, deliver me, and set me free. From this hour, I will serve You with all of my heart. Amen.

Now you can truly begin to know Him…Now you are on the road to a Better Life.

YOUR GOD-GIVEN KEY FOR TODAY:

Now say it:

"I know God, and I am in Him… And He is in me."

[Monday]

KEY: *I Will Use My Inner Resources of Prayer and Faith.*

Jesus said, *"Men always ought to pray and not lose heart"* (Luke 18:1).

The feeling you get when you enter a rushing stream is to go with the current instead of against it. That's the human, natural feeling. Jesus says, however, that you should not do that. You ought not to faint. You ought not to give way and go with the current or the way the world goes. Instead, you should pray. You should stay in faith and use the faith that you have.

Now, using your faith means centering your believing upon God as a Being, believing that His power is superior to all other forms of power. You put your mind upon God, rather than upon something negative.

As a matter of fact, a Christian who knows God's ways does this. He makes Christ the center of his life. The Bible says, *"Looking unto Jesus, the author and finisher of our faith"* (Hebrews 12:2).

Have you ever thought about your faith having an origin? Faith has a beginning. Faith actually starts. Yes, perhaps you have. But have you thought about its ending? Christ is the author and FINISHER of your faith. The faith that He began in you, He desires to finish. In order to have faith, one must look to God. In order for that faith to be finished, to become a fact, one must continue to look to God, looking to Christ, the author and finisher of our faith.

Now, who the real supplier of life? Who is it who intervenes on your behalf? Who is it who takes people and things and moves them into proper place so that they touch your life exactly right?

It's GOD.

The Apostle Paul said, "God shall supply all your need." (See Philippians 4:19.) Not someone else, not something else, but God.

What I am saying is:

God is the One who makes your Christian experience work.

Prayer and faith help us to reach God. Expectancy keeps our minds tuned in to God so that we look to Him for all our needs to be met and our entire lives to be used for His glory. This causes God to release His power in us, so that our faith can be completed.

As a young boy, I used to watch my parents read and study the Bible. Frequently, they would pause to mark a passage. They would become so absorbed that they would be completely oblivious to their surroundings, even when I was running and playing throughout the house. Even my shouting didn't seem to disturb them. Once in a while, they would look up from their reading, and I would see tears in their eyes.

WEEK 6: MONDAY

Once, I asked them why they cried when they read the Bible. They said, "Son, someday when the Lord Jesus is real to you as a person... When you feel Him standing by your side, when you know He is closer to you than your very breath, you will know and understand why we cry."

I was nineteen when I received Christ as my Lord and Savior. And the first thing I did was to get out the Bible my parents had given to me and began to read it for myself.

You see, when I accepted Christ into my heart, I did not just embrace an idea or a philosophy. I embraced a person... Jesus Christ. Today, Jesus is the most real person I know... I know Him better than anyone else.

And I came to know Him best by reading the Word of God, especially focusing on the four Gospels, Matthew, Mark, Luke, and John, as well as the Book of Acts. As I read them, I could literally see Jesus rising up out of the pages. Through the Word, I followed Him down the dusty roads of Galilee, and among the sick as He ministered to those with deep problems... And I began to find the answers to my own problems.

But I didn't stop with the Gospels and Acts. I read through the entire Bible quite a number of times. And each time I read a verse now, even today, I find something new and exciting that helps me in my walk of faith with Christ.

So I suggest to you, if you do not have a Bible, get one. The same way your body needs food, your spirit needs food. Be sure to get a Bible that's yours and yours alone. Also, be sure there is room enough in the margin to write and make notes. Yes, it's all right to write in your Bible. Pretty soon, it will become like an old friend to you, and it will help you and comfort you in your time of need. So as you read it, underline those verses that seem to leap out at you. Make notes in the margin as God speaks to your heart.

In times of discouragement or loneliness or confusion, read your Bible often. It always helps to read the Word of God. Reading it gives you strength, courage, and a stronger faith. At a time when you're tired, even the touch of a Bible is wonderful. The feel of it will give you confidence, for I know and believe that it is true and eternal. Things may be going to pieces all around you, but the Word of God is sure and steadfast. It is an anchor for your soul.

The passage I read over and over when I feel weak is Luke 10:19, which says, *"Behold, I give you the authority to trample on serpents and scorpions, and over all the power of the enemy, and nothing shall by any means hurt you."* This always reads well when you are attacked by the enemy, and have feelings of inadequacy.

When I feel bad in my body or mind or spirit, and the devil would have me believe God is making me feel that way, I turn to Luke 9:56 and read it until satan no longer can keep me from believing it. *"For the Son of Man did not come to destroy men's lives but to save them."* Anything that would destroy me, such as sickness, oppression, or fear, is not sent from God. He came to save, not destroy.

And when I still need help along these lines, then I read John 10:10. It's perhaps my favorite scripture in the entire Bible. *"The thief* (satan) *does not come except to steal, and to kill, and to destroy. I* (Jesus) *have come that they may have life, and that they may have it more abundantly."* God wants us to be happy, healthy and normal, and to enjoy life more abundantly. He wants us to have a Better Life.

When I'm struggling to pay bills, I quote 3 John 2, and it always helps me. *"Beloved, I pray that you may prosper in all things."* God is interested in our material needs being met, and He gives us this promise in Philippians 4:19: *"My God shall supply all your need according to his riches in glory by Christ Jesus."*

Psalms chapters 1, 23, 91 and 103 are especially inspiring to me when I need strength and confidence, and I quote them every day of my life.

Matthew 8 is another chapter I frequently read, especially in times when sickness attacks me, and when I need healing—as well as when I need healing faith, as I pray for others.

All of us come up against situations which may appear hopeless to us. Mark 9:23 is my verse for this. *"If you can believe, all things are possible to him who believes."*

Reading the Bible like this helps me to think and believe in a positive manner. It strengthens my determination and increases my faith.

The Bible says in Romans 10:17, *"Faith comes by hearing, and hearing by the word of God."* Nothing can take the place of the house of God, His Church. Now, in a sense you are hearing the Word of God as you read it. However, nothing can replace the hearing of faith. That's why going to church is so important to you.

When the preacher is anointed by the Spirit of God, he or she handles the Word very skillfully. They seem to say just the right thing to help you believe and release your faith. They put you in a better attitude… a faith attitude. When you leave God's house for your home or your job, you carry a new strength, an inner light, a deeper knowledge, a stronger determination, and a greater faith, which enables you to stand up to the tricks and strategies of the devil… and to win over him. Remember, the Bible says in 1 John 4:4, *"He who is in you is greater than he who is in the world"* and **the gates of hell shall not prevail against the church** (Matthew 16:18).

YOUR GOD-GIVEN KEY FOR TODAY:

Keep your Bible near you… And read it often.

[Tuesday]

KEY: *God Loves Me, and He Will Never Give Up on Me.*

Have you ever felt you had so miserably failed that there was no way for you to start over? No place to begin again? Your friends and loved ones had deserted you and there was nothing to live for? And even worse, it seemed either God was dead, or He didn't care about you at all?

Well, don't feel like you're alone. I receive letters from people every day who feel exactly like this.

But I have good news for you... God is not through with you... He never gives up... He loves you... He loves you... He loves you... Yes *You*, just like you are!

There was a man in the Old Testament who was a prophet. His name was Jeremiah. He was called "The Weeping Prophet," because he wept so much over the spiritual condition of the nation of Israel. In one place in the Bible, he said, *"Oh, that my head were waters, and my eyes a fountain of tears, that I might weep day and night... for my people"* (Jeremiah 9:1).

But one day, he discovered that crying about the problem, and feeling sorry for his people, wasn't going to get the job done. Just about the time he thought God was through dealing with man, the Lord drew him up short and said, "Jeremiah, go down to the potter's house ..."

It's a good thing that Jeremiah was sensitive to the voice of God. He didn't ask any questions; he just went.

When he walked in, he saw the wheel spinning and the clay on it, and the potter's hands skillfully working. And Jeremiah said to him, "What are you doing?"

He said, "I'm making a beautiful vessel."

And Jeremiah said, "With that little bit of shapeless clay on the wheel?"

He said, "Yes."

"Well, how do you know it's going to be a beautiful vessel?"

"Because I have a plan, and a dream, for this tiny bit of clay. I have a design for it."

As Jeremiah watched, he gained a new appreciation for man in his heart, and for God's great design for every human being. He began to realize that every human being is unique and irreplaceable, and that every person is a person of great worth.

As the potter was shaping the mass of clay, according to his own design, and trying to make of it a beautiful vessel, suddenly his face changed, and he stopped.

Jeremiah said, "Potter, why are you stopping?"

He said, "I've just discovered a defect, a flaw in my clay. It's marred. There's something wrong."

Jeremiah began to realize why God had sent him down to the potter's house, because He, too, realized something was wrong with man. Man was doing all those wrong things because something was wrong inside him. There was a flaw... a defect in human hearts.

As Jeremiah watched the potter begin to reshape the clay, he realized that the potter was not going to give up. And it came to him that *God is not going to quit*. God has never given up on man, even though we are flawed, even when we make mistakes. God has never given up on you. And God won't quit. As long as you have a breath in your body, God won't quit on you.

What did the potter do next? Well, it was an amazing thing. He pulled the clay off the wheel, and with his hands he began to break it. He smashed it; then he began to knead it together again.

Jeremiah said, "Potter, what are you doing now?"

The potter said, "I am breaking the clay in order to remake it." So he crushed it, kneaded it, and worked it until it was pliable again, and he worked out the flaw. He put the clay back on the wheel and began to spin it. And with his skillful hands, he began to reshape it according to his design and plan.

Jeremiah looked up with a smile on his face, and he knew that he had a message of hope to take back to the nation of Israel.

And that message is:

God's skillful hands are upon you… just a bit of clay… because He has a design for your life. He has a plan for you. Yes, no matter how your life is marred… regardless of the flaws… He has something wonderful for you. He's going to make a beautiful vessel out of you yet.

And friend, I believe that with all my heart.

I can almost hear you saying:

But you don't know how bad the flaw is…

I may not know how bad your flaw is, but…

I KNOW THE POWER OF THE FLAW-REMOVER.

God made you, and He can make you brand new, all over again.

GOD WON'T QUIT.

GOD LOVES YOU.

HE HAS A PLAN FOR YOUR LIFE.

YES, YOURS!

Remember, God specializes in clay vessels… All you have to do is let yourself become pliable in His great hands.

YOUR GOD-GIVEN KEY FOR TODAY:

Remember this, and say it out loud.

"God loves me… Me… Me… And He will never give up on me."

[Wednesday]

KEY: *I Can Walk with Jesus Every Day.*

It's so easy, when things go wrong, for someone to say to you, "Trust in God." But people are always saying to me, "Richard Roberts, how do I trust in God?"

This is especially true for new Christians. They have received Christ as Savior and Lord, and now, it seems the problems start coming, and they begin to wonder. They want to trust God as their Source to see them through these problems, but they wonder "how."

I want to share with you, from the Word of God, how you can learn to trust God.

The Apostle Paul tells us in 1 Peter 5:7, *"Casting all your care upon Him, for He cares for you."*

God is concerned about you… the person. He is concerned about your loved ones… He is concerned about every situation in your life. You can TRUST God. You can trust Him, because God is the Source of your total supply (Philippians 4:19).

You see, God lays the riches of His glory, end to end, in Heaven, and says, "According to these, I will supply your need."

Now, man cannot say that, and earth cannot give such an abundance of supply, but God can. He is the Source of your total supply. And He is the roadmap to your Better Life.

Trust is a commitment. Commitment is like sitting down on a chair, but it's more than sitting on the chair. It's resting your full weight upon the chair, and it's relaxing. It's believing that the chair will support your weight.

One of the most powerful and dramatic examples of how to commit your whole weight upon God is found in Matthew 14.

Here, the story is told of how Peter attempted to walk upon the water. Now, Peter had been raised around the Sea of Galilee. He knew what it was like to be in and out of water all the time, and to fish in his boat. But he had never walked on the water.

However, during a storm, one night when the disciples were out there in the boat, and they were about to lose their lives, Jesus came walking to them upon the water. They looked up and saw Jesus out there, perfectly balanced on the waves. It was like liquid pavement beneath His feet. But there they were, over there in the boat, which was shaking to pieces. It looked like it was going under any minute.

Peter said, "Lord, if it's really You, tell me to come to You on the water."

And Jesus said, "Come... Come on out of that sinking boat." That is, "Come out here to Me where it's safe."

Peter leaped out! And with his eyes upon the Lord, his Source, he began to walk on the water. He began to walk above the problem that was about to take his very life. Then, in his ear, he heard the winds blow. He looked around and saw the waves. He no longer was looking at God, his Source, or trusting in Him. And as a result, he immediately began to sink.

There's another part of this story that is seldom told. Peter began to sink but he cried, "Lord, save me... I perish." A very short prayer, but if he had prayed longer, he might have drowned! I know one thing. It's not the long prayer that gets the job done. It's how you are reaching out to the Lord on the inside, and whether you are using your faith.

Well, I can just see Peter as he starts going under. Picture it in your mind. He goes under once and comes back up and yells, "Jesus!"

He goes under the second time, and he comes back up crying, "Jesus, Jesus, I perish!" By this time, he's not trusting in the waves or in anything else… By this time, he has his eyes back on his Source. Each time he came up, he saw Christ. He had put his eyes back on Jesus again.

Jesus reached out His hand and took Peter's hand in His. That's one thing you can really feel. You can feel when the hand of the Lord is upon you. I mean, when your hand is in His hand, you know it. There's a big difference when He is reaching out His hand to you and when He's not. Jesus took Peter by the hand and lifted him up, and he stood there beside Jesus.

I can see them now as Jesus and Peter begin walking together, arm-in-arm, back to the boat.

Peter did walk on the water, but he didn't walk on it by himself. And God never asks you to do anything by yourself. You don't have to feel alone, because God is closer to you than your very breath. He is with you—and never leaves you nor forsakes you (Hebrews 13:5).

You know, it's all very simple when you get right down to it. I said, "simple," but I know it isn't easy. To keep your trust in God, your Source, you must keep your eyes on Him… and Him alone. Just as soon as you start looking to someone or something else to meet your need, you'll begin, like Peter, to sink beneath the problem. And before you know it, the problem will be on top of you.

I know… because it has happened to me many times in my life. But I also know that just as soon as I get my eyes back on God, my Source… when I remember who my Source is, then I begin to climb up out of the problem and get on top of it. Then I can sit back and relax and trust God, who is my Source, because I know that He has never failed me and He never will.

YOUR GOD-GIVEN KEY FOR TODAY:

I can walk with Jesus every day, because He will never, ever let me down. My hand is in His hand, and I'm not letting go.

[Thursday]

KEY: *Jesus Has Walked This Road Before Me... All I Need to Do Is Follow Him.*

There's something that I believe will really help you... knowing the difference between conversion and discipleship.

I was converted to Christ at age nineteen, just a few weeks before my twentieth birthday. It was a single, heartfelt act of repenting of my sins, and believing on Christ to save my soul. It was something I did in my parents' bedroom. As I told you earlier, I had been running from God for a long time, knowing that there was a call on my life, but I had wanted to make my own way.

But now, everything had changed. God had healed me, several times. A prophetic word had been spoken over me by my father, of what I was to do with my life, and I knew it was God.

It was a struggle for me, at first. But the more I thought, and prayed, and realized that Jesus Christ, God's only Son, had died for me, the more I knew I wanted to be a Christian. Now, as I said, I was a late teenager when I gave my heart to the Lord, and now, I'm in my sixties. Through God, I have more good years ahead, for I fully expect to live all my days, as He has planned.

The point is this: It is one thing to come to an act of receiving Christ as your personal Savior. It is entirely another to become a disciple, or a faithful follower, of Jesus Christ.

WEEK 6: THURSDAY

Your conversion and your becoming a disciple are two different things. Your conversion is what Christ does for you... Your becoming a disciple is what you do for Him, in the days and years of the rest of your life.

The act of your conversion was probably like mine—a struggle for you to get yourself to repent, and believe on Jesus, so He could do for you what no one else could... and that is to save you from your sins and give you His salvation.

So, you may be wondering, "How do you become a disciple?"

Becoming a disciple is not a single act. It is something you do, as a way of life, for the rest of your life. Jesus explained it: *"If anyone desires to come after Me, let him deny himself, and take up his cross daily, and follow Me"* (Luke 9:23).

The key word here is D-A-I-L-Y. Not one act... in one day... of turning your life over to Christ, but more, much more than that. It is being willing, daily, to follow Christ and become His disciple. It is going from your start, as a baby, born into the Kingdom of God (see John 3:3–5), growing into an adult in Christ, into Christian maturity, in which the living Christ is being daily formed in you (see Galatians 4:19).

It means you take on Jesus' own life and lifestyle, discover daily His way of doing things, and do them joyfully and continuously. Every day is a new day. Every day, you try to give God your best, then ask Him for His best, which is what seed-faith is really all about.

Yes, you can look back fondly at the act of your conversion, which was your spiritual birth and your starting time with Christ. But you go on living for Him daily, letting Christ take over your thoughts and deeds... your very life. It is taking up your cross. And what is the cross?

The cross, to Jesus, was the giving of Himself in sincere love and concern, in doing good to people, giving of His time and talents and efforts, giving of His resources, until one day, everything He had and everything He was would all be given. For, you see, the

Cross of Calvary was actually the last of Jesus giving of Himself. He had been doing it from the beginning (see Acts 10:38), but He finished that total, complete act of giving on the Cross. I think this is very important for you to know and understand.

"Seed-faith giving" as a way of life is taking up your cross daily. Why is it a cross? Because you and I, as human beings, have been taught by the world to get and not to give. Many of us don't like to give at all, because we feel like we lose something when we do. When we give to God, we are taught by some people not to expect anything back from Him.

That's the way people lived before Jesus came, but He opened up a "new and living way" (Hebrews 10:20) — the way of giving and giving first, of giving cheerfully and finding God's love coming back to us in the form of our need (see 2 Corinthians 9:7). I'm talking about giving not as a debt owed, but as a seed sown—giving with the expectation of a harvest that would come back to us—giving for a desired result.

Discipleship, as Jesus teaches in the Bible, is to take up our cross daily and gladly follow Him. Learn of Him and His ways and F-O-L-L-O-W. This is seed-faith, which will move you into a new life of expectation and receiving your most needed miracles. This is the road to a Better Life.

Here is an easy formula for discipleship (walking with Christ daily):

F- FOLLOW CHRIST DAILY

O- OBEY JESUS' WORD

L- LOVE HIM

L- LEAN ON HIM

O- OPEN UP AND START GIVING

W- WALK DAILY WITH HIM

YOUR GOD-GIVEN KEY FOR TODAY:

Now, no matter how rough it gets, keep saying:

"Jesus has walked this road before me… All I need to do is follow Him."

[Friday]

KEY: *One of the Greatest Seeds I'll Ever Plant Is Forgiveness.*

Jesus gave us two impossibilities… perhaps even more… but two in particular. First, He said in Matthew 18:7, *"It is impossible but that offenses will come."* By that, He meant we're going to offend somebody, and somebody is going to offend us… It is going to happen. It's impossible for it not to happen in the stresses and strains of our daily lives.

The second impossibility Jesus mentioned is… "Unless we forgive, we cannot be forgiven" (Matthew 6:14–15).

This means, unless I forgive someone else for what they've done to me, I cannot be forgiven for what I have done to them or to someone else. Now, those are two impossibilities.

There's something about offending someone or living in the stress and strain of that offense, and being unforgiven, that is, evidently, too heavy for human beings to bear. Somehow, it throws us off balance.

Think about it for a moment… Forgive, and you shall be forgiven. Once again, remember what Jesus said… *"Unless you forgive, you will not be forgiven by your Father in Heaven"* (Matthew 6:14).

Sometimes, some of us don't seem to care whether someone else forgives us or not. Or perhaps we have offended someone and we even say, "Well, so what?" But remember, there is someone else we deal with, and that is God. God has so constructed us that we cannot live successfully when we have committed offenses and have not made them right.

I remember many years ago, when our children were little, I did something that hurt and offended my wife Lindsay, as well as our three daughters. Now, I'm the type of person who can oftentimes be oblivious when I've done something wrong. However, when I realize my mistake, I can't wait to go to the person and try my best to make it right. So in this case, when I realized what I had done and that I had hurt my family, I gathered Lindsay and the children together in our living room and sat them down in a circle. And here's what I said.

"Lindsay and girls, I've done something that's wrong. I realize that I'm wrong. And I want you to know that I have asked God to forgive me. And now, I repent before you and ask you to forgive me. Please forgive me. And I give you my word, I will do my best that this situation will never, ever happen again."

All of them unanimously forgave me. And I believe a great burden was lifted off of the five of us as I did it. They felt better and I know I felt better.

There is a remarkable story in the Bible (Matthew 9) of a paralyzed man who needed, and received, forgiveness.

Four of his good friends brought him on a journey to Jesus because they believed their friend could be healed by Him. But when they arrived, the crowd in the house was too big. They climbed up on the roof, lifted up their friend, tore off the tiling, and let him down into the midst of the crowd, right in the presence of Jesus.

Now, let me stop in the middle of the story and remind you that when you're sick or afflicted or bowed down in any way, Jesus is in tune with you. What I mean by that is, He is right at the point of your need.

When Jesus looked at this man, He saw his paralysis. But He also saw something else, and compassion flowed out of Him for the man. Jesus knew that there was another kind of sickness beyond the paralysis that had gripped the man's inner-self. It was troubling him, and it was a terrible weight.

Our Lord knew that the man was sorry. So He said to the paralyzed man, "Son, your sins are forgiven you... You are forgiven of all the bitterness you built up over your affliction... all of that striking back at people and striking back at whatever it was that caused you to be ill... all of what you have held inside. You are forgiven."

How difficult it is to be sick and not be bitter. How hard it is not to strike at the very ones you love and who love you. How difficult it is when such deep resentment builds up inside of us. But Jesus said to the man, "You are forgiven."

FORGIVEN!

How many of us are forgiven? Are you forgiven? Am I forgiven?

Jesus said, *"Son, be of good cheer; your sins are forgiven you"* (Matthew 9:2–4).

Notice that Jesus dealt with the man's soul first. He dealt with the unforgiven sin. Then, Jesus followed it by a dramatic physical healing. "Take up your bed and walk," He said. And the man was able to do it. He received a miracle on the inside, as well as a miracle of physical healing!

You see, apparently when we are unforgiven, it can often paralyze our inner-man, causing us to have great difficulty in functioning. And it appears to me that humans are greatly affected by forgiveness, whether we have it or whether we don't have it.

Whether anyone ever forgives you or not... you forgive... for that's what Christ did on the Cross. He said, *"Father, forgive them, for they do not know what they do"* (Luke 23:34).

You see, Christ could have ruined it all there on the Cross by striking back at the very people who had hurt Him, beaten Him, and nailed Him to a cross in order to kill Him. But He reached down into the innermost part of His being and said, "Father, forgive..."

Many of them never responded. But the important thing was that He responded... He forgave.

I love Jesus Christ today, because He forgave me, and He keeps on forgiving me. He is teaching me to forgive and to keep on forgiving.

Maybe you feel something in your heart that should be brought up. Maybe you have an urgency to say something to your wife, or your husband, or a child, or a parent, or a brother, or a sister, or someone else. I'll tell you this, it will be one of the greatest seeds of faith you've ever planted, and I believe that God will multiply it back to you... And through forgiving, you will also be forgiven.

Yes, I understand it's tough to forgive, especially when you feel like the other guy is the one who should ask forgiveness. Well, maybe I can help you out. Here's what I do:

No matter how I have been wronged, I just say: "Lord, I forgive that person as a seed I plant." Then, the burden of the whole thing is no longer on my shoulders. When I forgive as a seed I plant, I believe God will straighten everything out better than I could ever have thought of.

So remember this and say it out loud:

One of the greatest seeds I'll ever plant is forgiveness.

Now, if you really mean that, write down on a piece of paper the biggest wrong someone has dealt you. You can put down their name if you want to. God knows. Remember, you're not just forgiving them for what they did; you're forgiving *them*, and that makes the difference.

Now, once you've written it down... Throw it away just like you're planting a seed in the ground... And look for God's harvest to come back to you.

WEEK 6: SATURDAY

YOUR GOD-GIVEN KEY FOR TODAY:

Say it again so you'll remember it: *"One of the greatest seeds I'll ever plant is forgiveness."*

[Saturday]

KEY: *I Am Obeying God and Expecting Him to Bless Me.*

My father gave me the greatest advice I ever received. He said, "Son, stay little in your own eyes, and God will bless the world through you."

I'm sure he gave me that advice because he knew it would be a difficult assignment for me. Then he gave me a second piece of advice. He said, "Son, always obey God."

Now, my dad didn't say that to me just one or two or three times. He said it to me often, especially as I was young. Over these many years, what he said to me lodged in my heart, and I've done my best to follow it.

We all must learn obedience… one way or another.

When I was a teenager, I heard a story about the training process of the beautiful Arabian horses in the Middle East. In that desolate part of the world, there are hundreds of miles of trackless desert. And in the past, the Arabian horse was the way that most people traveled.

This breed of horse was regarded very highly, and men would pay great prices for them. Their training put them through a highly specialized school, and the trainer would put the horses through all types of tests.

There was one test that was most severe. When it came near the time for graduation, the trainer would withhold water from the horses, and he would have the horses do without water as long as possible without dying of thirst. Sometimes, the temperature in those deserts would reach 130 degrees. Imagine what the horses must have endured. Imagine going a long period of time without water in conditions like that.

All the while during the test, the trainer was leading these horses to water. Of course, as they drew near the water, they could smell it. Soon, they would break loose, and with the last strength they had, they would run to the water to plunge in. But just as they got there, the trainer would blow his whistle—a signal they were supposed to respond to. The horses that stopped without drinking, turned around, and trotted back to the trainer graduated. They were perfectly obedient horses. The others who plunged into the water were sent back to school.

Now, why is such a test… such obedience… necessary? Because the life of a man on that horse is entrusted to the horse. Imagine yourself out on the trackless desert, on the back of a disobedient horse, a horse that will not obey the signals you give him. You could both easily die.

Christianity is tough. It's not easy, and it was not intended to be, because man has to learn obedience. If he does not learn to obey God, then he will obey man or he will obey the devil. He will learn some kind of discipline, whether he wants it or not. He may have to learn it by the law, and there are some who are behind prison walls today who are being subjected to the learning of discipline. Whether they willingly obey or not, they obey.

Each one of us has to learn for himself the meaning of Christ's words, *"If anyone desires to come after Me* [be my disciple]*, let him deny himself, and take up his cross daily, and follow Me"* (Luke 9:23).

Follow Me. We must become sensitive to the promptings of the Holy Spirit… open-minded to whatever the Lord would have us do. We must be willing to obey.

WEEK 6: SATURDAY

Are you living in obedience? Are you under the authority of God?

I can relate to any person today who wants to be a law unto himself, or who wants to have his own way... to rebel against his parents, against society, against the Church, against God Himself. I can relate, because that's what I did. Yes, it brought heartache to my family, and to me as well.

But the day came when I recognized that I was totally out of the will of God, and I made a decision that I would come under the authority of God, because I gave my heart to Christ.

Now, today, I still don't obey all the time, as I should. Sometimes, I think I'm obeying, and then I realize I'm not obeying. Sometimes I slip back into a disobedient spirit. I rebel, and I don't want anyone to say anything to me. Sometimes, I don't want to listen to God or to those who love me and are trying to help me.

That's the way we humans are in our own natural state without God's grace. But I do know this. The only way to live a successful Christian life is to come under the authority of God... and to be obedient to Him. Sometimes, I slip and fall or make mistakes, but each time I do, I get back up, repent, tell God how sorry I am, ask Him for forgiveness, and get back on that road to a Better Life.

Now, let me ask you this question: Are you living in obedience to God?

Have you accepted God's authority to such an extent that you are willing to give up your way and take God's way instead? To give up your will and take God's will?

Even Jesus had to say, "Not My will but Yours be done" (Luke 22:42). The Bible tells us in Hebrews 5:8 that Jesus learned to be obedient by the things that He suffered. Imagine that. Jesus Himself had to learn obedience and to do what God told Him to do.

Eventually, Jesus had to face the things that God wanted Him to do, for *"He [Jesus] had offered up prayers and supplications, with vehement cries and tears to Him who was able to save Him from death"* (Hebrews 5:7).

Jesus did not want to go to the Cross. He did not want nails driven into His hands. Can you imagine how that felt? Imagine having the flesh and bones of your hands crushed by those nails being driven through them, and then having nails driven through your feet.

But that was not the worst of it. Imagine being stripped and hung on a wooden cross and left to die. Jesus did not look forward to that. He wanted men to understand that He came to the world to save them. But they didn't understand, and He cried for God to grant Him some other way. But He knew that a seed has to be planted if you want it multiplied back to you. That's the law of God. That's the law of nature.

And so, Jesus had to give, and He had to obey God. The human part of Him didn't want to do it any more than we want to be obedient. But Jesus is our example in giving up His own way and taking God's ways. We can also say, "Not my will but God's will be done." And how glorious it is when we go through a struggle and endure the pain of it and come out with a resurrection miracle... with a seed multiplied... and the joy of the Lord flowing from our hearts with our needs met.

I ask you again, "Are you putting yourself under God's authority?"

"Are you living in obedience... disciplining yourself as Jesus did... taking God's will for yourself?"

If you are, then you're going to be blessed by God. Maybe you're not in perfect obedience. That's all right... This is something we grow into. The important thing is, are you trying to be obedient? Are you doing the best you can?

After all, we as Christians are not perfect, just forgiven and walking toward perfection.

WEEK 6: SATURDAY

YOUR GOD-GIVEN KEY FOR TODAY:

I'm obeying God and expecting Him to bless me.

WEEK 6 RECAP

- **Sunday:** I Know God, and I Am in Him... and He Is in Me.
- **Monday:** I Will Use My Inner Resources of Prayer and Faith.
- **Tuesday:** God Loves Me, and He Will Never Give Up on Me.
- **Wednesday:** I Can Walk with Jesus Every Day.
- **Thursday:** Jesus Has Walked This Road Before Me... All I Need to Do Is Follow Him.
- **Friday:** One of the Greatest Seeds I'll Ever Plant Is Forgiveness.
- **Saturday:** I Am Obeying God and Expecting Him to Bless Me.

WEEK 7

[Sunday]

KEY: *I Believe in Miracles…Today!*

Have miracles ceased?

That's the question many ask today. And there are Christians today who believe that miracles stopped when the Apostles died.

But I want to remind you, the Bible says in Hebrews 13:8, *Jesus is the same yesterday, today, and forever.* If Jesus *ever* performed a miracle, He is still performing miracles today.

As I write this book, I can report to you that in the last twenty years, we've received approximately 150,000 healing testimonies. These are people from all over the world who are describing miracles they have received in their lives through our prayers.

So, I want to say to you emphatically: **Miracles have not died out.** Jesus is still healing people today, just as He did some 2,000 years ago.

When I was in high school, I remember that our long-time friend, Reverend Billy Graham, invited my father, Oral Roberts, to attend the World Congress on Evangelism in Berlin, Germany.

I had wanted very much to go with my dad on this trip, but the Congress was during school for me, so I was unable to go. But something remarkable happened while he was there.

During my dad's time as a delegate, he was met by a pastor from India. He said to my dad, "Brother Roberts, I have a very difficult problem. I have never understood or believed in miracles or that God healed the sick, although I've preached for many years. I thought miracles had died out."

My dad said to him, "Sir, what is the problem?"

The pastor replied, "Two of my members rushed into the church one day with their child, who was dying. The doctors had given up. The parents thrust the little child into my hands and said, 'Pastor, please pray for God to heal him."

"I was in a dilemma. They asked me to do what I did not believe could happen... that is, for God to heal him. Before I realized it, though, I took the child in my arms and prayed for him. And to my utter amazement, God healed him!"

My dad chuckled and said, "Sir, then, what's the problem?"

The pastor said, "My problem is very serious, Brother Roberts. Did I do the right thing in praying for the little boy?"

My dad knew that this was a very important moment and started to say, "Of course, you did right." But he knew he had to have something to back up that statement so that this pastor could understand God's will and His Word in a deeper way.

Suddenly, the Lord gave my dad a word of wisdom. And here's what he said to him. "Pastor, why don't you ask the little boy if you did the right thing?"

The pastor thought for a moment and said, "Oh, oh. Why don't I ask the little boy? Oh, yes. You've given me the answer. Thank you so much, Brother Roberts. I'm going back to India after this conference, and I'm going to ask God to give me a healing ministry." And the Lord did.

All through these years of being a Christian, whenever anyone has confronted me with the questions, "Have miracles ceased? Do they still happen today?" I will often tell them this story and finish with the line, "Why don't you ask the little boy?"

That phrase did not come out of my father's mind. It came out of his spirit. The Holy Spirit planted that in his mind, and then he spoke it "Why don't you ask the little boy?"

When they asked the blind man in John 9:25 who had healed him, the man replied, "I don't know. All I know is, once I was blind and now I can see."

You see, anybody who has been sick and has received a miracle from God has no question in his mind about the rightness of believing God for a miracle... or whether God still heals today. He knows it.

The fact is, my friend, you can spend hours, days, even weeks in arguing whether or not miracles still happen today and get nowhere. If you really want to know, find someone who has experienced a miracle and ask them what they think. Or better still, believe God for the miracle that you need yourself. Once you or someone close to you has experienced a miracle, there will be no question in your mind.

The most important thing in your life is a miracle... especially when you need one.

Why? Because you have a seven-day-a-week life — with seven-day-a-week needs — and seven-day-a-week faith.

I believe God made miracles for you and you for miracles. Miracles are on the road to a Better Life.

YOUR GOD-GIVEN KEY FOR TODAY:

I believe in miracles... today... and I believe that they're still happening.

[Monday]

KEY: *I Will Not Take "No" for an Answer.*

All throughout my life, the Lord has spoken to me prophetically. Sometimes the word came through my father, Oral Roberts. Other times, the word came through ministers with prophetic giftings. Sometimes the word came through my wife, Lindsay, while other times the Lord spoke directly to me.

One night, I received a phone call from my dad. He was so excited! He said, "Richard, the Lord has spoken to me again and told me that healing is coming big time, and I think that you should begin to emphasize healing more on your TV programs."

Well, that certainly resonated in my spirit. "Healing is coming big time." Think about that for a minute. All throughout the Bible, you can find the healing power of God. From Genesis to Malachi in the Old Testament, and from Matthew to Revelation in the New Testament, healing is emphasized.

Through the prophetic word my dad shared with me, the Lord said, "Tell the people I want to heal them. Tell them not to take no for an answer. Believe Me and release their faith, for healing is their heritage." Wow, what a mighty and wonderful prophetic word!

The good news is, healing is just as real today as it was when Jesus walked this earth. That word was in total harmony with everything the Lord has shown me about healing all through these years, and it goes along with 3 John 2, where the Bible says, *"Beloved, I pray that you may prosper in all things and be in health, just as your soul prospers."*

In other words, it's God's will for you to be well in every area of your life—in your spirit, mind, body, family, finances, emotions, business, ministry, marriage... yes, in every area of your life. Now, that's healing, and that's the road to a Better Life.

WEEK 7: MONDAY

Let's look at Matthew 8. In this passage of Scripture, Jesus had just come down from the mountain, after He finished His great Sermon on the Mount. Suddenly, a leper came and fell at His feet and worshipped Him and said, *"Lord, if You are willing, You can make me clean"* (Matthew 8:2).

Can you imagine the audacity of this leper? In those days, lepers were considered unclean and forbidden by Jewish law to mingle with the rest of the people. A leper was supposed to stand afar off and cry, "Unclean! Unclean!" But this leper, no doubt, saw the love and compassion in the eyes of Jesus and knew that it was His will to heal people.

"If you will," cried the leper. Suddenly, he heard Jesus say, "I am willing. Be cleansed" (Matthew 8:3).

And the Bible says, "Immediately his leprosy was cleansed" (Matthew 8:3).

"I will." I've often wondered what would have happened if Jesus had said, "I won't." What if He had not been involved with human beings and their needs? What if He just made a garden and sculptured the mountains and made the earth a parade ground for His creation to see? What if He had said no? But He said, "Yes, I will."

You see, Jesus *is* involved. And as I like to say it, He is at the very point of your need.... right where you need Him the most.

Next, also in the eighth chapter of Matthew is the story of the Roman army captain coming to Jesus and kneeling there in the dusty road, saying, *"Lord, my servant is lying at home paralyzed, dreadfully tormented"* (Matthew 8:6).

Christ said these words: "I will come and heal him" (Matthew 8:7).

Here again, Jesus says, "I will."

You see, Jesus could have said to this Roman, who was an overlord there in Palestine—and who had bowed to no man but Caesar—"Look, you rough, rude, uncultured, paganistic, brutal solider. If you think you have any part of My kingdom, you're wrong. I don't have any time for you. Why don't you take your soldiers and go back to Rome?"

But Jesus didn't have that attitude toward the man. Instead, He was involved with the need and the desperation the man had for his military aide. Jesus was concerned when the Roman centurion said, "My servant is lying at home dreadfully tormented."

So, the Lord said, "I will come and heal him… I will…" There are those words again.

I want you to know, my friend, there's nobody outside the reach of Christ's human and divine love. Neither you, nor anyone else, is outside of it. You are within His circle of concern and love, for He is concerned about you. Let this truth settle down into your spirit.

You see, the position of Christ is a very positive one towards you. "I will come and heal …"

Your position must be a powerful and positive one toward Him, as well. Let yourself take this position by faith. In fact, say it out loud right now…

"Yes, Lord, I will to be healed. I want to be healed. I will not take no for an answer. I will release my faith. I will believe You for a mighty miracle in my life. Healing is my heritage. I will not give up… I will not let go… I will hold on… and I will expect Your touch on my life."

YOUR GOD-GIVEN KEY FOR TODAY:

I will not take no for an answer. I will release my faith and believe God for my miracle.

[Tuesday]

KEY: *God's Works Mean a Miracle to Me.*

As a general rule in the New Testament, Jesus refers to miracles as the works of God or the works of the Father.

Now Matthew, Mark, Luke, and John continually said that Christ performed miracles, but Jesus called them the works of God. For example:

"The works which the Father has given Me to finish—the very works that I do—bear witness of Me, that the Father has sent Me" (John 5:36).

In other words, Jesus said, "I do the works of my Father."

Jesus is talking about doing the works of God. In John 10:37–38, Jesus said, *"If I do not do the works of My Father, do not believe Me; but if I do, though you do not believe Me, believe the works…"* Jesus was saying, "If you cannot believe that I am the Son of God, believe these works… these works of God."

Jesus indicates a miracle is not a sometime or a one-time thing. It is not some sort of magic. He places a miracle in the category of the works of God. Now, the moment you stop calling them miracles and put them into the area of the works of God, then you see that Jesus Christ has only come to do what God has been doing all through the centuries and will continue to do forever. Jesus came to do the works of the Father. He is carrying out the essential nature of His Father, which is to bring His works of life to the world.

He explains here that the Spirit of God is upon Him, and He's coming to do these mighty works of the Father.

Acts 10:38 says, *"God anointed Jesus of Nazareth with the Holy Spirit and with power, who went about doing good and healing all who were oppressed by the devil, for God was with Him."*

Jesus was anointed by the Holy Spirit. Then He went about doing good and healing all who were oppressed of the devil, for God was with Him. He was doing the works of God.

If the word "miracle" turns you off, don't worry. Just remember, Jesus emphasized that these miracles were really the works of God.

Jesus is still talking about the works of God in Luke 4:18 when He said, *"The Spirit of the Lord is upon Me, because He has anointed Me to preach the gospel to the poor."* Jesus was really saying, "God has sent Me with good news to the poor, and that good news is, you don't have to be poor anymore."

Jesus went on to say,*"He has sent Me to heal the brokenhearted, to proclaim liberty to the captives, and recovery of sight to the blind, to set at liberty those who are oppressed; to proclaim the acceptable year of the Lord"* (Luke 4:18–19). These are the works Jesus is doing. These are the works of the Father. These are what the gospel writers call miracles or wonders.

In 1 Corinthians 12:10, we learn that one of the nine gifts of the Spirit is the working of miracles. Here again are "works"—the works of our Father.

In John 14:12, we read, *"He who believes in Me, the works that I do he will do also; and greater works than these he will do, because I go to My Father."* Greater Works will *YOU* do.

In Acts 3, the story is told of how the apostles brought healing to the lame man who was carried daily and placed at the gate of the Temple in Jerusalem.

Peter and John came by one day, and by faith, the man was healed. Because of this healing, they were persecuted.

The temple leaders called Peter and John to a meeting, where they commanded them not to speak at all, nor teach in the name of Jesus. But Peter and John answered and said unto them, *"Whether it is right in the sight of God to listen to you more than to God, you judge. For we cannot but speak the things which we have seen and heard."* So *when they* [the temple leaders] *had further threatened them, they let them go, finding no way of punishing them, because of the people, since they all glorified God for what had been done* (Acts 4:19).

The apostles returned unto their own company and they prayed. *"Now, Lord, look on their threats, and grant to Your servants that with all boldness they may speak Your word, by stretching out Your hand to heal, and that signs and wonders may be done through the name of Your holy Servant Jesus"* (Acts 4:29–30).

This was after the Ascension of Christ. Christ was no longer on the earth in the flesh at that time. He'd been crucified and resurrected, and had ascended back to His Heavenly Father as the glorified Christ and God had sent the Holy Spirit.

His disciples were still doing the same works and even greater works than He had done. They were being persecuted for it.

Peter and John returned to their group of fellow believers to pray. They called upon the Lord not to deliver them from persecution, but to grant that they would speak His words with boldness by stretching forth His hand to heal… by letting them continue to do the works of God.

What I am saying is this. This beginning of miracles, or this beginning of the "works of God," is what Jesus, our Lord, did for us (John 2). His time on earth was not an ending of the works of God, but a beginning of the works of God. These works of God carried over into the lives of His followers, and they are in the lives of His followers today, if we will only accept them.

So, when you have insurmountable needs, needs that are so baffling and so terrible that they require something beyond the natural—beyond the ordinary—you have recourse to God and His wonderful works.

Now, *that's the road to a Better Life*, for there is power in God's wonderful works. I believe He has a miracle for you, and I want you to believe it too.

YOUR GOD-GIVEN KEY FOR TODAY:

God's works mean a miracle to me. (Say it over and over again.) *"God's works mean a miracle to me."*

[Wednesday]

KEY: *I Can Claim My Family to Be God's Property Now… for There Is No Distance in Prayer.*

When our middle daughter, Catherine Olivia, was a little girl, she was attacked in her body by the E.coli virus. She was hospitalized and quarantined because of the concern that the virus might spread to others. We prayed her through all of that, and by prayer and the good work of the doctors, she was healed.

However, in the ensuing months, her doctors were saying that she had developed lupus and also the early stages of crippling arthritis. She actually broke her ankle because of the weakness in her bones.

Naturally, we were all still praying for a miracle.

I was scheduled to minister in South Korea, and Lindsay felt that I should not cancel the trip, but that I should go and count it as a seed for our daughter's complete healing.

When I arrived in Korea, I got the news that Olivia could only get around on her crutches and that it was very difficult for her to go up and down the stairs in our home. She actually began to sit backwards on the steps and go up one stair at a time. She cried with the pain in her ankle and foot.

Suddenly, I got angry at the devil! Here I was, trying to minister to others, while my own daughter was struck with a satanic attack. It was as though he was trying to discredit the healing ministry and God's desire to heal people.

Then I remembered that Lindsay had said to me, "Honey, there's no distance in prayer. You can send the healing Word of God to Olivia, claim her to be God's property, and believe for her healing."

So I began to pray with that in mind. Lindsay put Olivia on the phone, and I took authority over lupus, arthritis, and the break in her ankle.

I said out loud to the devil, "This is my family. This is my daughter, Olivia. She belongs to God. You cannot have her. In the name of Jesus, I break this satanic attack against her. Lupus, come out! Crippling arthritis, come out! Break in the ankle, be healed! Amen."

Although the Pacific Ocean stood between us, God bridged the distance in prayer. Suddenly, Olivia was running up and down the stairs, no crutches and no pain. Praise God!

By the time I got back home, there was no trace of lupus or arthritis, and the break in her ankle was completely healed. We learned that we could declare by faith that we were God's property and that the devil has no rights over our lives, because we belong to God. Our daughter was gloriously healed, and she's still healed and serving the Lord today. I'm so proud of her.

When you say, "My family and I are God's property," you are saying something powerful. You're saying, "The devil has no part of me or my family."

YOUR GOD-GIVEN KEY FOR TODAY:

Seal off the devil and his demons by affirming…

I can claim my family and me to be God's property, for there is no distance in prayer.

[Thursday]

KEY: *When I Pray for Someone Else's Healing, I Have an Opportunity for God to Heal Me.*

Many years ago, a woman named Marie worked for our ministry. She discovered she had an advanced stage of cancer. The doctor said she only had a matter of months to live.

Marie was a strong, Spirit-filled Christian. She loved the Lord with all of her heart. She wanted to live and not die (Psalm 118:17).

After the initial shock began to wear off, she went to prayer and God spoke to her. The Lord told her to find every person she could who had cancer and pray for them. And He reminded her of James 5:16, which says, *"Pray for one another, **that you may be healed.**"* So, for weeks, she did everything in her power to locate people throughout our city who had cancer. She called or visited them and prayed for their healing.

Then something unusual happened. At her next exam, the doctors could not find any cancer. She was completely healed! She credited her miraculous healing to the fact that she obeyed the Lord and prayed for someone else's healing, believing that as she did, God would not only heal them but also heal her.

Marie lived for quite a number of years after that and continued working in our ministry.

WEEK 7: THURSDAY

As many of you know, I have conducted healing crusades all over the earth. I've also preached for many pastors' conferences and leadership seminars.

One of the things that I always do, as I teach people how to pray for the sick, is to remind them that one of the most powerful healing prayers ever prayed is when we pray one for another, believing for their healing and expecting healing to come back to us. I have seen it happen over and over again all around the world. When I get people praying one for another, invariably the person who does the praying begins to receive a touch from the Lord.

Now, let's examine James 5:16 one more time... *"Pray one for another that you may be healed."* The emphasis here is upon the one doing the praying.

Sometimes when I pray for someone, I suggest a two-way prayer... That is, I ask him or her to pray for me first before I begin praying for them. I do this to help the sick person plant the seed of concern and healing prayer for someone else, according to James 5:16.

Now, let's look at this from Jesus' standpoint.

First of all, He's saying that you pray for someone else to be healed so that you may be healed also. Secondly, He is saying to put the seed in first, so He can have something from your heart to work with.

I believe that God is trying to get you and me to open up on the inside. For the truth is, many of us, deep down on the inside, are inhibited. We are tense, and we don't often let the real person come out. Many of us have been taught from infancy not to reveal our inner-heart because people might misunderstand or betray us. We fear that they might think less of us if we are totally frank and really turn loose and pray for their healing.

When we need healing in any area of our lives, we are dealing directly with God, and He's saying to us, "Open up. Open up. Pray one for another that you may be healed." It's another way of saying, "Give, and it shall be given unto you" (Luke 6:38). It's another way of seeding for a miracle.

YOUR GOD-GIVEN KEY FOR TODAY:

Make a note of James 5:16 and keep saying it to yourself.

"When I pray for someone else's healing, I have an opportunity for God to heal me."

[Friday]

KEY: *When Nothing Less Than a Miracle Will Do*

As I have said before, when I was a boy, I traveled all over the United States and Canada, as well as overseas, in my dad's crusades. It was a thrill to sit in the front row and hear him preach those firecracker healing sermons, and then watch him lay hands on the sick and see miracles happen right before my eyes! Sometimes, he would even call me up on the platform to stand by him.

I especially loved to go with him into the invalid room, where people who were too sick to stand in the prayer line would wait for him to come and lay hands on them and pray for their healing.

One of the greatest miracles in my father's ministry occurred in the early 1950s in Roanoke, Virginia. There was a little boy about six years old who had suffered with Perthes Disease in his hip. One leg was two-and-a-half inches shorter, and he could not walk without crutches.

His parents brought him to the crusade that night, but they couldn't get in because the overflow crowd was too big. It was snowing outside and quite cold, but somehow, through the help of an usher, they managed to get into the building and stand over on the side.

It was the last day of the crusade, and my father had laid hands on thousands of people that day. As he came down the hall, ready to return to the hotel and catch a flight back home, he noticed a little boy sitting in a room by himself. As he passed the door, he couldn't help stopping to see what was going on. He asked the boy a question: "Son, what are you doing in there?"

The boy replied, "I'm waiting for Oral Roberts."

"You are?"

"Yes."

"What's your name, son?"

"Willie. Willie Phelps."

"Well, Willie, I'm Oral Roberts."

"You are?"

"Yes, I am."

"Well, Brother Roberts, I heard you preach today, and I'm supposed to be healed."

My dad would later tell me this story, and how he felt as if there was electricity in the air because God's power felt so strong and present at that moment. Somehow he knew in his heart, if he laid his hand on young Willie Phelps, God would do a miracle.

He laid his hands on Willie and prayed a brief prayer, then turned and left the building. But he didn't hear the rest of the story for another 18 months.

Willie turned to his mother and said, "Stand back. I'm going to walk." He took off his built-up shoe, threw down his crutches, and instead of walking, he ran... healed by the power of God!

About a year and a half later, my dad returned to Roanoke for another crusade, and that was when he learned of the great miracle testimony of

Willie's healing. "It's one of the greatest healings of my ministry," my dad would always tell me. His eyes would tear up as he told the story.

I've shared this story many times all over the world. I would have been three or four years old at that time... just a couple of years younger than Willie. But hearing my dad tell the story made me feel like I was really there, after all.

My friend, there are times in our lives when nothing less than a miracle will do.

When you and I can learn to have faith like a child... like little Willie Phelps... when you and I can be fully emptied of doubt and believe God with all of our heart, soul, mind, and strength... then I believe we get into the right place to receive.

I've always felt that children can believe for miracles so much easier than we adults, because they are so fresh out of heaven. So, when you need that special miracle, and when nothing less than a miracle will do, use your faith and try to become like a little child. Then hang on to this truth:

YOUR GOD-GIVEN KEY FOR TODAY:

When nothing less than a miracle will do for me, I will use my faith like a child and believe God for the supernatural to touch my life.

[Saturday]

KEY: *God Is My Healer.*

God has taught me that everyone is sick in some way. This sickness is anything that throws any part of a person out of harmony with the rest of himself.

WEEK 7: SATURDAY

Above all, God has taught me that sickness is an inside job. You see, the first thought that goes through your mind when sickness strikes is that you will never get well. In fact, that's what the devil is really good at… telling you that this sickness will continue, and you'll never recover.

But remember, the Bible says that the devil is not only a liar, but he is the father of lies (John 8:44). Therefore, he is not capable of telling you the truth. So, if he is telling you that you won't be healed, you can know beyond any doubt that God wants you well… He wants you to be healed in every area of your life.

Back when my dad was seventeen and suffering with tuberculosis, they thought that he was going to die… that he would never get well. And in fact, the idea that he "would die" shot through his mind until his sister, my Aunt Jewel, came in and said seven words that changed his thinking completely. Here are those seven words. "Oral, God is going to heal you."

My dad heard those words with his ears. Those words got in his mind, and then they got into his spirit. Suddenly, for the first time, he believed he was not going to die. He was going to get well.

The same is true today. When satan comes to you trying to steal, kill, and destroy your life, you can know that his lies are from the pit of hell and that God wants you well in every area of your life.

Many people today wonder where God is when sickness strikes. Well, I want you to know He is at the very point of your need, and that's where you look for Him. He's always been there, and He's there right now for you too.

I believe that healing begins with an attitude change. It is us as human beings saying, "I open myself up to a miracle because I believe that God wants me well and not sick."

That kind of attitude helps you to believe that Jesus Christ, God's only Son, came to make you whole, to heal you from your head to your feet, inside and out, to make you a new creature, so that you can come alive in Him (2 Corinthians 5:17). That's healing for the whole man! And my friend, that's the road to a Better Life.

Just as sure as Jesus healed my father from tuberculosis all those many years ago, He is on the job to heal you today. In fact, let me pray a healing prayer over you right now:

"Heavenly Father, I come to You, not in my name or my strength, but in the mighty, everlasting Name of your Son, Jesus, Who came that we might have life and have it more abundantly... and to have it in every area of our lives."

"I rebuke every sickness, every disease, every fear, and every doubt. I command the devil to take his hands off of your life, and I pray for healing to come into your life... in every area of your life, from your head to your feet. Satan, I command you: Take your hands off of God's property! And my friend, I pray for you right now, believing in God for a miracle. I release my faith for it. And I'm not coming out of this prayer of agreement with you until the miracle is manifested. In the authority of Jesus' name, I pray and I believe. Amen and Amen."

YOUR GOD-GIVEN KEY FOR TODAY:

God is my healer.

WEEK 7 RECAP

- **Sunday:** I Believe in Miracles...Today!
- **Monday:** I Will Not Take "No" for an Answer.
- **Tuesday:** God's Works Mean a Miracle to Me.
- **Wednesday:** I Can Claim My Family to Be God's Property Now... for There Is No Distance in Prayer.
- **Thursday:** When I Pray for Someone Else's Healing, I Have an Opportunity for God to Heal Me.

- **Friday:** When Nothing Less than a Miracle Will Do.
- **Saturday:** God Is My Healer.

WEEK 8

[Sunday]

KEY: *When I Act, My Faith Begins to Work.*

All power has a point at which you make contact. In your car, you turn the key and the motor turns over. If you flip a light switch, there is an instant contact with the electric company that causes the power which gives you light...

There has to be a point of contact... the light switch, the accelerator in your car... any source of power you can name must have a point by which you make contact with it.

However, the important thing is not the point of contact. The important thing is that you release the power. The power is the thing that you want released. We put the point of contact in its proper context of usefulness. It is not an end in itself, but it is a very useful instrument to help you release your faith, believing God for a miracle.

In Matthew chapter eight, a Roman army captain had a very definite need of healing for his military aide who was grievously tormented with paralysis. Eventually, the captain went beyond the army doctors and went directly to Jesus.

He bowed before Christ and called Him "Lord." Literally, he switched his allegiance over from Caesar to Jesus Christ, God's only Son. He did it because first of all, he had a need that could not be met by any power that he knew about.

Secondly, the captain had come to see Jesus as the embodiment of life itself.

Then he bowed. It was literally force bowing to meekness—an armed might before the unarmed. It was the proud uniform of war bowing before the seamless robe of the Carpenter from Nazareth.

First, the Centurion told Jesus the story of how tormented his military aide was. Jesus responded immediately by saying, "I will come and heal him." In other words, Jesus was saying, "I'll walk the miles up to the Roman encampment and lay my hands on your aide and make him well.

But the man said, "No, that's not necessary, because I recognize that you have authority above all authority. You just speak the word right here, and my military aide will be healed." In other words, You don't have to come to my house. Just stand here and send the word, and he'll be healed.

Isn't it amazing that sometimes you find faith where you least expect it and sometimes, when you look to find it in places where you would expect it, it's not there? Here is the commanding power of faith when it is released. The point of contact was to speak the word. Why?

Because this is a man who recognized authority and power... Jesus' power. And the man needed that power to be released for a miracle.

Jesus responded by saying, *"Go your way; and as you have believed, so let it be done for you."* On the way back to the Roman garrison, the army captain heard or received word that his military aide had been healed at the same moment that Jesus spoke His healing word.

This is one of the greatest examples of the point of contact in all the Word of God.

Now, what does the point of contact do?

The first thing it does is to recognize God. It recognizes Him as the Source of all the power. The second thing is, the point of contact sets the time for you to release your faith. It does not necessarily set the time for the healing or for the miracle to happen... but it does set the actual time for you to release your faith and believe for it.

WEEK 8: SUNDAY

Now, you can do several things with your faith. One thing you can do is to keep your faith inside of you.

One man said to me, "I have all the faith in the world."

I said, "Sir, that's your problem. You still have it."

Faith must be released to God. It doesn't do you any good just welled up inside you. You have to let it go.

Someone says, "Well, how do I know that I have faith?" You know it because the Bible says you have it. *"God has dealt to each one a measure of faith"* (Romans 12:3).

God has a certain measure of faith, and a part of it is given to every person. You have it. I have it. Every person has it. But you might not use your faith. What Jesus is seeking is for you to release the faith that you have, so that it becomes an act.

For example, in order for you to have faith in a chair, you have to act on your faith, and sit down on the chair. For your faith to be useful, it has to become an act. You have to act on it. That is to say, you must release it.

The point of contact works best for people who believe in the authority of Jesus—that He is not only their Savior, but He's also their Lord. He's over every situation they'll ever face.

This is the road to a Better Life… It's a practical level of living daily under the Lordship of Jesus, where you see that everything of a negative nature must yield to Him. You never say, "God can't do that." You never say, "That's impossible." You cut the word impossible out of your vocabulary. You come into a relationship with Christ until you believe that He is "all in all" and that He can do anything and there's nothing too hard for Him.

The second point of contact… the laying on of hands… was used by Jairus, a ruler of the synagogue of the Jews. Jairus was not a rabbi, but he was a leader in the synagogue and held a very high and responsible position. His little daughter became so ill that she was about to die.

Jairus had heard of Jesus, and knew that Jesus could heal his daughter. Therefore, he asked Him, saying, *"Come and lay Your hands on her, that she may be healed, and she will live"* (Mark 5:23).

I've found that the laying on of hands is best used by an individual who is more influenced by another person's faith, who wants to feel the warmth of another person, who wants the intimacy of human contact. This was certainly the case with Jairus.

This point of contact... the laying on of hands... set the time for Jairus to release his faith. And it's important to zero in on that moment we release our faith to God, because circumstances will often arise to test our faith. Knowing we have believed God already helps us to stand firm. While he and Jesus were on the way to the little girl's bedside, some people met them and said to Jairus, *"Your daughter is dead. Why trouble the Teacher any further?"*

Jesus immediately said, *"Do not be afraid; only believe"* (vs 35–36). That is, keep your point of contact. Don't turn loose of it. You want the laying on of hands, and that's your point of contact. Hold on to it.

When Jesus arrived at the house, the little girl had apparently died. But because the point of contact was made prior to her death and Jairus held onto the point of contact, never giving up, Jesus did lay His hands on the little girl and she revived.

Another point of contact was used by the apostles of the Lord and especially by the Apostle Paul.

Paul was preaching one day, and there was a crippled man in the crowd. Paul saw the faith that the man had, and cried out, *"Stand up straight on your feet"* (Acts 14:10)! That's all Paul said: *"Stand up straight on your feet!"* That's the spoken word. He spoke the word, and the crippled man responded to that type of point of contact. He leapt and walked.

The same man, the Apostle Paul, used the laying on of hands while he was on the Island of Malta, and great healings came to people there (Acts 28).

So, various points of contact were used in the New Testament. The particular one used was usually a good fit for the background of the person who needed the healing power of Christ.

In other words… God loves you so much that, in a sense, He accommodates Himself to the way you respond. And the thing that will help you establish your point of contact is usually honored by God.

Receiving Holy Communion is another point of contact. Taking the bread, which symbolizes the body of Christ, broken and bruised for your healing, and drinking the cup, symbolizing His shed blood for the remission of sin, is a very powerful way to receive healing and blessing in your life.

The Holy Communion has, through faith, not only great power to deal with your soul, but also with your body. It is indicated in 1 Corinthians 11 that some of the Corinthians who were taking the cup and the bread were taking it unworthily. That is, they were not grasping the meaning of what Jesus did on Calvary. They were just eating and drinking without using their faith, and they were missing what it was all about.

As a result of their misunderstanding, they were not able to take Communion in faith for what Jesus had done for them. The sicknesses they had were not being healed. Some of them were dying before their time. They were not taking advantage through faith of the bread and the cup.

First, they were not grasping the meaning of the body of Christ in that they were not looking up to Him in thanksgiving. Second, they were not grasping the meaning of His body in their relationships with one another. In other words, there was bickering and division. There was quarreling and fussing and fighting among the Christians in Corinth.

When they took communion, their faith, the faith they had in their hearts, was not being released. And because their faith was not being released, the healing that the Lord wanted to bring them was not coming to them. It was like they were being cut off... like they were dying of thirst while standing in front of a great fountain of fresh water!

But Paul said to them, "When you eat of the bread and drink of the cup, do it in faith, do it in love, and do it in expectation."

Now, here's something very important. When you make anything you do toward God your point of contact, you're planting a mighty seed of your faith. And you can always depend upon God to multiply the seed back to you in the way you need it most.

The point of contact is so important. Let me summarize it in this way...And I promise, according to the Word of God, that if you will follow these truths step-by-step, you can expect to see a difference in your prayer power.

1. A point of contact is something you do. And when you do it, you release your faith.

    Faith is inside you. God has given to every man the measure of faith, according to Romans 12:3. Faith is something you have... But until you release it, it is as though you have none. Faith has to come out of you. It has to become an act... a single act of believing.

2. Every power must have a point of contact to release it.

    With electricity, for example, you flip the light switch to release the power to the bulb, which in turn lights the room. In the same way, your point of contact releases your faith to God, which releases His power back into your life.

3. A point of contact helps you to recognize your Source... God.

4. A point of contact sets the time for the releasing of your faith. It does not necessarily set the time for your healing. It sets the time for the releasing of your faith for miracles to meet your needs.

5. The point of contact may be many things. It may be…

the spoken word…

the laying on of hands…

taking Holy Communion…

my letters to you, or your letters to me…

the prayer time during our television programs and Facebook videos, when I stretch out my hands to pray for your healing…

or anything that helps you to turn your faith loose of all doubt, and believe God for a miracle.

Believe me, releasing your faith helps put you on the road to a Better Life.

YOUR GOD-GIVEN KEY FOR TODAY:

When I act, my faith begins to work.

[Monday]

KEY: *Jesus Is Unlimited, and There Is No Distance in Prayer.*

One thing I've learned for sure is the fact that there is no distance in prayer. This is because Jesus is not only omnipotent (all-powerful)… He is not only omniscient (able to know everything)… But He is omnipresent, which means He is everywhere at the same time.

My father emphasized that truth with me when I was little. He would be somewhere preaching, and sickness would strike our family. He would get us on the phone and pray for us from where he was, and we would receive healing where we were.

Lindsay and I emphasized that as well with our children, Jordan, Olivia and Chloe, so that no matter where we were in the world, we could call home and pray, and believe for God to heal our family. It did not matter that I was not physically present with them, because I was present with them by faith. And by faith, miracles happened.

I cannot begin to count the number of times that I've written a letter or an email, prayed for someone over the phone, left a voice message, or prayed a prayer on a Facebook video, only to receive a testimony from someone who was healed as I sent the Word. That's because Jesus is unlimited, and there is no distance in prayer.

This was dramatically brought home some years ago through the miracle of a nine-year-old girl named Emily. Emily is from Alabama, and she was born with crooked, turned-in feet. This condition made it very difficult for her to walk, run, and play with her brothers and other children.

One night, she and her family were watching Lindsay and me on television. Our special guest that night was our long-time friend, Billye Brim, from Branson, Missouri. Billye and Lindsay and I have been friends for a long time. When it came time for healing prayer, I stretched out my faith toward the camera and said, "There is no distance in prayer. I'm going to pray here, and I want you to release your faith, and believe God with me right there where you are… Believe God for a mighty miracle."

I began talking about God making crooked places straight, and for bones and muscles to come into alignment. As I prayed this prayer, I had no idea about little Emily or the condition she was in. But as she and her family watched the program, she looked down at her feet during my prayer and watched them as they literally turned straight.

Her mom and dad immediately contacted us and gave us the story. And it wasn't long until she gave her testimony on our television program. We sent our video team to Alabama to record this great miracle.

I did not lay hands on Emily. I sent the Word through my prayer on television, because there is no distance in prayer. As I write this book, Emily is in her early twenties, and she is still perfectly healed… normal in her feet and legs in every way.

Friend, we serve a mighty God, who is all-powerful, all-knowing, all-seeing, and who is everywhere at the same time. Jesus is unlimited. And we can reach out to Him, no matter where we are, and believe God for a miracle.

YOUR GOD-GIVEN KEY FOR TODAY:

Jesus is unlimited, and there is no distance in prayer.

[Tuesday]

KEY: *I Can Have a Point of Contact with God.*

In the Bible, there are many points of contact. For example, a laying on of hands, a prayer cloth, and the anointing oil.

A point of contact is something you do. And when you do it, you release your faith.

I want to stress that. It's something that *you do*. It's an action, not an object.

When I was a boy, I had 22 warts on my left hand. Being left-handed, they really bothered me... And they were spreading.

My mother was going to take me to the doctor and have them burned off. But my dad said, "Let's pray first before we do that."

He took me into the other room and closed the door. Then he said to me, "Richard, I'm going to lay hands on you and pray. And I want you to release your faith when I do."

I said to him, "Dad, how do you release your faith?"

He said, "Through a point of contact. That's something you do. And when you do it, you release your faith and believe God for a miracle."

My dad saw that I was having difficulty understanding, so he pointed to the wall and said to me, "Do you see that light switch?"

"Yes," I said. "I do."

Dad said, "That light switch is a point of contact."

I said, "What do you mean, point of contact, Dad?"

"Richard, a point of contact is something you do. When you do it, you release your faith." I sat there, trying to understand.

Then he said to me, "Son, that light switch on the wall has no power, but it is hooked up to the electric company where the power is. When you flip the switch, you touch the electricity and the lights come on."

Then he said, "The faith in your heart is just like that light switch. In itself, it has no power. But when you release it to God, you touch God's power... And a miracle can happen. So, when I lay my hands on you, let your faith go up to God."

I answered, "Okay."

He began to pray for me. Then he said, "In Jesus' name, Richard, release your faith, and believe God to heal you."

I didn't know exactly what to do, but with all my strength I began to say, "Faith, get up there to God. Get up… get up… get up there to God."

And the older I get, the better it sounds… "Faith, I release you. And I expect a miracle from God."

I looked down at my hand, and every wart was still there. I looked up at my dad, and he said something I'll never forget. He said, "Son, we've released our faith. Now, let's expect a miracle."

My mother decided to delay going to the doctor for a few days, and each morning when I woke up, the first thing I did was look at my hand.

The first day my hand was the same. The second, third and fourth days, the warts were still there. On day five, six, seven, eight and nine, there was no change.

But when I woke up on the tenth morning and looked at my hand, every wart had totally disappeared! I mean, they were completely gone, every one of them.

It was a miracle! I had used a point of contact to release my faith to God, and I had received a healing.

But something even greater happened. I learned how to release my faith for a miracle.

Throughout my ministry, I have taught this principle to people all over the world.

Remember, a point of contact is something you do. And when you do it, you release your faith to God. Then, you believe Him for a miracle, and you never give up or stop believing. *This is the road to a Better Life.*

Through this experience and many others like it, I have learned to flip that switch of faith to bring God's healing power into my life.

And if I can use a point of contact to release my faith, then so can you.

YOUR GOD-GIVEN KEY FOR TODAY:

Release your faith to God, and expect a miracle.

[Wednesday]

KEY: *I Am Focusing My Faith on Jesus.*

Some time ago, I was preaching in Calgary, Alberta, Canada. During the service, God gave me a word of knowledge about backs being healed.

A number of people came forward to give testimonies of being healed through that word of knowledge, while others came forward, hoping that I would lay hands on them and pray, because their backs had not yet been healed.

I remember one man who came forward was suffering in his back so much that he could hardly walk. The stiffness in his back made it very difficult for him to move at all, and he winced with every step.

When I came to him, he said, "Richard, would you lay your hands on me and pray for my healing?"

I replied, "Of course I will." I put my hands on his back, and began to call on God for healing. Immediately, in my spirit, I knew something had happened. I felt a warmth flow down my shoulder and into my hand, and then go directly into his back.

I said to him, "Sir, did you feel what I felt?"

He said, "Yes, I did."

I said to him, "What are you able to do?"

He said, "I think I can bend over a little." And he did... but not very far.

WEEK 8: WEDNESDAY

Then I said to him, "Can you try again?" He began to bend a second time, and this time he went much further down.

I said to him, "Do you think you could try one more time?"

He said, "I believe I can." And this time, he bent all the way down and touched his hands to the ground. He looked up, smiled, and said to me, "Richard, it's been twenty-five years since I've been able to do that." Everyone in the crowd was rejoicing.

Now, the most important thing for you to know in this story is that I did not do anything special. I just prayed. My hands are a point of contact to help people like you to release their faith, and to get on God's road to a Better Life.

When I prayed for this man, something instantly began to happen. But he had to join his faith with mine and believe for the ultimate miracle. In those three times that he bent down, each time he expected more from God... And he received it.

Because as you act on your faith in God, the devil gets the idea that you're serious. And he will flee in terror (James 4:7).

Now, here's an easy way for you to think of it. Just picture a camera. You know, you have to look through the viewfinder, and unless your lens is right on target, the image is fuzzy. You then have to adjust the lens until the image comes into focus.

All right, now picture in your mind God coming to you through His Son, Jesus. The image may be fuzzy at first, but as you think and pray on it, it becomes easier.

Picture Jesus coming to you at the point of your need.
FOCUS YOUR FAITH ON HIM.
A miracle comes through FAITH IN GOD.
A miracle comes when you ACT UPON YOUR FAITH,
when we *DO* SOMETHING.

Your God Given-Key for Today:

As you work at this, say to yourself out loud:

"I am focusing my faith on Jesus."

[Thursday]

KEY: *I Will Touch and Agree for My Need to Be Met.*

Back in the 1970s, when we were doing our television programs at the NBC Studios in Hollywood, my father, Oral Roberts, was often asked to be a guest on what, at that time, were the major television talk shows. And whenever he went, he always took me with him, and said, "My son will also sing."

As I look back on it now, it's funny…

I was never asked to be on those shows, and yet I wound up on them. We were on the Mike Douglas Show, the Dick Cavett Show, the Merv Griffin Show, the Johnny Carson Show, and a number of others.

One day, when we were on the Mike Douglas Show, as the interview was winding down, Mike asked my dad one more question: "Oral, I can understand your prayer for people face-to-face and their responding and receiving help. What I cannot understand is how you do it on television."

My dad said, "Wait a minute, Mike. To me, that camera is a living human being. In fact, when I stand before that camera, I feel so close to the viewer, I feel like I can just reach out and touch him, or touch her. And I believe that people can feel that."

"How?" Mike said.

WEEK 8: THURSDAY

My dad replied, "By our closeness. By thinking about what Christ can do. Jesus said, in Matthew 18 and 19, 'If two of you shall agree on earth as touching anything that they shall ask, it shall be done for them by my Father, which is in heaven.'"

Now, you must understand that this was the early 1970s, and my father's crusade days were over. His practice at that time was to stretch out his hands toward the people on television, and to ask them to touch the area of their body that needed healing, or lay hands on the person they were with, in faith… touching and agreeing, as the Bible says.

As all this was going on, I was sitting over on the side, listening to every word and learning. I was young in ministry at the time. I had not yet felt a call to preach. I was singing on the programs. The preaching time would come later, and the healing ministry would come as well. But I was listening, and I was synthesizing all that my father was saying. In other words, it was getting down inside me.

And here we are, all these years later. When I'm on television or Facebook or my Saturday evening live telephone conference call, I stretch out my hands and pray according to that same scripture in Matthew 18:18–19. I believe that as I stretch out my hands and pray that the power of God and His anointing will flow right through my hands, through the television camera, through the Internet, through the telephone, and touch people—bring healing, health, and wholeness in every area of their lives.

This is something that I believe.

This is something that I do.

This is something that I'll stake my life on.

At this writing, in the past nearly twenty years, we've had approximately 150,000 healing testimonies that have come pouring into our ministry headquarters. And those are just the people who shared their good news with us. That does not count those who have received healings and have not told us about them.

Back in those days, my father was extremely excited about being on television. And in these days, I'm just as excited… except we have more outreaches now. My father did not have the opportunity to do live conference calls or Facebook videos. But I do. And I'm so grateful to be on television and on social media and on conference calls, preaching, teaching, and bringing God's healing power to people in need.

Yes, there's a spiritual excitement about it. And when it comes time to do television, I can hardly wait to stand in front of that camera. I feel an extreme closeness to the individual person and his or her need. I, and the person watching, can come together there by faith, in the quietness of their own home, or wherever they are watching.

When I'm on Facebook, I can share in the same way. I can reach out my hands and pray, according to the Word of God. I can touch and agree through our telephone conference calls, and believe for the Lord Jesus to bring healing and wholeness. This is an extremely effective means that God has given us to help people get their needs met.

Actually, this is another form of a point of contact. Even if you are alone and have no one to touch and agree with, it's just as effective to touch yourself and pray for your needs to be met.

As I mentioned earlier, Jesus said in Matthew 18:18–19, *"If two of you agree on earth concerning anything that they ask, it will be done for them by My Father in heaven."*

So, when you're watching me on television, or live on Facebook, or listening to our Saturday evening conference calls, or receiving a letter from me, that's your point of contact. I am one; you are two. And you and I, along with God, make a majority.

YOUR GOD-GIVEN KEY FOR TODAY:

When you pray, say:

"I will touch and agree for my need to be met, and then expect a miracle to happen to me."

[Friday]

KEY: *I Will Plant Seeds of Faith, Hope, and Love Every Day.*

A partner of ours had a job that required him to drive 120 miles round-trip daily. Within walking distance of his home was a large plant that paid good wages and offered good working conditions. Besides saving wear and tear on his car and himself, if he worked there, he could come home each day for lunch.

For several years, he had applied regularly for a job there, but was turned down each time. During this period, the company hired hundreds of new employees. He couldn't understand why he couldn't get a job there, and finally gave up trying.

One day, he heard my dad and me speaking on the Key Principles of Seed-Faith.

First, look to God as the Source of your total supply.

Second, give as a seed, and it will become seed-faith for God to multiply back to you in the form of meeting your need.

Third, by looking to God as your Source and giving as seed-faith, it's the evidence on which your faith can act. So, expect a miracle from God's heavenly supply.

In my dad's message, he made the statement: "A rejected opportunity to give is a lost opportunity to receive." In my message, I said, "The greater the sacrifice— the greater the blessing."

These statements are in harmony with Jesus' Words in Luke 6:38, *"Give, and it will be given to you: good measure, pressed down, shaken together, and running over will be put into your bosom. For with the same measure that you use, it will be measured back to you."*

This man saw that receiving follows giving. A miracle follows believing. It's just like "breathing in–breathing out." The harvest follows seed-sowing and soil-tending.

In 2 Corinthians 9:10, we read, *"Now may He who supplies seed to the sower, and bread for food, supply and multiply the seed you have sown and increase the fruits of your righteousness."*

In other words, if you have a heart to give, God will put seed in your hand.

Well, this man and his wife became partners with our ministry and began sowing regularly, each month. As time passed, they began learning how to look to God as their Source, and to put Him first in their lives.

About four months later, we heard an amazing story.

One morning, as the man sat at breakfast, he looked at his wife and said, "Honey, God has become our Source. We're giving as Jesus has told us to. And I believe God is going to start multiplying it back. How? I don't know. But I believe He will do it in His own time and His own way. And I know He's going to open up a new and better job for me. I am expecting it."

Then the woman said to her husband, "I think you should go down there to that company down the street and apply again."

He said, "You know, you're right. I believe I'll do it. Why not? God is alive, He's here, and He's at the point of our need. We've given Him our best, and we're going to expect Him to give us His best back."

The next morning, he got up early and headed toward the head office at the plant just down the street. Pretty soon he was back, shouting words to his wife. "Honey, I got the job! Honey, I got the job!"

She said, "How? Tell me all about it."

He said, "Well, when I walked in, I told them my name, and said that I had come to go to work. The man actually acted as if he had been waiting for me. He told me they would be ready for me as soon as I could come. Then he signed me up, and told me to hurry back and report to work."

The man said to us, "This is my dream come true. The thing I like best is that I can walk to work, and walk home for lunch if I want to. Each day, I give thanks to God, for truly He sent a miracle to us."

Now, you can call this coincidence…

You can call it positive thinking…

You can call it an accident, if you want to…

I call it God multiplying seeds sown. Now that's seed-faith in action. And that's the road to a Better Life.

It proves God is where the need is. And when seeds of faith are sown, God multiplies them back in the way we need it most.

If you've been faithfully practicing seed-faith and putting the Three Miracle Keys to work, it's time for your miracle. You can say, just like that man and his wife in this story, "Well, why not?"

Whatever your lifelong dream may be, I believe it's time for your miracle harvest. Why not? Because… and say it… "I've planted my seeds in faith, expecting."

YOUR GOD-GIVEN KEY FOR TODAY:

I will plant seeds of faith, hope, and love every day… and expect miracles.

[Saturday]

KEY: *Seed I Have Planted Is Ready to Be Harvested Back in the Form of Miracles to Me.*

It was back in 1954 that my dad stretched his tent for a healing crusade in Baltimore, Maryland. I was five years old, and because it was summer, I got to go.

I was surprised when my dad asked me to sing. He stood me before a crowd of some 10,000, and put a mic in front of me. I sang the old gospel song, "I Believe." I'll never forget it.

Something else that happened on that crusade was the opportunity to meet Dr. Myron Sackett. At that time, and for years to come, Dr. Sackett was the director of our ministry outreach to the Jewish people in Israel.

During the 1950s and 1960s, Dr. Sackett was responsible for raising funds to purchase New Testaments in the Hebrew language, and to bury them in copper cases in the caves of the deserts of Israel.

He knew that the Bible says that after the Rapture and the rise of the Antichrist, the Jews will literally head for the hills when they realize that the Antichrist is against them. While there, they will hide out in places where our ministry, along with others, have planted Bibles in Hebrew.

And in those days to come, many Jews will come to a saving knowledge of Jesus Christ as God's only Son, and their Savior. Praise God!

As I grew older, I got to know Dr. Sackett well, as well as his precious wife, May. As a matter of fact, for some years, she was a Prayer Partner in our Abundant Life Prayer Group.

WEEK 8: SATURDAY

During that crusade, I was standing with my dad when Dr. Sackett came and said, "Brother Roberts, someone just gave me three one-hundred-dollar bills to buy Hebrew Bibles, and I'm going to mail it off and order the Bibles."

Then the next day, he came back to my dad and said, "Brother Roberts, I feel led of the Lord to sow the $300 as seed into this ministry, believing that God will multiply it back into a much larger amount to buy even more Bibles."

The next day, he came to my dad and said, "Brother Roberts, a man just came by and handed me a gift of $1,000 for Bibles, and I'm going to send the money overseas for Bibles in the Hebrew language." He said to my dad, "Just think, Brother Roberts. I had $300 and I sowed it, and God has already turned it into $1,000 in just a matter of days!"

In those days, my father called that Bible principle "The Blessing-Pact Covenant with God." Later, he renamed it "Your Seed-Faith Covenant with God."

Even as a child in that crusade, listening to Dr. Sackett and my father talk, the principles of sowing and reaping were getting deep into my heart. And the older I got, the more I understood it.

By the time I was age nineteen and had given my heart to the Lord, I fully committed myself to sowing my seeds each month unto Him, plus offerings on top of that, and then expecting Him to use it for His glory, and to multiply it back to me in the way I needed it most. It was my start on a road to a Better Life. And it's just as powerful today as it was then.

The good news is, if it will work for me, it will also work for you. God will take every seed you sow, use it for His glory, then multiply it back in the way you need it most.

YOUR GOD-GIVEN KEY FOR TODAY:

Seed I have planted is ready to be harvested back to me in the form of miracles.

WEEK 8 RECAP

- **Sunday:** When I Act, My Faith Begins to Work.
- **Monday:** Jesus Is Unlimited, and There Is No Distance in Prayer.
- **Tuesday:** I Can Have a Point of Contact with God.
- **Wednesday:** I Am Focusing My Faith on Jesus.
- **Thursday:** I Will Touch and Agree for My Need to Be Met.
- **Friday:** I Will Plant Seeds of Faith, Hope, and Love Every Day.
- **Saturday:** Seed I Have Planted Is Ready to Be Harvested Back in the Form of Miracles to Me.

WEEK 9

[Sunday]

KEY: *I Talk to God, and He Talks to Me.*

There is one thing about Jesus that stood out to His disciples… and that was His prayer life. They noticed that when Jesus prayed, something happened. Now, it wasn't like that when they prayed… Something might or might not happen. Perhaps some of them did not even enjoy praying.

There was something about Jesus' prayer that was exciting, and when Jesus prayed, His disciples wanted more.

One day, they came to Him and said, "Lord, teach us to pray …" (Luke 11:1).

And Jesus began by saying:

"In this manner, therefore, pray" (Matthew 6:9).

Jesus was not indicating that this was to be the disciples' only prayer or that those words were to be the only words that were ever said in prayer. And it was not to be a substitute for their own personal prayers. But Jesus meant that this prayer would be sort of an outline… a way to fashion their prayer in such a way that they could expect God to answer. Today, we call it The Lord's Prayer.

"Our Father in heaven, Hallowed be Your name.
Your kingdom come.

Your will be done.

On earth as it is in heaven.
Give us this day our daily bread. And forgive us our debts,
as we forgive our debtors. And do not lead us into temptation,

but deliver us from the evil one. For Yours is the kingdom and the power and the glory forever. Amen"
(Matthew 6:9–13).

I'm going to break this prayer down into parts this week. Each day, I'll take different parts and show you what it means to me, and hope that it will mean something to you as well.

Our Father...

Jesus began the prayer with "Our Father." Now, the word "Father" as it pertains to God was not used in a personal way by the people of the Old Testament, although God was sometimes referred to as a father. It was first used in a personal way by Jesus. The term *Father* signified the closeness they had together. It meant that He and God the Father were immediately and personally related.

This was the new dimension that Christ brought out of the Old Testament into the New Testament. He tells us to call God our Father, suggesting the closeness of our relationship with Him.

Many years ago, I read a story about President Abraham Lincoln and his son, Tad. One day, Tad was outside the White House playing in the yard, while his father was busy with the affairs of the nation. Little Tad apparently got into a fist fight, and came out the loser. He ran into the White House with his lip cut, his nose bleeding, and his clothes torn.

When he got to his father's outer office, there sat several members of the President's Cabinet waiting to see him. The little boy, sobbing, said, "I want to see my father... I want to see my father."

The Secretary of the Treasury, in sort of a spirit of laughter, spoke up and said, "You wish to see the President of the United States?"

And the little boy said, "I want to see my FATHER."

"Well," he said, "I will take you in personally to see the Chief Executive Officer of the United States."

But the little boy again said, "I want to see my FATHER."

Then the Secretary of State spoke up and said, "Look, I'll take care of this little boy. Son, I'll take you into the presence of the greatest diplomat in the world, the head of our nation."

The little boy just kept sobbing, saying, "I want to see my FATHER."

Finally, the Secretary of War said, "Son, I'll take you in to see the Commander in Chief of the Armed Forces of the United States of America."

And the little boy said, "I just want to see my FATHER. I just want to see my FATHER."

Everything these men said about Lincoln was true, but to the little boy, the Head of State, the Great Diplomat, the Commander in Chief of the Armed Forces was his father. And he knew if he could just get in there to his dad with his cut lip, bleeding nose, and torn clothes, his father would put his arms around him, hug him close, and things would be all right again.

Jesus indicated that this is the relationship we have with God in prayer. We are to think of Him as *our Father.*

As I grew up, I was very close to my parents, and I loved them with all my heart. But there was a special bond between my dad and me.

As I came up under him in the ministry, learning how to preach, teach, and bring God's healing power to people in need, I sought the anointing that he had on his life.

And I would say to him, "Dad, I want a double portion of your spirit."

My dad always said to me what Elijah said to Elisha: "Son, you've asked a hard thing, but if you see me when I go, you'll have it."

And the day came when that double portion anointing came upon my life.

I'm so grateful for my parents, and I'm so grateful for my relationship with my dad... my father.

When you pray, say, *"Our Father... Our Daddy."*

YOUR GOD-GIVEN KEY FOR TODAY:

I talk to God, and He talks to me.

[Monday]

KEY: *God Is… in Heaven.*

"God is…" Jesus said, when you pray, pray to someone who is… who never changes. The weather changes… People change… Circumstances change… But God never changes. He exists… because HE IS.

Listen. Say it to yourself over and over again. "God IS… *God is.*"

Say this out loud, "If He is not here now, then He has never been here."

Say, "He is willing to help me now."

Say, "If He's not willing to help me, He has not been willing to help anybody, but He is… and He will."

"Which art…" This means God is in your total life…physical, material, spiritual, from the crown of your head to the soles of your feet. You have a seven-days-a-week life… seven-days-a-week needs… and you have a seven-days-a-week God. God is with you every moment, every day, everywhere. Which art … means GOD IS.

Jesus said, "Which art in heaven."

He was not trying to locate God. He was using this term to express the ability and power of God to take care of us and our needs.

On another occasion, Jesus said, *"I have come that they may have life, and that they may have it more abundantly"* (John 10:10).

When Jesus spoke these words, the world was filled with impossibilities. All around Him, Jesus saw people hemmed in by circumstances, disease, discrimination, poverty, fear, and failure. And He knew that "in heaven" there were resources for man's needs.

Water for his thirst.
Food for his hunger.
Strength for his weakness.
Riches for his poverty.
A kiss for his sorrow.
Gladness for his misery.
And love for his loneliness.

So, Jesus reached up and took heaven and kissed the earth with it, and opened it, and gave it to the children of men. He came with outstretched hands, filled with God's blessing, with an open heaven behind Him. He came into people's lives at the point of their need, performing miracles and setting them free, in His mighty name.

So, Jesus tells you that when you pray, remember that God, your Father, is… and that He is *in heaven*. And IN HEAVEN, there are no shortages. God's riches are laid end to end across heaven, waiting to be given to you.

It's the road to a Better Life, and we'll discover more as we continue with the Lord's Prayer this week.

YOUR GOD-GIVEN KEY FOR TODAY:

"God is… in heaven…"
Say it over and over and over and over again.

[Tuesday]

KEY: *I Will Honor the Name of the Lord.*

In The Lord's Prayer, Jesus used the phrase, "Hallowed be Your name."

Jesus had a deep feeling about the name of God. He never used it irreverently… nor in vain… nor as an obscenity. Or a word to swear with. In fact, Jesus never used an obscenity. He reverenced the name of the Father with great honor and love. And He says to you and me, "When you pray, be sure that you have reverence for the name of God."

To reverence God simply means to show loving respect for Him and His Word. He is holy, and He desires and deserves your reverence.

How would you act if you were invited to a meet a king? Would you run into the throne room laughing and talking? Or maybe eating a bag of chips and drinking a soda? Or would you tread lightly, being very careful what you say and where you stand and what you do? Good question, isn't it? Well, I found myself in a position like that once.

Some years ago, I was conducting a crusade in the Southern African Republic of Swaziland. During that trip, I was invited to meet with the Queen Regent. Her husband, the king, had died, and she had been named regent because the eldest son was not yet old enough to take the throne.

My wife and I, and our team, were ushered into her home. I was very careful what I said and what I did. And I was told that my head could not be higher than hers. So therefore, I bowed as I walked and sat down on the floor before her.

And I did not speak until she asked me a question.

It was the most interesting experience. She actually asked me to preach… and sitting on the floor, I did just that. Then I gave an invitation, and nine members of the Royal Household gave their hearts to the Lord.

Then the Lord spoke to me and said, "Get up and go lay hands on her." I said to the Lord, "I can't do that. My head cannot be higher than hers." And the Lord was so kind, He said, "Just ask if you can."

So I said, "Your majesty, the Lord has impressed me to stand and lay my hands upon you. Is that acceptable?"

She smiled and said, "Yes, it is." And she lifted her hand, gesturing for me to stand.

So I walked over to her, stood next to her throne, laid my hands on her, and prayed a prayer of blessing. It was quite a day, let me tell you.

The Bible says in Exodus 20:7, *"You shall not take the name of the Lord your God in vain, for the Lord will not hold him guiltless who takes His name in vain.*

Be very careful what you say about God. God is God... and God alone. There is no other. Because we are thankful to God for His great works for us and in us, we worship Him and Him alone. As the Bible says in Exodus 20:3, we will have no other god before us.

He is sovereign, and He has the right to demand of us whatever He desires. And He never does it in a cruel way, but in a loving way. Thank God we can worship Him in spirit and in truth and hold up His name.

YOUR GOD-GIVEN KEY FOR TODAY:

I will honor the Lord's name and hold it in high reverence.

[Wednesday]

KEY: *God's Kingdom and Will on Earth and in Heaven Is Important to Me.*

Jesus was and is very concerned about the nations... the kingdoms... that exist on the earth, but He was and is even more concerned about another kingdom... a higher kingdom... God's kingdom. He taught us to pray, "Your kingdom come, your will be done on earth, as it is in heaven."

When I was a boy in elementary school, I read the story of a British team of mountain climbers who were trying to scale Mt. Everest. While they were climbing, their leader, whose name was Mallory, slipped and fell hundreds of feet to his death.

This, of course, broke up that particular team and they went back to London to give their report. As they spoke to a packed audience, there was a screen behind them showing pictures of Mt. Everest and the different levels where they had climbed and the exact spot where Mr. Mallory lost his life.

They talked about their great leader, the hardships they had undergone, the cold, the wind and the snow. Then the man who was doing the most talking turned toward the picture of Mt. Everest on the screen, and began talking to it as if the mountain were alive.

He said, "Mighty Mt. Everest, we tried to conquer you once and you beat us. We tried to conquer you the second time and you beat us, but we are going to conquer you, because *you cannot get any bigger. But we can.*"

I believe this sort of sums up what Jesus is saying. We live in earthly kingdoms. These kingdoms are only going to be so powerful... They are limited. Jesus lived in the days of the Roman Empire, a kingdom of men that had spread over the known world at that time. It had conquered the nations and had control over all the people who lived in them.

But Jesus said that these kingdoms of men are not going to fully conquer everybody. These earthly kingdoms are not going to get any bigger, but God's kingdom is. Through Him, you and I can get bigger too. As we do His will, it begins taking us on the road to a Better Life.

In fact, every time we pray this prayer, The Lord's Prayer, we are praying a revolutionary and radical prayer. We are praying for a new kind of kingdom to come into being. We are praying that what is in heaven will come to earth…will come to be… down here in the earth. That starts with God's will in heaven being lived out by earthen vessels like you and me.

Some people fear the will of God, but actually I can't think of anyplace better to be than in His perfect will. His will for your life will never restrict it. It will open your life up to the greatest possibilities. When you begin to do God's will, you really begin to live… That's the road to a Better Life.

YOUR GOD-GIVEN KEY FOR TODAY:

I want God's kingdom to come and His will to be done in my life.

[Thursday]

KEY: *God Will Meet My Daily Needs.*

When Jesus said, "Give us this day our daily bread," I believe He meant give us this day our material needs.

Jesus knew all about our physical necessities of life. He knew the worth of a widow's mite (Luke 21:1–4) and what the loss of a coin might mean to a person. He knew about clothing that needed mending and about not having a place to sleep at night (Luke 9:58).

Even after Jesus' resurrection, He showed concern for His disciples' physical needs. The day He walked home with two of His friends, He sat down at the table and broke bread with them (Luke 24:13–35).

Several days later, when the disciples had been out all night fishing, Jesus knew that they would be hungry, so He prepared breakfast for them (John 21:9–13).

I'm glad that Jesus did not tell us to pray, "Sell us this day our daily bread," because we could never pay God. Instead, Jesus said, "God, give us this day our daily bread."

You see, Jesus is saying that we can't get away from our Source. God is the Source of our total supply, and we can never be very far away from our Source, who is God. The only true bread… the only true supply of our material needs comes through Him.

Jesus is talking about bread… **about God's bread**. He's talking about a supply of our needs that really satisfies… about clothes that satisfy… about an automobile that runs… about a house that becomes a home. He's talking about God meeting our needs.

God is concerned about your bread. He's concerned about the money that you need… and the clothing you need and the home that you need. He's concerned about your physical heath. He does not want you to die before your time. God wants you to have peace. He wants you to live out your days in health and happiness. He wants you to live in the knowledge that He is the Source of your total supply, seven days a week, 24 hours a day, every day of your life. And when the day comes that you stand before Him face-to-face, I believe His arms will be wide open, ready to receive you.

Now, friend, that's the road to a Better Life.

YOUR GOD-GIVEN KEY FOR TODAY:

God will meet my daily needs.

[Friday]

KEY: *Forgiving Is the Great Stress Reliever.*

Jesus said forgive us our trespasses… then after Jesus concluded The Lord's Prayer, He added these words… *"For if you forgive men their trespasses, your heavenly Father will also forgive you. But if you do not forgive men their trespasses, neither will your Father forgive your trespasses"* (Matthew 6:14–15).

Jesus indicated that the human race is guilty of trespasses. Each of us is a trespasser.

We *do* things we ought not do.

We *say* things we should not say.

We *think* things we should not think.

We commit trespasses, and our forgiveness must come from God. There is one Forgiver and one only… and that is God. Men may or may not forgive us, but God will forgive.

A man once said to John Wesley, "I'll never forgive." Wesley replied, "Then pray that you will never sin." In other words, the only way you are ever going to be forgiven by God of your own trespasses is to forgive the one who has trespassed against you.

Back in 1972, my father and I, and our television team, made a prime time TV special in London, England. Several special guests joined us as we sang songs along the River Thames, in front of Big Ben, in Trafalgar Square, and other historic sites. My father preached his message at the Old Coventry Cathedral, and just before he preached, I sang a solo titled, "When I Survey the Wondrous Cross." I sang it walking through the ruins of that cathedral.

You see, Coventry was one of the earliest sites to be bombed by Nazi Germany in WWII because it was an industrial city. They almost bombed it off the map, and they didn't spare the churches.

A bomb struck Coventry Cathedral… a tremendous edifice which, at that time, was hundreds of years old and beyond price. The church was literally destroyed. Only a little of it was left standing.

When the war was over, the people rebuilt the cathedral, but they left the old, scarred, bombed-out part like it was. They picked up three hand-forged nails from the ruins, put them together in the form of a cross, and wrote on them… "Father, forgive."

How could they forgive the Nazis? How could they forgive a people who had killed six million Jews? How could they forgive a people who burned up their city and destroyed their church?

In their hearts, they reached a place where they said, "Father, forgive…" Do you see? They might have harbored some trespasses themselves also. They might have been hating back just as much as the Nazis had hated them. So I believe it was a double prayer, "Father, forgive them… as You forgive us."

I believe that forgiveness is a great stress reliever. For when you harbor an offense in your heart, it eats at you. It literally tears you up on the inside, and there's great healing in forgiveness.

And by the way, whether the person you forgive responds back to you or not is not the point. The point is, when you forgive them, it releases you. That puts you on the road to a Better Life.

YOUR GOD-GIVEN KEY FOR TODAY:

In forgiving others, I am forgiven also.

[Saturday]

KEY: *God Is Leading Me, Delivering Me, and Setting Me in His Kingdom by His Power and Glory.*

When Jesus said, *"And do not lead us into temptation, but deliver us from the evil one,"* I believe He was saying, "God, don't forsake us when the going gets rough. Help us to get through those situations that seem bigger than we are, even when it seems like the water is over our heads."

Help us to be strong in the Lord and in the power of His might... which is the joy of the Lord, because that's our strength.

A man came to me once for prayer and broke down and began to cry. As he tried to regain his composure, he apologized, saying, "Richard, I'm so sorry, but I can't help crying." I encouraged him to let his tears flow. I told him that they were a release for his spirit and an expression of his prayer to God.

Tears are not a sign of weakness. Jesus cried. He cried when His friend Lazarus died, and His tears brought Him to action, and He raised Lazarus from the grave. He cried in the Garden of Gethsemane, "with strong crying and tears" (Hebrews 5:7).

In whatever way we express this sincere desire of our heart to God, He will understand. He will help us, and He will never lead us into temptation. Sure, we're all tempted, because we're human beings. Even Jesus was tempted. That's the devil's business.

But we can say, "No," in the name of Jesus. "I won't go there. I won't say that. I won't do that." And we can call on God to deliver us from every evil thought and evil action.

And when Jesus said, *"For Yours is the kingdom and the power and the glory forever. Amen,"* I believe He was talking about the kingdom of God in our hearts, with access to all of God's power and glory, not just here on earth, but forever.

As Jesus said these words, He was living in a province of the Roman Empire. The Roman soldiers, in their barbaric cruelty, were everywhere putting their burdens upon people. They were acting like they were going to rule forever... that Rome would always be the master kingdom. But Jesus looked beyond Rome... beyond every other kingdom that would arise on the earth. And He said, "Yours is the kingdom."

Jesus was saying that there is something bigger, better, and more stable than this or any other earthly kingdom... And that kingdom is ruled by the king of Kings and the lord of Lords. The good news is, when you receive Christ into your heart, you receive God's kingdom into your life, here on earth.

And in doing so, you're not alone. You're surrounded by the kingdom of God... an incomparable power that sets you free... a glory that can fill your heart... So, why settle for just the things of this world, when you can have the permanent kingdom of God within you?

You can have the limitless Spirit of Jesus Christ helping you to receive health again. You can receive salvation for your soul. You can have your material needs met, and this can start today.

Just for starters, you can think of The Lord's Prayer this way, even as you say the words, "Our Father, which art in heaven ..." Just think of that opener as God's "front porch," and when you get on the front porch, you can start knocking, asking, and expecting God's blessings in your life. This is why you can say to yourself every day:

YOUR GOD-GIVEN KEY FOR TODAY:

"I will be led by God in every area of my life… on my road to a Better Life."

WEEK 9 RECAP

- **Sunday:** I Talk to God, and He Talks to Me.
- **Monday:** God Is… in Heaven.
- **Tuesday:** I Will Honor the Name of the Lord.
- **Wednesday:** God's Kingdom and Will on Earth and in Heaven Is Important to Me.
- **Thursday:** God Will Meet My Daily Needs.
- **Friday:** Forgiving Is the Great Stress Reliever.
- **Saturday:** God Is Leading Me, Delivering Me, and Setting Me in His Kingdom by His Power and Glory.

WEEK 10

[Sunday]

KEY: *God Is Concerned About My Daily Needs.*

In John chapter 6, we find the story of 5,000 men, plus women and children, who were hungry to the point of fainting. They needed bread… and through a miracle, Jesus gave it to them. When the multitude had finished eating, they gathered up 12 baskets full of fragments. All this, and Jesus began the miracle with only a boy's lunch of five loaves and two fishes.

This is a very important point in this story. This is Jesus Christ, who is concerned about people having bread. These people were out of bread. They followed Him so long and so far into the desert that their food ran out. It was growing late, and it would soon become hard for them to find food and shelter. The disciples suggested that Jesus send them away to buy bread, but Jesus said, "Let us feed them ourselves." Jesus immediately became concerned about these people, and their need for bread.

Bread represents the totality of man's need. Everyone needs bread. We need bread for our bodies. We also need clothes for our bodies, houses, cars, money for our needs, and things to be taken care of in our families. We need these things right down here on earth… and our Heavenly Father knows that we need them.

As I said earlier concerning The Lord's Prayer, Jesus told us to pray, "Give us this day our daily bread." Then He said, *"For your heavenly Father knows that you need all these things"* (Matthew 6:11 and 32).

Now, let me make something very clear. Jesus is not against our having things; He just doesn't want things having us.

Jesus says we are to pray and ask God for the things we need... He says that God is concerned about our well-being. Jesus was there in the midst of thousands of hungry people, and He did something about it.

Thank God He is concerned about the body I live in. He's concerned about the mind I have to think with. He's concerned about my soul and my spirit. He's concerned about the house I live in. He's concerned about my needs being met. He's God. I'm a human being, and He loves me, and I love Him.

There's another very important statement here that we should not miss, and here it is... Jesus knew what He would do.

Right in the midst of those five thousand people being hungry, yet not having any bread and not being able to send them away for fear they might faint by the wayside, the Bible says Jesus knew exactly what He would do. In other words, He had a plan. Jesus needed someone to put in a seed to match the need. That person turned out to be a little boy.

The Bible says, *"Unless you are converted and become as little children, you will by no means enter the kingdom of heaven"* (Matthew 18:3).

That is to say, we must become uninhibited like a child. Just look up and ask, and let God be who He is. That's what a little child does. He is so uninhibited about God, he believes God can do anything and there's nothing too hard for Him.

This little boy had a small lunch which he voluntarily gave to our Lord. That little lunch became a seed to match the need.

Sounds crazy, doesn't it? Certainly, your mind might say, "How could Jesus take a little boy's lunch and multiply it to feed 5,000 hungry men, plus women and children besides?"

Sometimes, it's difficult for our minds to take in the way God works. That's because His ways are above our ways, and His thoughts are above our thoughts. He takes the things that the world calls foolish and uses them to confound the wise. (See Isaiah 55:8–9 and 1 Corinthians 1:27.)

Now, there are some people who just don't believe this miracle happened. But you know, I've seen God take small things and multiply them to answer a prayer in my own life. I've seen it happen in other people's lives, as well.

In fact, I remember the day that we received a prayer request from a woman who was a partner in our ministry. First, she was facing surgery. Second, she needed a new home. Third, she was believing God for a wife for her son. That son loved his mother very much and planted a seed of faith in our ministry, believing for all these prayers to be answered. Well, guess what? When she got prepared for the surgery, the doctor said, "The growth is gone." The surgery was canceled. The next thing you know, she was living in a brand-new home that her family built for her. Third, her son met a wonderful young lady and got married.

Now, someone could say, "Well, that probably would have happened anyway." But it certainly had not happened up until then. I believe it happened because her son put seed in to meet the need.

The good news is, when you sow, you have a Bible right to believe that God will use it for His glory and multiply it back, good measure, pressed down, shaken together, and running over (Luke 6:38).

Oh, by the way, guess who got the 12 baskets full of leftovers? The Bible doesn't say, does it? But in my heart, I believe it was the little boy.

Let's go on planting seeds, and remember that every seed you sow is a seed that God can use for His glory and multiply it back to you.

YOUR ROAD TO A BETTER LIFE

YOUR GOD-GIVEN KEY FOR TODAY:

God is concerned about my daily needs.

[Monday]

KEY: *I Will Pray and Tell God Exactly How I Feel.*

What is prayer? Prayer is the sincere desire of your heart. Prayer is the key that unlocks the throne of God's mercy. Prayer is just simply telling God how you feel. *"The effective, fervent prayer of a righteous man avails much"* (James 5:16).

Sometimes people say to me, "Richard, I really don't know how to pray."

I always respond, "Well, how do you feel?"

Sometimes these people look at me amazed, and say, "What do you mean, tell God how I feel?"

And I always say, "Well, why don't you try it?"

Sometimes the words that come out of people's mouths when they pray are not very pretty. But after a while, after they begin to empty themselves of those negative thoughts on the inside, something changes. They begin telling God how much they love Him and how sorry they are for things that they have done, for sins that they have committed, for offenses against other people. Before long, tears are flowing down their face, and they have a real encounter with God because they told God exactly how they felt.

I remember once when the devil struck hard at our family with sickness. Lindsay called my dad to come down to our house and pray. I was so angry at the devil. I stood up and shouted and virtually cursed at him. Lindsay was embarrassed, but my dad said to her, "Lindsay, let him get it out of him."

Soon, all of that came out of me, and I was able to pray the right kind of healing prayer over our family. My dad joined in that prayer, and things began to change. Sometimes you have to get things out of your system. You know what? God doesn't get offended easily when we do that. He allows us to talk out of our hearts. Sometimes it isn't pretty. And sometimes it's not very pretty when it comes out of my mouth. But the time comes when I always say, "God, I'm sorry. I didn't really mean that, and I repent."

Always remember, God is a big God. And He can take what we throw at Him.

If you're scared, if you're anxious, don't be like some people who refuse to admit it. Be honest. Tell God how you feel. Tell Him you're scared. Ask Him to give you the inner strength to stand up strong. We all get scared at times. If you study the Bible, you'll find lots of times where people were scared.

Consider, for example, when Jesus was asleep in the boat. He had told the disciples they were going over to the other side. But when the storm struck, they forgot that Jesus was in the boat, and that they had a divine appointment on the other side of the lake. They awakened Jesus and said, "Don't you care that we're about to drown?"

Jesus didn't criticize them. He just simply woke up, walked to the bow of the ship, and spoke to the winds and the waves, saying, "Peace, be still." And the Bible says there was a great calm (Mark chapter 4).

Telling God how you really feel helps relieve the stress and the pressure of daily life. Telling God about your frustrations, your hopes, and your dreams can be a powerful force in your life.

One more thing. You can always tell God anything because He's your Source… your Source for faith… your Source for deliverance from fear… your Source for salvation from sin… your Source for healing and deliverance.

Don't worry about formulating the right kind of words. Can you remember just how easily you could understand your little child when he or she first started to talk? It may have made no sense to everyone else, but you knew exactly what they were saying.

You're God's child. He knows you and understands you perfectly. Start talking to Him in your own way, and pretty soon you won't be hung up anymore about how to talk to Him. Remember, prayer is a two-way street. It's not just you talking and Him listening; it's you talking and Him talking back to you.

YOUR GOD-GIVEN KEY FOR TODAY:
I will pray and tell God exactly how I feel.

[Tuesday]

KEY: *God Loves It When I Pray Because His Business Is Me.*

During the 1970s and 1980s, many outstanding Christian leaders came to visit my father. It was always a joy when I got to be in those meetings.

One such visitor was Corrie ten Boom, a dear woman who had spent years in a German concentration camp, literally surviving because she lived on her faith and sending prayer messages to God.

She told us about one time when she was really low in her spirit, wondering if this would be the day they would come and put her in the gas chamber. She said, "I got down on my knees and spread my Bible out in front of me, and I still often do this as I pray. I point to God's Word and remind Him of the promises to His children." Then Corrie smiled and said, "God likes it when we do that."

I can only imagine what she must have gone through in those years. What a powerful woman of God she was... so loving, so considerate, so kind.

Regardless of your method of sending messages (prayers) to God, you can reach out and touch Him... in the silence of your life...in your deepest emotions. You can touch Him when you're in a crowd... or if you're alone... if your bills are piling up, and you can't seem to pay them... if you're troubled in your mind and in your heart... if you're young or old... if you're scared and frightened... God is always there to hear you.

Someone might say, "But God is so busy." Well, sure He's busy. His business is you. And you'll find Him on the road to a Better Life.

Have you ever gotten too busy to listen to your own child? You may have occasionally, but usually your child is so insistent that you will finally stop and listen. Doesn't it always please you when your child takes you at your word?

Believe me, God is interested about every area of your life, spiritually, physically, financially, emotionally, in your family, in your business, in your ministry, in your job... in every area from your head to your feet.

It's like the old saying I used to hear: "If God gets too busy and runs out of time, He'll just make some more time, for after all, He made it in the first place."

YOUR GOD-GIVEN KEY FOR TODAY:

God loves it when I pray, because His business is me.

[Wednesday]

KEY: *I'll Do the Praying and Leave the Miracles Up to God.*

As you probably know, I receive prayer requests from people all over the world. They call as a result of our television programs, our podcasts, and live videos on Facebook, as well as other outreaches of the ministry. It is always my joy to receive the prayer requests and to pray, believing God for His miracle hand to touch their lives.

Many years ago, I made a commitment that I would rise up early in the morning, before dawn, and spend time in prayer. I do that for my family, as well as all of our partners and friends. It's such a blessing to be able to do it … And what a way to start the day.

Recently, I received this prayer request and a testimony from Alberta who is in Ohio:

> Dear Richard, thank you so much for your prayers. My daughter had been diagnosed with cancer after a biopsy showed a cancerous result.
>
> I said, "We are not going to accept this report." Then I called the Abundant Life Prayer Group. I left a message with my address, and I sowed a Seed-Faith gift to the Lord against my need. At that moment, I felt that my daughter was healed, and I could stand in faith for it.
>
> Soon, I received a letter from you saying that you were praying, and you encouraged me to expect a miracle for my daughter. I took that in faith and kept believing God for my daughter's healing.
>
> When my daughter and I went to our next doctor's appointment, he did a thorough examination, but he

could not find anything. There was no cancer! We give all the glory to God.

Now, these are the types of testimonies I receive… physical healings… spiritual healings… financial healings… In fact, all types of healing testimonies come into our ministry each day.

If you have never contacted the Abundant Life Prayer Group, here is your opportunity. The number to call is 918-495-7777. When you call, you'll reach one of our outstanding, well-trained prayer partners who have my spirit, and who believe in healing the way that I do.

On a personal note, the Abundant Life Prayer Group was founded back in 1958. As a matter of fact, I was in the room when the first phone call came in. I was just 10 years old, and I stood there and listened as my mother, Evelyn Roberts, answered the first call and prayed.

If I were you, I would write that number down. Here it is again, 918-495-7777. The Abundant Life Prayer Group is always open for prayer, seven days a week, 24 hours a day. Sometimes, you may get a voicemail, because of a backlog of calls. If so, while you're on hold, you'll hear my wife, Lindsay, and me, reading healing scriptures. It's not unusual that people testify to us that they received healing as they were listening to us read the scriptures. I pray the Abundant Life Prayer Group is a great blessing in your life.

YOUR GOD-GIVEN KEY FOR TODAY:

I'll do the praying and leave the miracles up to God.

[Thursday]

KEY: *God Is My Healer.*

Let it be established in your heart today that it's God's will for you to be well... well in every area of your life: spiritually, physically, financially, emotionally, in your family, your business, your ministry, your job, your marriage... That means all areas.

And I have a calling for the healing ministry in my life, and that includes you. In this chapter, I want to show you five reasons for you to believe that God will heal you.

1. God loves you as much as He loves anyone else.

He loved Moses even as his face shone like the sun.

He loved David, whom He called a man after His own heart.

He loved Elijah, who called fire down from heaven, saying, "Choose this day whom you will serve."

He loved Peter, who said, "You are the Christ, the Son of the living God."

You may say those were special people in the Bible. Well, they certainly were special people, but no more special than you. God created you, and you are unique and irreplaceable. There is no one like you. No one has your DNA. And God sent His Son for salvation and healing for you.

2. God has compassion for your hurts. He sent His Son, Jesus, to go to a cruel Cross to be crucified, so that you and I might be saved, healed, and delivered in every area of our lives. John 3:16 says, *"For God so loved the world that He gave His only begotten Son, that whoever believes in Him should not perish but have everlasting life."*

My father, Oral Roberts, taught me that compassion is an irresistible urge to remove the problem. In Matthew 14:14, Jesus went forth. He saw a great multitude. He was moved with compassion toward them, and He healed their sick. Compassion is different than sympathy. Sympathy says, "I'm so sorry. I wish I could help." Compassion, however, gives you the urge to reach into the person's life and pull out the sickness, the disease, the problem... whatever it is, compassion wants to get rid of it, in the authority of Jesus' name.

3. You can know that God wants you healed. His Son, Jesus, took upon Himself your sicknesses and diseases as well as mine. He bore them for us, so we might be free of them. Isaiah 53:5 says, *"But He was wounded for our transgressions, He was bruised for our iniquities; the chastisement for our peace was upon Him, and by His stripes we are healed."* Isaiah said this centuries before Jesus came on the scene. It was a prophetic word, but it's just as true today as it was when Jesus sacrificed His life on the Cross for you and me.

4. *Jesus Christ is the same yesterday, today, and forever* (Hebrews 13:8). **What He did in Bible days, He's still doing these days.**

If He can heal the woman with the issue of blood in Luke chapter 8, then He can heal you.

If He can heal blind Bartimaeus, who sat by the roadside begging in Mark chapter 10, then He can heal you.

If He can heal the military aide of a Roman army captain in Matthew chapter 8, who came to Jesus saying, "Just speak the word and my servant will be healed," then He can heal you.

If He can heal Peter's mother-in-law, who was sick with a fever, with the touch of his hand, then He can heal you (Matthew chapter 8).

First John 3:8 says, *"For this purpose the Son of God was manifested, that He might destroy the works of the devil."* So if the Lord healed in the past, destroying the devil's works, He certainly will heal now, to do the same.

5. You can know that God wants you healed. He has given you the faith to believe for your healing. Romans 12:3 says,

"God has dealt to each one (every man and woman) *a measure of faith."* You don't have to have any extra faith. You just simply use the faith that you have right now, and believe Him for a miracle.

Let me tell you beyond any shadow of doubt... God is still healing today. What He has done before, He's still doing.

And I'm setting my faith with you right now, in the authority of Jesus' name, for the Lord to heal you in every area of your life. There's a stirring in me for miracles right now. And with all the compassion in my life, with all the faith in my heart, I believe for you right now. I command the devil to take his hands off of your life. I pray for your miracle, and I am expecting it to come. Amen.

Make no mistake about it. I believe the road to a Better Life is paved with miracles.

YOUR GOD-GIVEN KEY FOR TODAY:

I will remember that God is my healer.

[Friday]

KEY: *God Is Superior in Quality... Excessive in Quantity.*

Oftentimes, people ask me what my favorite scripture is in the New Testament. Or, sometimes when I autograph someone's book or Bible, they will say, "After you write your name, put down your favorite scripture." Invariably I will write down John 10:10, which says, *"The thief* (the devil) *does not come except to steal, and to kill, and to destroy. I* (Jesus) *have come that they may have life, and that they may have it more abundantly."*

Now to me, that is a poignant picture of the difference between God and the devil. The devil is against you. He comes but for three reasons: to steal from you, to kill you, and to destroy the memory that you were even born. God comes towards you with health, strength, life, wholeness, healing, miracles... in every area of your life. The devil is against you, and God is for you. *"He who is in you is greater than he who is in the world"* (1 John 4:4).

Every time I quote John 10:10, it supercharges my faith. It reminds me that God is bigger and better than anything in this world, and His ability to love us and His supply for miracles are endless. While the devil wants to wipe me out, God wants to lift me up. It reminds me that God is a good God and the devil is a bad devil, that there's no badness in God and there's no goodness in the devil. Jesus, God's only Son, came to take off you what the devil put on, to take out of you what the devil put in, to put back in you what the devil took out, and to put back on you what the devil took off.

Talk about getting into God's flow of miracles. Wow! I'm not just talking about healing from sickness and disease. I'm talking about healing of the whole person... body, mind and spirit.

Here is a testimony I received from Olive in Florida:

> I had a stroke and as a result, I couldn't raise my left hand. While I was watching *The Place for Miracles* one day, Richard Roberts had a word of knowledge from God and said, "Someone cannot raise their hands. Raise your hands and do what you couldn't do." I acted in faith and found that I was able to lift my left hand.
>
> That's not the only miracle I've had through the Oral Roberts Ministries. Another time, Richard and Lindsay were planning to have a communion service on *The Place for Miracles*. I put notes all over the house so I would remember to participate. The morning of the communion broadcast, my back went out. I

couldn't bend. I couldn't sit. I was walking in pain, but I got ready for communion anyway. When Richard started praying, I put my hands on the TV screen and I prayed with him. When he was done, instantly I could bend. I could walk without pain. It was amazing!

Also, my grandson was doing very poorly in school. He was failing so badly that his teacher wanted to hold him back a year. I called the Abundant Life Prayer Group for prayer, and he began to improve right away. Now he is an honor student. Glory be to God!

The good news is what God did for Olive and her grandson, He wants to do for you. It's His greatest wish that you be in health even as your soul prospers (see 3 John 2). Remember, God is good and the devil is bad. Jesus is for you and not against you, and John 10:10 reminds us of that.

Read that scripture often. I do. It gives a great strength to my faith, as I travel on the road to a Better Life.

YOUR GOD-GIVEN KEY FOR TODAY:

Always remember that God is superior in quality and excessive in quantity.

[Saturday]

KEY: *I Will Release My Faith for Healing.*

In this chapter, I want to give you six steps to your healing. These are six steps that I believe will help you to release your faith and believe God for healing… in any area of your life where it's needed.

Here are the six steps:

1. Know that healing is a part of Christ's ministry today because the age of miracles has not passed.

Yes, it's true that there are many Christians today who believe that the age of miracles stopped when the apostles died, but you and I know it's not true. *Jesus is the same yesterday, today, and forever* (Hebrews 13:8). If He ever healed, He's still healing today. He's still performing miracles in people's lives, and we receive testimonies of healings every day through the Abundant Life Prayer Group… through letters, emails, and through other outreaches of this ministry. These testimonies are living proof that what God did in Bible days, He's still doing these days.

2. Know God's promises to heal in the scriptures, and be convinced that they are personally for you.

There are many scriptures in the Bible concerning healing, but what I'd like to focus on right here is Acts 10:38 where the apostle Peter says, *"God anointed Jesus of Nazareth with the Holy Spirit and with power, who went about doing good and healing all who were oppressed by the devil, for God was with Him."* It is said that Jesus was either on His way to heal somebody, or He was there healing them, or He was on His way to heal somebody else.

Get hold of a healing scripture. Study your Bible for them. Pick them out. Write them down. Quote them. Meditate on them. Most importantly, believe that they are for you personally.

3. Understand that God wants you well.

Only satan wants you to suffer. This goes back to John 10:10: *"The thief does not come except to steal, and to kill, and to destroy…"* Yes, satan wants you to suffer sickness, disease, fear, doubt, lack, and everything that is unlike God. But remember the rest of the scripture: "Jesus came so that you may have life and that you may have it more abundantly." On one side, you have satan, who only wants you to suffer. On the other side, you have God, who only wants you to be well. And God is bigger, more powerful and more loving than the devil ever could be. In a contest between them, God always wins!

4. Ask God to heal you according to His promises, and believe that He hears you when you ask.

There are a lot of people today who do not understand that it's God's will for you to be well, but notice 1 John 5:14–15—we have confidence that He hears when we ask according to His will. And what is His will? That we prosper and be well (3 John 2). So you can believe, according to these scriptures, that when you ask God to heal you, healing is His will for you. He hears that prayer and desires to answer it. He wants you to be healed in every area of your life. I want you not only to be healed, but I want you to believe that when you pray for healing, God hears you.

5. Believe when you pray that you have received what you've asked for.

Mark 11: 24 says, *"Whatever things you ask when you pray, believe that you receive them, and you will have them."* This is the scripture that Lindsay and I prayed when we began to believe God for a healing ministry. We asked Him for it, and we believed by faith that we received it long before we actually had it. Months passed, and we kept praying for people, and no one was being healed. But we did not quit believing God, and the day came when the healing ministry burst into our lives. That was 37 years ago, and it's been strong in us ever since. Believe that you receive it by faith and expect God to fulfill the manifestation, even if it takes time in arriving.

6. Praise the Lord for the answer, and act on His promise.

There's no substitute for praising God and thanking Him for what He is doing. As I said, you're not only thanking Him for the answer in advance, but you're acting like it has already happened. This is true faith — when we live our lives according to God's Word, not our circumstances.

Someone may say, "Well, I would be lying if I thank Him and act like the answer has already come." No. You're not lying because that's what God does. The Bible says, *"God calls those things which do not exist as though they did"* (Romans 4:17).

Now, let me summarize.

1. Know what God has promised you.
2. Ask God to do what He promised.
3. Act like God is doing what He has promised.
4. Use your faith.
5. Believe God.
6. Expect a miracle.

YOUR GOD-GIVEN KEY FOR TODAY:

I am releasing my faith for healing in every area of my life.

WEEK 10 RECAP

- **Sunday:** God Is Concerned About My Daily Needs.
- **Monday:** I Will Pray and Tell God Exactly How I Feel.
- **Tuesday:** God Loves It When I Pray Because His Business Is Me.
- **Wednesday:** I'll Do the Praying and Leave the Miracles Up to God.
- **Thursday:** God Is My Healer.
- **Friday:** God Is Superior in Quality… Excessive in Quantity.
- **Saturday:** I Will Release My Faith for Healing.

WEEK 11

[Sunday]

KEY: *I Can Communicate Directly with God...Because He Helps Me.*

All throughout this week, I want to share with you concerning speaking in tongues. What does it mean to be baptized in the Holy Spirit and to speak in tongues? How can you do it, and what are the benefits?

Well, those are all good questions. I began speaking in tongues on the day I gave my heart to Christ in October of 1968, and I've been praying in tongues every day since then.

Now, when I say praying in tongues, I'm talking about the prayer language of the spirit. I use the terms synonymously... speaking in tongues, the prayer language of the spirit, and praying in the spirit all mean the same thing.

In the Bible, Jesus said, *"It is expedient for you that I go away: for if I go not away, the Comforter* (the Holy Spirit) *will not come unto you; but if I depart, I will send him unto you"* (John 16:7).

In the Greek language, the word "Comforter" is "Paraclete." The word Paraclete is translated "comforter" in the King James Version of the Bible. It means "one called alongside to help"... or "one who warns"... "one who admonishes"... "one who helps us over our rough spots." So, the Divine Paraclete is the One who gives us what we need at the time we need it.

Another way of saying it is, the Comforter (The Holy Spirit), is Jesus' other self. Let me explain what I mean by this.

If I were to give you a dollar and you were to give me a dollar, you would have the same buying power with that dollar as the dollar that you just gave me. You would be just as well off as you were before. In the same way, Jesus was saying to His disciples, "If I go away, I will send you another Paraclete...another called alongside to help. I've been by your side physically. I have been everything to you. I have helped you. Now, you are distressed because I'm physically leaving the earth. But when I go back to my Father, I will send you another Comforter."

When Jesus physically left the earth, He said He would send another Comforter...another one called alongside to help. And He said we would do better with our lives with that Helper than if He (Jesus) had remained physically with us.

Having the Holy Spirit... the Divine Paraclete... the one called alongside to help is like having Jesus walking beside you in the flesh. Except it is better, because He is in His invisible, unlimited form. Jesus, in His physical body, could only be in one place at one time. The Holy Spirit can be anyplace, anywhere, all at once.

I believe this is the key to the beginning of understanding the Baptism of the Holy Spirit and the prayer language of the spirit, and what it means to have the Holy Spirit working in our lives.

Keep reading in the next chapter, and you'll discover that the prayer language of the spirit is not a language of your intellect.

YOUR GOD-GIVEN KEY FOR TODAY:

The Holy Spirit is called alongside to help me.

[Monday]

KEY: *I Can Pray with My Spirit and Not Just My Intellect.*

Your spirit communicates directly with God without the aid of your mind, through what the Bible calls other tongues, another language that you have not learned... a language given to you by the Holy Spirit. As you pray in the spirit, your spirit talks to God out of the depths of your inner being. Your spirit is now able to talk to God freely, because the Holy Spirit has come in to help you communicate your deepest needs to God. And by the fusion of your spirit with the Holy Spirit (much like your two hands joining together), the tongues, or the prayer language of the spirit, is produced.

You see, through Adam's fall, man's mind became blurred. He no longer could see God clearly. As someone has said, man's mind now acts as a censor, and too often, it censors out what God is saying to him.

A censor blocks certain things we would otherwise be able to see and hear. For example, if a prisoner writes a letter, that letter is intercepted by a censor to read, and portions of it may be deleted so that the person who receives the letter may or may not receive the entire letter as it was written.

In the same way, when Jesus was on the earth talking to His disciples, they listened to Him, but their minds censored out parts of what He said. Their minds intercepted lots of things that Jesus said and did not let those godly truths get down into their spirits. Therefore, they did not understand all that Jesus was saying.

But on the Day of Pentecost, when Jesus baptized them in the Holy Spirit and the Spirit got down into their spirit, they were able to speak in another language... a tongue that their minds had not learned and did not understand. This new tongue could not be censored by the mind because the mind does not understand what the spirit was saying. So, once again, man could communicate directly with God from his spirit and mind as Adam first did, before he fell.

In other words, the prayer language of the Holy Spirit restores our ability to communicate directly with God in a way that is pure, complete, and uncensored by the effects of sin.

As humans, we cannot look upon God. We are not at ease with God. We cannot talk freely to God. Somehow our understanding, our ability to grasp God, to communicate with Him, to understand life as God intended it, has been blurred. Something negative has happened to it.

Adam—the first man—had perfect communication with God. But he lost that full communication.

You see, God made man a spiritual being. God made man's spirit to be supreme over his mind and his body.

God did not make man physical. He just gave him a body.

God did not make man mental. He just gave him a mind.

God made man spiritual.

God put everything in man's spirit that had to do with the life of God, and the spirit, then, was to use the mind and the body as instruments. (See 1 Corinthians 6:19–20.) Through his spirit, man would talk and walk with God, subdue the earth, and enjoy his life as a whole person.

God loved man and put him together as a perfect being. But the devil sought to separate man and disintegrate his total personality, so that he would lose contact with God and would depend only on his powers of reason. That way, the devil could get in and influence man's life.

The devil knew if he ever got man to die spiritually, if he were successful in disintegrating the inner part of man, then he could cause the spiritual likeness of God to disappear from the spirit of man. Then...

Man would be left with a mind and a body, with the ashes of his spirit scattered around him. He would be like a ghost walking through the world... not knowing where he was going... not knowing how to talk with God... running into problems and not knowing how to solve them... getting into darkness and not knowing how to create light. Man would find all kinds of knowledge but would have little wisdom to use it.

Certainly we see in the world, which is operated by the mind of man, much knowledge but very little of the wisdom of God. As a result, things seem to be getting worse and worse.

Adam and Eve saw that the Tree of the Knowledge of Good and Evil had to do with their intellect. It had to do with their minds. God had told them they had the power to say yes, but He also said, "The day you eat of the tree, you will die..." That is... your spirit will die... the real part of you will disintegrate. It will be dead.

When Adam and Eve ate of the tree, the Bible says, "They knew..." They knew.

This is when the mind took ascendancy over the spirit. For the first time since God had created man out of nothing, the mind became the boss. It was no longer a servant of the spirit. It now began to suppress the spirit, to put it down until it was like a ghost. It was literally without the life of God.

When Adam chose to eat of the Tree of the Knowledge of Good and Evil, he was saying to God, "I want to do what I want to do. I'm going to elevate my mind and make the pursuit of knowledge the main thing in my life" (Genesis chapter 3).

The spirit of man died that day. His spirit was pushed down, and his mind rose up and took charge. The mind became supreme, and from that moment on, knowledge has been man's goal... his god.

But knowledge by itself is not an end. It cannot solve anything... It has to be based in something greater than it is... and that is the wisdom of God. To have the wisdom of God, you must be awakened by the Holy Spirit and born again... until the spirit which God made you to be comes alive, and you become a living soul again.

YOUR GOD-GIVEN KEY FOR TODAY:

The Holy Spirit is coming alive in me today by God's power.

[Tuesday]

KEY: *The Holy Spirit Now Lives in Me.*

When you are converted (saved, born again, received Christ as Savior...these terms all mean the same thing), the Holy Spirit brings you to Christ. The Holy Spirit gives you a new birth. In the same way that the Holy Spirit conceived Jesus, you were born again. You were born the first time of the flesh through your parents, but now you must be born the second time of the Holy Spirit.

Why? Because that spirit of yours is not alive. Your spirit has to be born again — it has to come into existence a second time. Jesus said, *"Most assuredly, I say to you, unless one is born again, he cannot see the kingdom of God"* (John 3:3). How do we have this experience? The Bible says, *"Repent, and let every one of you be baptized in the name of Jesus Christ for the remission of sins; and you shall receive the gift of the Holy Spirit"* (Acts 2:38).

The word "repent" means "change your mind."

I want you to notice how this all goes back to the mind of man. What happened in the Garden of Eden was that man chose some-

WEEK 11: TUESDAY

thing mentally. Man used his mind to choose knowledge. When God sent the Messiah, Christ, He was to bruise the head, or mind, of the devil, so when the Bible tells us to repent, it literally means to change our minds.

God doesn't tell you to change your spirit because your spirit is dead. In order for God to get into your spirit, you must open your mind and change it. How? By saying, "I am wrong." These are the three hardest words that you will ever say… "I am wrong." Repentance means "I am wrong, or I have sinned."

Not only must you say "I am wrong" as a first act to be born again, but you must also continue to say it the rest of your life. You must live in a state of repentance because you will be wrong again… and again… and again… and again. And so will I.

Repentance begins with the mind, and the Holy Spirit is the one who renews your mind. *"Do not be conformed to this world, but be transformed by the renewing of your mind, that you may prove what is that good and acceptable and perfect will of God"* (Romans 12:2).

Jesus became the second Adam. His purpose was to liberate you and me, to bring us into a union with God… beginning with our spirit. Jesus came so that the mind, which took dominance and supremacy over the spirit and the body, and made knowledge its pursuit in life, could now resubmit itself to God. In this way, the spirit of man could become dominant and supreme again. Man could once again become a spiritual being.

He would be able to discern spiritually.

He would be able to understand spiritually.

He would be able to see that every problem he has begins in his spirit, and every solution to that problem begins in his spirit.

Through the power of the Holy Spirit indwelling us, we are discovering that no matter what the problem feels like, it originates in our spirit. It may seem to be a mental or physical or financial or marital or some other kind of problem, but it all begins in our spirit. But thank God, that's where the answer also begins, in our spirit.

YOUR GOD-GIVEN KEY FOR TODAY:

I will allow my spirit man to dominate my life, rather than allowing my mind to dominate me.

[Wednesday]

KEY: *The Holy Spirit Lives Deep Down Inside Every Believer.*

One of the works of the Holy Spirit in your life is to help you with the things you face as a human being.

The Apostle Paul, who gave us most of the teaching that we have on the Holy Spirit, said, *"The Spirit also helps in our weaknesses* (our problems, our needs). *For we do not know what we should pray for as we ought..."* (Romans 8:26).

That is, we often just don't know how to pray. Our mind—our intellect—doesn't have the power. The mind is not a creator. It is only an instrument of the Spirit. The creative part of us is in our spirit.

"Now He who searches the hearts knows what the mind of the Spirit is, because He makes intercession for the saints according to the will of God" (Romans 8:27). When we reach the place that we just don't know how to pray... or the words to say when we pray... or even what to ask God for, we must not surrender. We must not give up and say it's hopeless. We must not say I can't do it. We must understand that within us is the Holy Spirit.

WEEK 11: WEDNESDAY

He is like a river of living water, and He's there flowing, 24 hours a day in the life of every believer. Jesus said, *"If anyone thirsts, let him come to Me and drink. He who believes in Me, as the Scripture has said, out of his heart will flow rivers of living water." But this He spoke concerning the Spirit, whom those believing in Him would receive; for the Holy Spirit was not yet given, because Jesus was not yet glorified"* (John 7:37–39).

Then Paul said in Roman 8:27: *"Now He who searches the hearts knows what the mind of the Spirit is."* The Holy Spirit is a person, and a person talks. He has an intellect, and in the mind of the Holy Spirit is all knowledge. In the Holy Spirit's mind is the understanding of all languages. In the Holy Spirit's infinite mind is the ability to communicate with God. So, the Holy Spirit searches our hearts and finds what is troubling us.

The Holy Spirit's greatest function is to intercede for you through the prayer language of the Spirit, according to the will of God.

He really wants to pray on your behalf and to help enable you to enter into His prayer for you. The Holy Spirit is within you, and He's down there searching your heart... searching out what the real problem is... searching for that thing that you feel deep down inside of you, which Jesus called "the belly or your inner man." I'm not talking about your stomach. I'm talking about your solar plexus area, your belly. That's where the Holy Spirit is living.

The Holy Spirit goes into the deepest level of your being... finding things that may have started years ago... finding things that gave you problems when you were in your teens... finding something way back in your marriage that hurt you... finding that problem that was so severe, it looked like it would strangle you to death and crush you out of existence...

The thing is there inside you, and with all of your praying in your mind, your intellect, you have not been able to bring it up. You have not been able to locate that thing that is troubling you and to pray according to the will of God for it. Now, the mind of the Spirit finds that problem and gathers all that up and begins to pray... to intercede with God, according to the will of God, for you.

The Holy Spirit prays on your behalf according to God's will, in tongues—in words that your mind has not developed or created. Praying in the prayer language of the Spirit first, and then praying with the understanding, also puts us, at least partially, on the level with Adam. (See 1 Corinthians 14:14–15.)

Our spirit and mind are no longer strangers. They are brothers, and they belong together. They are now one unit again.

Now, through the power of the Holy Spirit, we can pray with the spirit and we can pray with the understanding also. We get on a level where we can communicate with God, where we lose our fear, we can talk with Him and walk with Him in a different way than we have ever been able to before. We can become truly creative. We can discover new knowledge, combined with wisdom and understanding. We can come into a oneness with God and into a deeper love with one another. We can come into the renewing (or blossoming) of our minds by the Holy Spirit.

YOUR GOD-GIVEN KEY FOR TODAY:

I will pray with my spirit and with my understanding also. I will pray in tongues, then pray with my own language and begin to get understanding.

[Thursday]

KEY: *If You Trust the Holy Spirit, He Will Never Let You Down.*

As I've shared earlier, I gave my heart to Christ in my parents' bedroom. It was just two weeks before my twentieth birthday. When I prayed that prayer and repented of my sins, Jesus not only forgave me but gave me a feeling on the inside… a bubbling in my spirit… that I had never known before.

I was so excited about my new relationship with Jesus! He was no longer just a person that I heard about from my parents. Now He was in my heart by the power of His Spirit, and I wanted to tell everyone about what had happened to me.

Later that evening, I was back in my dormitory room when I heard a group of young men across the hall praying.

I knew that quite often that group would get together for a prayer meeting. I had been invited a number of times to come in, but up until then, I had refused.

That night, I didn't wait for an invitation. I just knocked on the door.

When they answered, I said, "What are you doing?"

They said, "We're praying in tongues. Would you like to pray in tongues?"

Well, the word had already begun to spread that earlier that day I had given my heart to Christ, and the guys in that room were very excited about it.

One of them said to me, "Why don't you just don't join in this prayer as we pray in the spirit?"

And I said, "I don't know how."

They said, "It's so easy. What did you feel when you got saved this afternoon?"

I replied, "I felt something bubbling up in my spirit."

"Yes," he said. "That's the Holy Spirit in you. He took up residence in your heart the moment you gave your heart to Christ."

He said, "Just start praying in tongues with us."

I said, "Well, I don't want to mimic you."

And he replied, "You will not be mimicking us. We'll just be priming your pump."

"Priming your pump," I said.

"Yes, we'll help you get started," he replied.

Suddenly, I remembered when I was a boy living on a farm. We had an old water pump, and we had to prime the pump to get water to come out. We put in a little water to get a lot of water. I understood that concept. What he was saying was, "Start praying in tongues with us, and the Holy Spirit will take you into your own prayer language."

It sounded so simple. As they began to pray in tongues, I just joined them. Pretty soon, a couple of unintelligible syllables came out of my mouth. It made no sense to me. Then they stopped praying and said, "Now pray in English."

As I opened my mouth and started to speak in my own language, a few words came out that I knew did not come from my mind. They came from the Holy Spirit.

They said, "Let's pray again." The next time, more unintelligible syllables came out of my mouth. Then we stopped, and I prayed in English again. This time, more came out in English... words that I knew did not come out of my mind, but came out of my spirit.

Over and over again that night, I did it like that until I could pray in tongues and then stop and pray in English. However, over the years, I found that generally speaking, I only prayed in tongues at

WEEK 11: THURSDAY

moments of great happiness or moments of deep sadness. And that's a trap that many Christians fall into. They don't pray in tongues and then pray with their understanding on a daily basis.

It wasn't until after I married Lindsay that I came into the fullness of the Holy Spirit which I enjoy today. After we got married, each night when we went to bed, we would pray together. Lindsay would immediately begin to speak in tongues, but I didn't have the same fluency. As I told you earlier, I only prayed in tongues when I was very happy or when I was very sad, but seldom when I was in the middle. Yet she could pray in tongues any time she wanted to. At first, I was jealous. Then I realized she was able to do something I wanted to do very much.

I said to her, "Honey, how do you pray in tongues any time you want?"

She said, "Let me help you." She began to lead me into praying in tongues on a regular basis. Each night, we would pray in tongues and then stop and pray in our own language. We did that so much that it became a daily thing with me to pray in tongues and then pray in English.

As I did, invariably several things would happen. As I prayed in English, I would begin to get God's response back to me. I would begin to say things in English that had been deep down inside me that I did not know how to express. More than anything, I began to get understanding, insight, new ideas, new concepts, and new and innovative ways of doing things. It literally transformed my life. My special thanks to Lindsay for teaching me how to do that. After all these years of marriage, we still pray in tongues together quite often.

The prayer language of the spirit…or tongues…may be the single hardest hurdle you will ever leap over, because the battleground is your intellect. Your mind wants to be supreme. It does not want to bow to the deepest longings of your heart and soul.

On the other hand, you may have already received this experience. If you have, that's great! Just keep on talking and praying to God in this manner.

If you haven't—believe this. It is for you. As you study this book along with your Bible, I am praying that this experience will come into your life. Whichever way it comes, remember, praying in tongues, or praying in the Holy Spirit, is to help you. You can pray in your own language, sure, but when you are overcome with a problem that you just can't even formulate the words to express it, then the Holy Spirit can move in. When you pray in tongues, and pray with your understanding (your own language), you'll be amazed at what comes out of your mouth as you speak.

The good news is, you can pray in tongues quietly at any time…not as a badge that someone will think you believe you're special because you speak in tongues. No, not that at all…but to get understanding.

I pray in tongues often…when I'm happy…when I'm sad…when I feel up…when I feel down…when I am excited…when I'm hurting. I pray in tongues on a daily basis, and I pray over everything I do. I don't do it as a demonstration to show how great I am. As a matter of fact, I do it because I need help. The good news is, if I can do it, you can do it too. Praying in tongues ups the speed limit on the road to a Better Life.

YOUR GOD-GIVEN KEY FOR TODAY:

I can communicate directly with God by praying in tongues on a daily basis—and I will do it.

[Friday]

KEY: *The Prayer Language of the Spirit Puts Me Together.*

The Holy Spirit was active throughout the Old Testament times. When our Lord Jesus — the second Adam — came, it seemed that only then was the Holy Spirit's personality fully revealed. We are now faced with the glorious prospect that our entire personality… spirit, mind, and body… can be reintegrated.

What we have lost — the gift of language which originates in the Spirit, by which we can talk directly to God — can be restored.

We reach down into the inner recesses of our being with the Holy Spirit in us and start speaking a language which, according to Paul, is "unto God" (1 Corinthians 14:2). This language is "speaking in tongues" or the prayer language of the Holy Spirit.

It's so difficult for our reasoning, our intellect, to understand that which is spiritual. In 1 Corinthians 2:14, we are told *"But the natural man does not receive the things of the Spirit of God, for they are foolishness to him; nor can he know them, because they are spiritually discerned."* That is, one has to get down inside his spirit to understand the things of God.

Now, there is a difference between your spirit and your intellect… your mind. Even though they exist together, there are times when they act almost independently of each other.

St. Paul said, *"For if I pray in a tongue, my spirit prays, but my understanding is unfruitful"* (1 Corinthians 14:14).

I believe Paul is saying here that he actually is praying with his spirit, but his mind is not necessarily part of that prayer. That is, his mind is not creating the prayer. Paul even goes so far as to say that his mind doesn't even comprehend it at all. It is in an unfruitful or inactive state for his mind, but not his spirit. It is as though his mind were an observer, but it's not comprehending the words or the sentences that the Spirit is putting together, because what is being voiced by the tongue is not originating in the intellect. It's coming from within... from the Spirit. It is as though the mind has been temporarily suspended from its activity.

This communication is as perfect as Adam and Eve could ever have spoken to God, according to the will of God, when they were in their original perfect state.

This is not to say that if one does not pray in tongues, he or she cannot pray at all. We often do pray with our minds, and we should. It can be productive to pray this way when we know exactly what the will of God is, and how to pray for it. Many people have never prayed with tongues. I would be the last person to say that they have not prayed, because many such people have a marvelous prayer life. It remains to be seen what could happen to their prayer life if they went deeper into the Spirit and were able to understand that they could pray with their spirit independently of their minds.

As a matter of fact, Paul indicates in the very next verse, *"What is the conclusion then?"* (Or in other words, what will I do?) *"I will pray with the spirit, and I will also pray with the understanding. I will sing with the spirit, and I will also sing with the understanding"* (1 Corinthians 14:15).

I believe the ability to express ourselves to God, both by the intellect and by our spirit, is exactly what God is trying to get us to develop. Now, through praying in the spirit as well as with our mind, we are going to give fuller expression of our total selves.

I think the Lord is trying to say that we can pray in the spirit to God and never be disappointed. We never have to be wondering whether or not God will hear us or afraid that God will not receive us, but we can talk to Him for who He is... our Father. He will talk back to us as His children...as His son or His daughter...as co-heirs with His Son, Jesus Christ. (See Romans 8:17.)

WEEK 11: SATURDAY

YOUR GOD-GIVEN KEY FOR TODAY:

Praying in the prayer language of the spirit helps me to give fuller expression of my total self to God. Plus, I get His response back to me.

[Saturday]

KEY: *Praying in the Spirit Is Part of Our Spiritual Armor.*

In Ephesians chapter 6, Paul speaks concerning our spiritual warfare and how to overcome the attacks of the devil with God's Word. *"Finally, my brethren, be strong in the Lord and in the power of His might. Put on the whole armor of God, that you may be able to stand against the wiles of the devil. For we do not wrestle against flesh and blood, but against principalities, against powers, against the rulers of the darkness of this age, against spiritual hosts of wickedness in the heavenly places"* (Ephesians 6:10–12).

Notice that Paul says we are in a spiritual warfare. It is a warfare first with the devil, and then with the princes of the devil, which could be translated demons.

You can't see the devil. You can't see these demons. They are fallen creatures… spiritual beings.

God, Who is Spirit, and the devil, who is spirit, and the human being, who is spirit, are locked in a battle.

The battle is between God and the devil. It's not between you and me or you and someone else. Behind every conflict we face in life is not another human being… although a human being may be involved. Everything that comes against us from a destructive point of view originates with the devil. It originates in these evil spiritual forces.

So, Paul is saying that because of this, you must be strong in the Lord. You must have the strength and power of God in you. You must put on the armor of God so that you may be able to stand and resist the attack. Otherwise, you will not stand; you will become discouraged and you will give up.

Paul likens the battle of life to a wrestling match. Have you ever watched a wrestling match? Have you seen how the wrestlers grapple with one another? How they turn, and twist, and lunge forward, and then draw back, trying to find the other's point of weakness? They throw themselves to the mat, or one picks up the other and throws him as far as he can. Sometimes, they get down on their knees and they grapple with one another as if it were a matter of life and death. This is the picture that Paul paints of our spiritual warfare with the devil.

It's a spiritual battle; therefore, we need to take on the whole armor of God. In Ephesians 6:13–18, Paul gives us seven pieces of that armor, all of which are extremely important.

Therefore take up the whole armor of God that you may be able to withstand in the evil day, and having done all, to stand.

Stand therefore, having:

1. girded your waist with truth

2. put on the breastplate of righteousness

3. shod your feet with the preparation of the gospel of peace

4. Above all, taking the shield of faith, with which you will be able to quench all the fiery darts of the wicked one

5. and take the helmet of salvation

6. and the Sword of the Spirit, which is the Word of God

7. praying always with all prayer and supplication in the Spirit.

Here, Paul likens our spiritual armor to the armor used by the soldiers of that day.

WEEK 11: SATURDAY

He speaks of the breastplate, which covers the entire chest area, so that an arrow could not penetrate and pierce the heart. He also mentions the shield of faith, which covered the entire body. It was held on the arm, and was used to ward off arrows of the enemy. By moving it around, the soldier could protect his entire body. Paul called this the shield of faith. He says we are to be so full of faith that we can repulse the attacks of the devil.

He lists several other pieces of the armor. Then he also mentions "praying always, with all prayer and supplication in the spirit."

*Praying always…*1 Thessalonians 5:17 says, *Pray without ceasing.*

How do we fight a spiritual warfare? We can't see the enemy. We feel the enemy. We feel the attack of a human against us, either physically attacking us or mentally attacking us. Or lying to us. Or disappointing us. Or, we are disappointing someone else. It works both ways.

How are we to fight this spiritual warfare? Paul says we are to pray without ceasing, and to pray in the spirit always. The key words are, "in the spirit …" We find these words repeated two other times: *"For he who speaks in a tongue does not speak to men but to God, for no one understands him; however, in the spirit he speaks mysteries"* (1 Corinthians 14:2). *"But you, beloved, building yourselves up on your most holy faith, praying in the Holy Spirit"* (Jude 20).

There is something about the spirit taking charge of the vocal cords, and bringing up what is down inside us… bringing it up over our tongue to God in another language. Praying in the spirit is most important in winning our spiritual battles.

Through the prayer language of the Holy Spirit, we can pray without ceasing. And as we do, we build up our inner man. We get stronger and deeper, and the flow of the Spirit through us increases. We are literally enriching our own lives. Then, by praying in the spirit, and afterwards in our own language, God can respond back to us.

The ultimate purpose of this prayer language of the spirit is that it goes up to God. God gets the prayer that originates in our spirit.

YOUR ROAD TO A BETTER LIFE

It is carried to Him by the power of the Holy Spirit. It is a prayer prayed in the will of God. It's a prayer prayed without the inhibitions of the intellect. The mind was in a completely unfruitful state. It's a prayer that originates in our spirit by the Holy Spirit. This is why God responds... Always.

How does God respond? How does this take place? Paul makes it clear in 1 Corinthians 14:13: *"Therefore let him who speaks in a tongue pray that he may interpret."*

After you pray in tongues... or in the spirit... just stop a moment and ask God to give you the interpretation...to speak back to you in your own understanding. Then, begin praying again in English or in your own language. In the process of praying in the spirit, the Holy Spirit has enriched your mind, and you will find God's response comes back to your mind. I have discovered that what I have said with my spirit now becomes what I say with my intellect, and so I'm able to pray with the understanding.

When I pray, I start in my spirit or in tongues (the prayer language of the spirit), and then I immediately go to my own language. I pray back and forth in tongues and then with my understanding until it's like they're one. It puts me together again. It reintegrates my entire personality... And I believe it will do that for yours, too.

All this week, I have shared with you as honestly as I know how concerning the value of the prayer language of the Holy Spirit and how it fits into the total Christian life. When properly used as a natural part of the expression of your deeper self to God, the prayer language of the spirit is so valuable and helpful that I cannot overemphasize its importance. It's something that I do every day of my life. Doing it literally supercharges my faith on my road to a Better Life.

To understand the true importance of the prayer language of the spirit, you should know this. It is to be immediately followed by your prayer with your understanding (in your own language). Praying with your spirit and with your understanding puts you together again. Your mind and spirit begin to function as one unit.

This is the essence of Paul's teaching and my own personal experience in my daily prayer life. I pray this has been a blessing in your life.

YOUR GOD-GIVEN KEY FOR TODAY:

I will pray with the spirit and with my understanding also.

WEEK 11 RECAP

- **Sunday:** I Can Communicate Directly with God…Because He Helps Me.
- **Monday:** I Can Pray with My Spirit and Not Just My Intellect.
- **Tuesday:** The Holy Spirit Now Lives in Me.
- **Wednesday:** The Holy Spirit Lives Deep Down Inside Every Believer.
- **Thursday:** If You Trust the Holy Spirit, He Will Never Let You Down.
- **Friday:** The Prayer Language of the Spirit Puts Me Together.
- **Saturday:** Praying in the Spirit Is Part of Our Spiritual Armor.

WEEK 12

[Sunday]

KEY: *I Will Be a Lifter-Upper.*

There are three types of people in the world. The first type says, "What's yours is mine, and I'm going to take it." The second type of person says, "What's mine is mine, and I'm going to keep it." And the third type of person says, "What's mine is yours, and I'm going to give it to you."

These three groups are illustrated in the story of the Good Samaritan in Luke chapter 10.

If you remember how it goes, a man traveled from Jerusalem down to Jericho, and fell among thieves. They stripped him of his clothing. They beat him within an inch of his life. They stole his possessions and left him for dead in the middle of the road.

This is what the world does. This group of thieves represents the devil who comes to steal and kill and destroy.

All of my life, I have faced these kinds of people... people who want what I have, even to the point of wanting my anointing.

Some months before my father went home to be with the Lord, he said to me, "Son, when I die, many men will rise up and say, 'I have Oral Roberts' anointing.'" Then he would chuckle and say, "But son, the double portion anointing is reserved for you." And then he would say, "The anointing is generational. It passed from Abraham to Isaac and from Isaac to Jacob and from Jacob on down to Joseph... and on down the line." Dad said, "No one can steal your anointing."

I've had people do things against me, say things against me, tell lies, try to steal my inheritance, try to steal my heritage, and, as I said, try to steal my anointing. I've had people write terrible and ugly things about me that were not true. I've never taken the time to defend myself, because you don't get anywhere doing that. You just have to let God be your defense. You'll always come across people who behave like the thieves in Luke 10.

Now, the second group of people is illustrated by the priest and the Levite who passed him up. Though they were capable of helping him, they did nothing.

Each of them came walking down the highway. When they saw the man lying injured in the road, they walked around him as far away as they could. They passed him up. They didn't want to get their hands dirty. This is the religious crowd, the crowd whose forebears put Jesus on the cross. These are the ones who act like they're spiritual, but they're not. They're just religious. Oh, they may go to church. They may have a Bible. They may attend Sunday School. But they have a hatred for other people. They think they're God's gift to the world. But when it comes to being a light to the world, as Jesus told us to be, they do not do it.

In my life, I've dealt with many such individuals. They are pious in their actions, appearing kind on the outside, but dirty on the inside.

The third type of person is illustrated by the Samaritan who came along, saw the man, and had compassion on him and lifted him up.

My father taught me that compassion is "an irresistible urge to remove the problem." It's different than sympathy. Sympathy says, "I'm so sorry. I wish I could help you." But compassion gets in there and gets the job done. Compassion does what is needed, even if it is not always easy or convenient, because that's who God is.

This Samaritan bathed the man's wounds, picked him up, put him on his donkey, and took him to a local hotel, where he said to the innkeeper, "Whatever it costs to take care of him, send me the bill." The Samaritan lifted him up.

WEEK 12: SUNDAY

Now, this Samaritan was the type of person who sees in every situation the opportunity to plant a seed. He sowed good seed into the life of this man who had been beaten and robbed and passed by.

The good news is, when we sow seed... whether it's our time, our love, money, prayers, smiles, compassion, a good word, no matter what it is... it's a seed sown as unto the Lord. And the Lord will use that seed for His glory, and then multiply it back to us.

I believe with all my heart that the Samaritan received a tremendous harvest, because he planted seed into the life of this man.

Now, the question is, which category do you fall into?

Are you one who simply takes from others and never gives anything in return? Do you beat them up with your words and your actions?

Or are you a part of the group that is so religious and high-minded that you wouldn't reach out and help anybody... even if you had the opportunity, do you just pass them up?

Or are you like the Good Samaritan who lifted him up and sowed seed into the man and saw to his well-being?

Good questions, aren't they?

I've chosen to be like the Good Samaritan. I want to be a lifter-upper. I want to sow seed into the lives of my fellow man. I want to win the lost to Christ all over the world. I want to help empower people with a taste and touch of the gospel. I want to impart the ministry that God has given me into the lives of others.

I ask again, are you a taker, or are you just a pious, religious person? Or are you a lifter-upper?

YOUR GOD-GIVEN KEY FOR TODAY:

I will be a lifter-upper. I will sow seed into the lives of my fellow man.

[Monday]

KEY: *God Is Alive, and Continuously Active in My Life.*

People often ask, "Richard Roberts, what do you do when you get discouraged? How do you handle it when you get depressed… when your ministry bills are piling up and you can't pay them … when you do all that you know to do, and it still doesn't seem to be working. What do you do?"

Well, it might surprise you to hear that these very things I'm describing happen to me… And they've happened to me a lot. Some people think I never get discouraged, that I never get down. But it's not true. I do. I know what it means to be discouraged… to really get low. I understand what it feels like when you think you're about to go under. I have faced it many times.

To be really honest and frank with you, when I get discouraged, I get downright scared. I get that sick feeling in the pit of my stomach that says I'm not going to make it. I know it's the devil. Still, I'm a human being. I get that same ugly feeling deep down on the inside as well. Then I get irritated, and sometimes hard to live with. I find that my words come out sharp and hard, even though I don't intend them to.

I'll find myself speaking sharp words to my wife, Lindsay, and to my children…words that I regret saying.

Now, they understand the stress and pressure that I'm under from time to time. But still, it's the wrong thing for me to do. Really, what I'm doing is, I'm acting out of my hurt.

That's when I get out my Bible. That's when I begin to pray in tongues. That's when I begin to ask God what He has to say about this situation I'm facing.

WEEK 12: MONDAY

Now, I love to read the Bible because it has a great deal to say to us human beings. To us who are down here on this earth struggling to be successful, God's Word has a lot to say about doing the best you can, but still feeling like a failure… about becoming so discouraged that you want to give up.

In Exodus chapter three, there is a story of a man who had tried and failed… who found himself inadequate for the task and fled to the desert. His name was Moses. I'm sure you remember his story.

Moses was born the son of Hebrew slaves. He was doomed to death (Pharaoh had decreed that all the baby Hebrew boys should be killed, because the people were multiplying too quickly.) But his parents hid him.

One day, the daughter of Pharaoh found little Moses hidden in the bulrushes of the river. She looked into the face of that little baby boy, and she loved him. She could not destroy him, so she adopted him. Moses grew up in the royal palace of Egypt, the son of the Pharaoh's daughter. But his real mother nursed him and cared for him as a young child, and she instilled in him his heritage…the knowledge of who he really was.

As Moses grew into manhood, he became more and more disturbed by the treatment of the Hebrews. One day, he came upon an Egyptian overseer beating a Hebrew slave. Suddenly, all the anger against the unjust treatment of his people rose to the surface. Looking around to see if anyone was watching, Moses grabbed a whip and, in anger, he began to beat the Egyptian until he killed him. Then Moses buried the Egyptian in the sand, but his act was witnessed.

Now, Moses thought that even if a Hebrew had seen what he did, that person would be glad. But he was wrong. Word of his deed was carried to Pharaoh. Finally, Moses had to run for his life from the land of Egypt.

Moses ended up in Midian… on the back side of the desert, tending sheep for a living. It was quite a come-down from the palaces of Egypt to a tent in the desert... from being honored as the son of Pharaoh's daughter to being a sheepherder. And all because Moses did what he thought was right. He had tried to help his people, and he failed.

So, there he was in the desert... with its endless sand, rocks, and bushes. For forty long years, Moses suffered disillusionment, disappointment, and depression because of his failure. He was in a negative cycle.

Round and round he went. Day after day, he watched the sheep and did the tasks of a shepherd. And he thought about his failure.

Does this sound familiar to you? Are you going around and around in a meaningless circle? Have you tried and failed to bring your dream to pass? Are you being daily devastated by this negative cycle?

If this sounds like you, let me tell you there's hope. You see... God exists. God is real. God is concerned about you. God cares about the cycle you're in. God knows the feeling you are experiencing right now... just as He did with Moses. And in tomorrow's chapter, I'll tell you what God did about it.

YOUR GOD-GIVEN KEY FOR TODAY:

God is real, and I know He cares about what I'm going through.

[Tuesday]

KEY: *God Knows the Feeling You Are Experiencing Right Now.*

Let me repeat to you what I said in the last chapter. God exists. God is real. God is concerned about you... yes, you, in the condition you're in, right now. He cares about the cycle that you're in. He knows the feeling that you're experiencing, just as he did with Moses.

So, God came to Moses out there in the desert. Isn't that a great thought? God came to him, and God will come to you… right at the point of your greatest need… right where you need Him the most. I'm talking about right in the middle of that negative cycle you're in…where you think nothing can ever change. Suddenly, God will come to you.

God came to Moses in a way that awed him at first… a way that Moses didn't understand. God appeared in a bush that caught on fire, and it kept on burning without being consumed. Naturally, Moses went out of his way to see this strange thing.

You see, first, God got Moses' attention. That's important. And God will get your attention and my attention. He didn't get my attention until I realized that there was a call of God on my life, and I had totally missed out on what God wanted me to do.

You see, I ran from God all through my teenage years. But the day came when I realized God had a plan for me that was better than my plan. Thank God, He got my attention. But even more so, thank God I finally paid attention.

I believe God is going to get your attention… one way or the other. When He does, it'll be a great day in your life. It will be a great day… for suddenly, you will see that God, your Source, is your only way out. He is the one who can break the cycle of bad things happening in your life.

I believe you will see that by trusting in Him, good things will begin to happen. That's why I can say "something good is going to happen to you." That's why I can say God wants you to have a Better Life.

One day, Moses saw a bush that was on fire. The fact that the burning bush was not consumed says something else to you and me as well. The bush speaks of the continuity of God. It says to us, "God is continuously alive and active in human affairs."

It said to Moses that, just as God was alive in the palaces of Egypt when Moses had been a prince, God was alive now among the rocks and sand and bushes of the desert. He was as much alive out there where Moses was like a tiny speck, lost in the universe, as He was when Moses was robed in royalty and walking the halls of the palaces of Egypt. God was in Egypt… and God was there in the desert when Moses was alone.

Now, that's a wonderful idea… to know that wherever you are and whatever condition you're in, God is continuously alive and active in your life.

God told Moses to take off his shoes, for he was standing on holy ground. It is always holy ground when you become aware of God. The awareness of God gives you the feeling that you are standing on holy ground.

God is a compassionate, caring God. He spoke to Moses from the bush and said, "I've seen the affliction of my people in Egypt. I've heard their cry, and I have come to send you to lead them out of bondage to a land of promise… a land flowing with milk and honey."

"I have heard their cry." This means:

God cares when you are oppressed.

God cares when you are beaten down.

God cares when you can't fling off the obstacles that are in your path.

God sees the afflictions, the torments, the needs, the problems, of you… of me… of every human being in the world.

God cares. And He sees every teardrop that falls.

Then God said, "I'm going to send you, Moses, to deliver my people."

WEEK 12: TUESDAY

Moses was so serious, he was almost comical. It's so much like the way you and I would probably have acted if we had been there. Moses asked, "You're going to send me back to Egypt?"

"Yes," God replied. "I'm going to send you back."

"Who am I, Lord? I've already tried and failed." Moses said, in essence, "Lord, I blew it." And that's a phrase we use today. "I blew it."

The next thing Moses said to God was, "I don't even know your name."

You know, Moses was down there in Egypt, trying to do God's work, and didn't even know who God was. A lot of people have never had an experience with God. They've never been truly saved by His grace or filled with His Holy Spirit. They're doing religious things, but it's not working. At least Moses was honest about it. He said, "I don't even know your name."

God said, "My name is I Am." That will be My name forever… I Am. I Am God… I Am now. I always was and I always will be. I Am."

Well, Moses kept piling up his excuses. He said, "If I go down there, they won't believe me. I'll stand up and tell them that You sent me, and they won't believe that You sent me. What will I do then?"

God said, "Tell them that 'I Am' sent you."

That didn't convince Moses, so God said, "What do you have in your hand?" Moses held a rod that he used to guide his sheep.

God said, "Throw it down." The rod became a snake. God said, "Take it up by the tail."

Moses did, and it became a rod again. It was a miracle.

God said, "Listen, I'll go with you in my miracle power."

That's what Moses had not counted on. He had merely counted on his own strength. He had not counted on the miracles of God.

Listen, there are miracles… and they're not in short supply. God's arm has not been shortened. He's still performing miracles, and

YOUR ROAD TO A BETTER LIFE

He's capable of bringing miracles and putting you on His road to a Better Life. He is the God of miracles. One miracle can do more in your life in five seconds than you can do in a lifetime.

In tomorrow's chapter, I'll show you how Moses, by God's anointing, delivered two and a half million Israelites out of Egyptian bondage to the Promised Land.

YOUR GOD-GIVEN KEY FOR TODAY:

God is my God of miracles.

[Wednesday]

KEY: *God Is a God of the Miraculous.*

I remember the words of an old song written by Ralph Carmichael:

"The God of miracles is reaching out His hand. The God of miracles is moving through the land. So, touch Him, believe Him, this moment when you pray. Now expect a miracle, and a miracle is yours today."

As I told you in the last chapter, one miracle can do more in your life in five seconds than you can do in a lifetime.

After Moses and God spoke in the desert about who God is and how He would be with Moses, Moses said to God, "I'm a stutterer. I can't talk good. I'm not eloquent. When I try to talk, the words don't come out right."

God said, "I'll be your mouth."

Moses finally became willing to go back to Egypt, because he understood now that he didn't have to go in his own strength… that he had a Source for his life. He had the great I AM—God—in his heart and by his side going before him... and above him... and beneath him ... and around him. Moses had a Source for his life.

Moses began to open himself up, and to give of his talent, his time, his life. It was a seed of faith that he planted which God could use for His own glory, and then multiply it back. Moses gave out of his own need of being delivered, his own need of freedom, his own need of having the miracles of God. Moses began to give for a desired result... And so can you.

Moses began to expect miracles. He knew that in the natural, when he went to Pharaoh, he would be no match for this great king. He knew that in his own strength, he couldn't lead two and a half million slaves out of Egyptian bondage. He knew he could not cross the Red Sea or bring water from the rock or lead them to the land of promise. He knew he would have to have miracles along the way, and he began to expect them.

The exodus of two and a half million Israelite slaves from Egypt is one of the greatest miracles of all time. It happened through a lowly shepherd who had been in a 40-year negative cycle of discouragement, fear, disillusionment, and depression...who finally opened himself up and despite his own shortcomings, let God have a chance to work in his life.

It's really my own story. I ran away from God. I ran away from my problems, and I ran away from myself. Even though I was raised in a Christian home, when I came back to face God, I really didn't know who He was. I was lost and undone without God or His Son. But how tenderly God dealt with me. I finally learned that God is my Source, and I'm continuing to learn how to put seeds of faith in...how to give...and how to expect miracles.

Can you see how Moses first got control of himself when he discovered God, and learned He was the true Source of his life? That's when he began to open up...not in discouragement and bitterness... but in giving of himself. That's when he really began to expect the mighty God to go with him... back to the scene of his failure. And right there, he believed God to start him on his road to a Better Life.

Think about that for a moment. The eternal principles of seed-faith have been in the Bible through the centuries, even in Moses' time. These *three miracle keys* changed the direction of Moses' life.

God became so real to Moses that nothing could stop him. Nothing can stop you when you grasp that seed-faith is real and workable in and through you.

YOUR GOD-GIVEN KEY FOR TODAY:

Say this confession—say it out loud:

"God is alive and continuously active in my life."

Say it out loud again: GOD IS ALIVE AND CONTINUOUSLY ACTIVE IN MY LIFE.

I believe when you latch on to that truth... and continue to say it out loud, you will be in the best position ever to receive His miracle touch in your life.

[Thursday]

KEY: *Seven Proclamations for Me to Make Every Day of My Life*

1. Something good is going to happen to me each day.

Each day confess... *"Surely goodness and mercy shall follow me all the days of my life; and I will dwell in the house of the Lord forever"* (Psalm 23:6).

2. I am walking in Christ's victory and holiness.

WEEK 12: THURSDAY

Confess... *"I am the righteousness of God, in Christ Jesus"* (2 Corinthians 5:21).

3. The mercy and grace of God is working in my life.

Confess... *"Let us therefore come boldly to the throne of grace, that we may obtain mercy and find grace to help in time of need"* (Hebrews 4:16).

4. The blessing of Abraham is working in me daily.

Confess... *"That the blessing of Abraham might come upon the Gentiles in Christ Jesus, that we might receive the promise of the Spirit through faith"* (Galatians 3:4)

5. I am healed by the stripes on Jesus' back.

Confess... *"But He was wounded for our transgressions, He was bruised for our iniquities; the chastisement for our peace was upon Him and by His stripes we are healed"* (Isaiah 53:5).

6. All my prayers are in the process of being answered.

Confess... *"And whatever things you ask in prayer, believing, you will receive"* (Matthew 21:22).

7. I am a soul winner and am increasing in the power of the Holy Spirit.

Confess... *"But you shall receive power when the Holy Spirit has come upon you; and you shall be witnesses to Me in Jerusalem, and in all Judea and Samaria, and to the end of the earth"* (Acts 1:8).

These confessions are really proclamations. I make them every day of my life. I suggest you do the same thing.

Quoting the Word of God is very powerful. When you quote the Word of God, your ears hear it. Then it gets down into your heart, and out of the abundance of your heart, your mouth will speak (Luke 6:45).

You'll never say what you don't believe. That's why confessing the Word is so important—because it gets into your heart, so you can begin to believe it. Each time you say it, the reality of God's Word becomes more powerful to you.

YOUR GOD-GIVEN KEY FOR TODAY:

I will confess these proclamations every day of my life. My faith in Jesus is growing.

[Friday]

KEY: *We've Got to Have Miracles*

Back in the mid-1980s, my father invited Dr. David Yonggi Cho, Pastor of Yoido Full Gospel Church in Seoul, Korea, to come to Tulsa and speak at our annual minister's conference.

I had read Dr. Cho's books, and I had followed his ministry. I knew that he pastored the largest church in the world, with over 700,000 members.

Dr. Cho had always considered my father to be his spiritual mentor. To see the two of them together brought great joy to my heart.

During Dr. Cho's visit, I was able to spend some personal time with him, and he invited me to come to Korea to conduct a healing crusade in his church. I was so excited to accept! When I arrived in Korea and walked into the church for the first time, the Spirit of God literally took my breath away.

Now, you must understand. If you count the sanctuary and all the overflow areas, they can seat almost 50,000 people at one time.

Dr. Cho escorted me in, and we sat on the platform. It was during the time when one of the associate pastors was leading in prayer. When those Koreans began to pray, the power of God hit me in my chest with such force that it drove me back into my chair.

The only way I could describe it is that it felt as if I was in a dragster and hit the accelerator with more than 1,000 horsepower.

WEEK 12: FRIDAY

Imagine how your body would be thrown back into the driver's seat. Well, that's what it felt like. I began to weep as the people prayed and prayed and prayed and just wouldn't stop praying. Finally, they rang a bell to get the people to stop praying.

By the time Dr. Cho introduced me, I was weeping. I had never seen that intensity of prayer in any country in my life. We had a marvelous three-day healing crusade with lots and lots of miracles. Over these many years, I have developed a friendship with Dr. Cho, and for some years now, I have served as a member of the Church Growth International Board of Directors, which meets every other year in Seoul, Korea. The last time I attended a conference, it was my thrill to be one of the main speakers in the great World Cup Soccer Arena, which seats 100,000.

Oh, and by the way, that stadium was filled with 100,000 people… and those were just Dr. Cho's leaders.

Some months ago, I was able to attend another Church Growth International Conference. While there, Dr. Cho made a powerful statement. He said, "We've got to have miracles."

Wow! Here's a man who pastors the largest church in the world, saying we've got to have miracles. Notice, he didn't say, "I'm so sorry that miracles have died out, and they don't exist anymore. They were just for those in the Bible." Instead, he said, "We've got to have miracles."

That means today, right now, in our lives, we must have miracles. We must have the saving, healing, delivering, miraculous power of God flowing into our lives. And we must minister that flow into the lives of others.

As I heard Dr. Cho speak, four things stood out to me.

Number one: People are sicker than ever before.

With all the medical breakthroughs, with all the great hospitals, clinics, diagnostic equipment, with all the tremendous doctors and nurses, people seem to be sicker than they've ever been. If ever there was a time for miracles, it's now.

Second: We must have the confirmation of the Word of God.

Jesus sent His disciples out preaching, teaching, and bringing His healing power to people in need. Just the preaching of the Word, as powerful as it is, is not enough. Just the teaching of the Word, as illuminating as it is, as fulfilling as it is, as heartwarming as it is, is not enough. We must have miracles confirming God's Word.

Third: These miracles are a sign to the unbeliever.

It lets them know that God has not fallen off the throne. He's a God who's alive, and He's still performing miracles as He did in Bible days.

And fourth: Miracles build faith for others to receive Christ. Some of the greatest healing miracles I've ever witnessed have come after the Word of God has been preached.

I remember preaching in a large church in Nairobi, Kenya. God performed miracles there. I went back into a private room for lunch. There, I was met by a woman in the final stages of AIDS. She had heard me preach, and her faith had risen. I stood up, laid my hands on her, and prayed. She was so weak that she could scarcely walk. The people with me helped her back to her car.

Some months later, I was back in Kenya for what would turn out to be the largest healing crusade of my life, with some 200,000 people in attendance on the last night.

Lo and behold, that woman was there that final night. She was healed, whole, and completely cleansed of AIDS. And it had been confirmed by her doctors. She stood before the crowd that night and gave her testimony. She later told me that when she first heard me preach months earlier, faith rose in her heart to believe for a complete miracle and for healing from AIDS. And she got it!

Dr. Cho is right. We've got to have miracles. That's what sets Christianity apart... *miracles*. I believe in miracles.

YOUR GOD-GIVEN KEY FOR TODAY:

We not only must have miracles, but in the authority of Jesus' name, we will have miracles because God is the same. He's never changed.

[Saturday]

KEY: *Lord, Help Me to Be Successful*

Most everyone on this planet wants to be a success. You do. I do. We want to do our best. Oftentimes, we measure our worth based on just how successful we really are.

Oftentimes too, people have a tendency to measure their success by a worldly standard, rather than a godly standard. Success by the world's standard could mean wealth or notoriety, what you possess, certain achievements, how famous you are, how beautiful you are, or how well you've been able to tap the resources of your brain.

But if the world's standard is the only measurement that we have to determine our success level, we will have an incomplete view of our own success. In other words, we won't get the whole picture, because God does not measure success according to what the world has to say.

I heard the story of a young man who went fishing at the lake, and as he stood there with his line in the water, he noticed the most successful man in town was also fishing just a little ways up the lake.

He eased his way closer and closer and closer to this elderly gentleman.

Soon, he was standing right next to him, and he just couldn't contain himself. He turned to the man and said, "Sir, may I ask you a question?"

The elderly gentleman looked at him and said, "Why, of course, son. What is it?"

"All my life, I've wanted to be a success. And since you're the most successful man that I know of in this town, would you please tell me how I can be a success?"

The man said to him, "Do you really want to know?"

The young man replied, "Yes, I do."

"Then put down your fishing pole." The young man put his pole down, and the elderly gentleman put his down. Then he promptly grabbed the young man by the back of his coat and threw him in the water.

Much to the young man's surprise, the elderly man jumped in on top of him, grabbed him by the back of his head, and held him under the water.

After the elderly gentleman had held the young man under for a long time, he lifted him up so he could get one breath. Then he pushed him back down under the water again.

He held him down, down, down… until it seemed the young man was going to drown.

Then the gentleman brought the young man up again, and threw him on the shore. He jumped on top of him again, and began to pound on his chest.

When the young man was able to speak, he said, "Mister, why in the world did you do this to me?"

And the man said, "Son, do you remember how bad you wanted that breath when you felt like you weren't going to be able to breathe again?"

"Yes, I sure do," the young man replied.

The gentleman said, "Son, when you want to be a success as bad as you wanted that last breath, you'll be one."

Now, it would be very easy for me to give you "three steps to success" or "four ways to be successful" or "seven things you must do to be a success in life." I could talk to you about becoming what you think about or deciding exactly what you want in life. I could talk to you about the price you'd have to pay and the commitment it takes to pay that price. I could talk to you about your work ethic, and living one day at a time. I could talk to you about never quitting and always giving your best. But I have something else in mind.

Let's look at the Apostle Paul. He had the most unusual success formula I've ever heard about, and it's found in Philippians 3:13–14.

Paul said these words: *"I do not count myself to have apprehended; but one thing I do, forgetting those things which are behind and reaching forward to those things which are ahead, I press toward the goal for the prize of the upward call of God in Christ Jesus."*

No matter what they threw at Paul, he just kept showing up.

Beaten with rods, he just kept showing up. Stoned and left for dead… he just kept showing up. Run out of town by criticism… he just kept showing up. Beaten with whips… he just kept showing up. Shipwrecked… he just kept showing up. Snake bitten… he just kept showing up.

Paul had the most unusual "never-give-up attitude" of possibly any man who has ever lived.

He knew how to put the past in the past, and how to press forward toward the success that God had in mind for him. He just kept moving forward on that road to a Better Life.

The day came when Paul said, *"I have fought the good fight, I have finished the race, I have kept the faith. Finally, there is laid up for me the crown of righteousness"* (2 Timothy 4:7–8).

That's what I want to be like. I want to be like the Apostle Paul. I want to leave nothing on the table, and give my very best for God.

I have a feeling that's the way you feel too.

YOUR GOD-GIVEN KEY FOR TODAY:

I will put my past in the past and press forward toward the great success God has for me.

WEEK 12 RECAP

- **Sunday:** I Will Be a Lifter-Upper.
- **Monday:** God Is Alive, and Continously Active in My Life.
- **Tuesday:** God Knows the Feeling You Are Experiencing Right Now.
- **Wednesday:** God Is a God of the Miraculous.
- **Thursday:** Seven Proclamations for Me to Make Every Day of My Life.
- **Friday:** We've Got to Have Miracles.
- **Saturday:** Lord, Help Me to Be Successful.

WEEK 13

[Sunday]

KEY: *No Weapon Formed Against Me Will Prosper…if I Keep My Spirit Right.*

We are beginning week 13 of this book. It's the last seven days and seven chapters. This week, we will talk about how to respond in a godly way to situations that hurt us, especially when what has happened to us is unfair. We will talk about the subject of how to handle criticism you deserve and criticism you don't. I will also deal with how to handle the blows struck against you by well-meaning people, and also blows struck against you by people who desire to injure and harm you.

I'll address how you can remain spiritually strong when there are lies told against you and there are ugly things that some people have both said and done. I'll share some of what I've been through and how I've handled it, so that you can use these tools in your own life to resist the devil when his attacks hurt the most.

I'm going to share seven rules with you which have helped save my life when attacks have come. And I believe that when applied properly, they will help save yours.

I doubt if anyone will ever reach the place where criticism and ugly words don't hurt, but I believe it is possible to create an attitude that will, in due course, take the sting completely away. I know, because I've burned with resentment at times over what some people have done to me, but God has shown me how to be an overcomer.

There's an old gospel song titled "Love Lifted Me." The first line of the verse says, "I was sinking deep in sin far from the peaceful shore..." Many times, when attacks come, it is tempting to give in to wrong thinking, wrong attitudes, and wrong behaviors. When what happens seems unfair or unjust or is based in a lie, we can respond with resentment and anger. We lack peace, and find ourselves tempted to do something that we know God would not be proud of.

In one situation I faced, I was accused of doing things I had not done. I was criticized and bad-mouthed, even though I was not guilty of their accusations. And honestly, it hurt me deeply. Like the song says, I was far from shore, lacking peace, and sinking fast.

I was fast reaching the point at which my resentment against my critics and those who had falsely accused me was turning into contempt and malice... and even hatred toward them. For a while, I wanted God to deal with them in the harshest way...I really wanted God to wipe them out... I think you know what I'm trying to say.

Perhaps you have been there too... or are there now... facing unfair accusations, harsh criticisms, unkind words from those who are seeking to hurt you. Keep reading, because I have some keys from God to help you!

First, let me share how far we can drift from God's ways if we're not careful. In my case, I actually developed a double resentment, because so much had come against me for which I was not guilty. But the most amazing thing is whenever I've been accused of something that I haven't done, God usually will not let me talk. Instead, He tells me to be quiet, that He is my defense, and I should keep my mouth closed. There are many scriptures that tell us God is our defender. Exodus 14:14 says, *"The Lord will fight for you; you need only to be still."* It's not always easy to be still when others hurt us. But it's essential to learn how to let God handle the situation instead of retaliating.

So, how can you resist the desire to retaliate, and instead trust in God to defend you? Remember God's goodness to you! Remember how He has blessed you! It worked for me... Rather than thinking of reasons for resenting those who have falsely accused me, and those who had sought to destroy me, I began seeking reasons why I should not be angry and resentful.

Now, I realize to the natural mind this strategy makes no sense, because the carnal mind wants to be angry and resentful. It's a challenge to be thankful to God when we are angry at others. But as I began to pray and trust God and be thankful for His blessings, God took the sword out of my hand. And by the time I was through seeking Him, I was free of resentment and contempt. He delivered me!

Yes, the hurts that people put on me had stung my very soul and had pierced my spirit, but those barbs began to be loosed, and I lost the urge to strike back. Then I remembered the scripture in Romans 12:19, which says, *"Vengeance is mine, I will repay, says the Lord."* I know that I had every reason to be upset, but no right in the spirit realm to respond the way my feelings tempted me to respond. Somehow in my spirit, I knew that God would handle those people in His own way and in His own timing, so I did not have to let myself be consumed by memories of what had happened.

Now, whenever I'm hit by criticism or attacked, I apply seven rules. Here is rule number one:

Rule 1 – When you are criticized and accusations are made against you, ask yourself this question: Is it true?

Don't ask, "Is it fair?" The question is whether there is truth in what was said, because truth is something you can learn from, and falsehood is something God can address. So ask these questions… Was it done by a person who seeks to help you, or by someone whose aim is to harm you? Is there a basis for the criticism or the attack? Have you given cause for them to have done what they did? Is it true?

By asking yourself if it is true, you can have a conversation with Jesus in the mirror. And then He can help you repent if necessary, change and grow more like Him. When we ask ourselves, "Is there any truth in what they have said or done," we are objectively facing life. Any other course is to escape from reality, which only stops our ability to walk closely with God!

So, if anything they have accused you of is true, then you must admit it and sincerely try to change.

By adopting this technique, you keep what they have done in perspective, and you keep your own heart pure. Remember, you're not responsible for their actions, but you are responsible for yours.

YOUR GOD-GIVEN KEY FOR TODAY:

I will not let what others have done to me destroy me.

[Monday]

KEY: *Truth Will Always Outlast a Lie*

Rule 2 – When the criticisms and accusations are not true, make a faith image of the power of truth over error.

The only way to conquer an untruth (a lie) is to take recourse in the changeless principle of the triumph of truth over error… right over wrong…and righteousness over evil. In many ways, this is the ultimate reality of our spiritual existence. God, who is truthful, good and righteous, triumphs over satan's lies and evil.

Here is one important thing to remember when you're facing an attack that involves other people. If the criticism and the accusations that people have made against you are not true, then they are based on a lie. Neither the universe nor the human spirit was created to accommodate a lie. Truth is built into the very nature of the way God created us, and telling a lie is against man's nature. It is something that God Himself will resolve, if you will trust Him and allow Him to do it.

This is the way of faith. If you are right and know it, you can afford to wait on God and see your salvation. (See 2 Chronicles 20:7, Exodus 14:13). It may be hard, but you can do it. And God will bless you for it.

Through the power of faith, you know something your critics and accusers don't know: truth crushed to earth will rise again. Just as surely as light banishes darkness because it is the stronger power, so truth will conquer a lie.

Jesus was crucified on erroneous testimony, misquotations, twisted meanings, and false accusations. But He just kept on loving God, giving of Himself to people, and expecting miracles. It was in the spirit of seed-faith that He went to the Cross. There He was crushed; but crushed truth has in it the seeds of resurrection. Death and defeat could not keep Him in the grave. The third day, Jesus arose, alive forevermore. It was the miracle of miracles. It was God reproducing the seed into the mightiest harvest of all… for Jesus' own life… and ours.

By holding steady and looking to God as your Source and by planting your seeds to Him, you can make a faith image of eventual triumph. Don't try to hurry things up and prove that the critics and accusers are wrong. Only those who are bound by fear can be panicked into striking back on the spur of the moment. Those who know their course is right are content to wait… to trust their Source, who is truth. They know truth will triumph. That means that your day is coming… and that's the road to a Better Life.

YOUR GOD-GIVEN KEY FOR TODAY:

What has been done against me for harm will be turned for my good, in Jesus' name.

[Tuesday]

KEY: *I Will Walk in Forgiveness.*

Rule 3 – Practice forgiveness, not resentment.

You can neutralize your critics and accusers when you practice forgiveness towards them. Resentment causes more resentment, but you can win through forgiveness.

Jesus forgave even while He was on the Cross. Not a thing His critics and accusers had said about Him was true. The passion of the people had been whipped into a flame by those who were prejudiced against Him. In Jesus' darkest hour, when seemingly He was isolated forever from His friends, when His cause seemed to be eternally lost, He did an astounding thing. He forgave them.

"Forgive them," Jesus cried. "For they don't know what they do."

Forgiveness is a powerful force for you. But unforgiveness is like drinking poison and expecting the other person to die.

One evening, some years ago, my wife and I were watching television. There was a man who was preaching. Lindsay and I were not paying that much attention until I heard him mention my name. Naturally I looked up to hear what he had to say. What he said was not true. It was a lie. He accused me of several things, and it really upset me. I knew that nothing he said was true.

I went to bed that night with a sick feeling in my heart, knowing that many people had seen that program and would no doubt believe what the man had said. It got to me.

First I was hurt. Then I got angry. And the anger turned to bitterness. For months, every time I thought of the man, I felt my hand clench into a fist. I wanted to take matters into my own hands. I wanted to confront him.

WEEK 13: TUESDAY

Some months later, I was invited to be a guest on a live television program. When I arrived at the studio, much to my surprise, the man who had said those wicked things against me was also there, and I really got angry.

I said to the Lord, "Why would you send me to this place and allow this man to be there?" And the next thought I had was, "I'm going to confront him right here and now, and expose the lies that he told about me."

Much to my surprise, the Lord spoke to me and said, "Go over there and ask him to forgive you."

I said to the Lord, "Forgive me? For what? I didn't say it. He said it. It was a lie, Lord. And You know it was a lie."

Again, I heard the Lord say, "Go over there and ask him to forgive you."

I said, "Lord, You go over there, and You ask him to forgive You." As you can see, sometimes when we get angry, we can say and do things that don't make sense... and we even risk striking out at the Lord. Thank goodness He is patient with us, even when we are not acting very much like Him.

A third time, I heard the Lord say, "Ask him to forgive you."

It took all my strength, but in obedience to the Lord, I walked over to the man, and here's what I said. "Sir, I've been holding something in my heart against you, and God has shown me that I'm wrong. I repent before God, and before you. And I ask you sincerely to forgive me."

His response surprised me! Big tears began to run down his face. He looked at me and said, "Richard, some time ago, I said some things about you on television. And I have since learned that they're not true. I'm sorry for what I said, and one reason I'm glad you're here tonight is because I want to make it right on this live television program."

Tears began to flow down my face too, as I realized the power of forgiveness to set me free!

He and I were reconciled, standing right there before we went on the air, live. He did exactly what he said he would do, and made things right publicly. That man and I became great friends.

Thank God for the spirit of forgiveness. Had I not done that, there's no telling what would have come against me. The seed of unforgiveness could easily have torn my life apart.

I discovered the rule that never fails, and that is to practice forgiveness. By this method, you are planting a seed that secures personal release and peace of mind again.

YOUR GOD-GIVEN KEY FOR TODAY:

I will forgive and let the person go... I will forgive and move forward with my life.

[Wednesday]

KEY: *Don't Let Hatred Get Hold of You, and Don't Strike Back.*

The next two rules are very easy to write about, but much harder to practice. But they are vital to overcoming when we are wronged or hurting. Here they are.

Rule 4 – Don't allow yourself to be drawn into the web of hate.

Rule 5 – Refuse to strike back.

All too often, we do not seek to overcome our resentments through forgiveness. We allow hate, like a spider, to spin its web around our souls.

WEEK 13: WEDNESDAY

Whenever an insect becomes entangled in the web, the spider immediately attacks, filling the insect's body with poison. Then the spider strengthens the web, preventing escape and making death sure.

Hate is like that. It fills the soul with negative feelings and sensations that arise from hate, setting off a chemical reaction in the body, poisoning the bloodstream and upsetting the nervous system. Some people believe it can even make your body and mind sick. Some who get immersed in hate never escape. You don't want this to happen to you.

Love is the only antidote for hate. The only way you can make love operative against hate is to remember that Jesus died for your critics and accusers, as well as He did for you. They, too, were made in the image of God—carrying a divine imprint on their souls. You may feel that you have every reason to hate them, but you have no spiritual right to it. For in hating them, you are really hating God who created them.

Henry Ford once said, "I shall never let anyone drag me down by making me hate them." We can learn from his wisdom.

Once love becomes active in your spirit, it will tear down the web of hatred, as well as destroy the spider of hate itself, cleansing your entire body from the poison and making you free. As you do this, you'll find yourself enjoying more peace, feeling more in control of your life, and maybe even physically receiving healing from sicknesses!

When the critics and accusers of Jesus came to arrest Him, Peter, one of Jesus' disciples, drew his sword and cut off the ear of the high priest's servant. (And I really don't think he was aiming at the man's ear!) Peter acted out of anger, and most of us would have cheered him on. But not Jesus.

Jesus healed and restored the man's ear. Then Jesus sharply rebuked Peter saying, *"Put your sword in its place, for all who take the sword will perish by the sword"* (Matthew 26:52). This is an eternal principle. Those who live by force shall surely perish by it.

To strike back is to meet force with force. This is the way that appeals to our fleshly nature, but it only leads to defeat and destruction. Living by force is to be motivated by fear. Fear makes a person feel so on the defensive that unless he strikes back quickly, he feels he will suffer loss.

In contrast, through your faith in God, your Source, you need never to use the sword to strike back. Faith strengthens your inner defenses by taking away the fear of what the critics and accusers can accomplish. Faith takes away tension and anxiety. Faith helps us stand strong, waiting on the Lord as He takes care of saving us from trouble.

Jesus did not seek to strike back by justifying His own course of action. He took a way of greater power through forgiving his enemies. And He won.

In effect, Jesus was saying to Peter, "You can win by refusing to strike back." By maintaining a loving, forgiving spirit, you can lift yourself from the lowest form of defense to the highest. I call this the seed-faith way of life... and it leads to a Better Life.

The seed-faith way of life lets you keep your self-respect. You have the knowledge that you could have attacked and shamed your opposers, and you know that they know it too. Yet you have dignified your own course by having confidence in its rightness, and at the same time you have kept your self-respect. No one can continually strike back without losing self-respect.

He who has lost self-respect has lost his way in life.

Believe me, I understand how challenging it can be to use self-restraint when we want to retaliate against those who attack us. Over the years, I've had many critics. I've also had many false accusations against me, and it's been very difficult. Doing God's will is not always easy. I've been accused of things that I haven't done. I have been lied about, lied to, stolen from, cheated, and misrepresented. I have had people say and do all kinds of hellacious things against me.

And yet, I have maintained silence, because God spoke in my heart and instructed me not to defend myself. Time after time, I would go to God and say, "Please, let me tell my story." And He would always say, "No, I am your defense. Keep your mouth closed."

Now, when you know you are innocent of accusations, that's a very hard thing to do. Perhaps you know all too well what this is like. But God can strengthen you to stand strong in Him, wait quietly on Him, and let Him take care of things. It's not always easy. But I've made it a way of life, and I believe that because God is no respecter of persons, He will help you to live this way, just as He has helped me.

I've also learned how to forgive those who have stood against me. In the natural, they don't deserve the forgiveness. But the forgiveness that I gave is not really for them. It's for me. It cleaned me out, and helped me to walk closer to God. I believe the same will happen for you as you forgive. Do it by faith, even if you don't feel very forgiving right now. Through a lifestyle of forgiveness, you'll feel lighter, freer, more peaceful.

And those critics and accusers… well, God will handle them in His own way, in His own timing. Therefore, we can leave them in His hands.

YOUR GOD-GIVEN KEY FOR TODAY:

I will walk in love and never strike back.

[Thursday]

KEY: *Quitting Is Not an Answer.*

Rule 6 - I will not allow discouragement to defeat me.

When you allow yourself to get discouraged because of criticism and accusations, you are permitting others to dictate your course.

Discouragement is one of the most dangerous feelings you can have, because failure and success are often separated by only the distance of that one word — discouragement.

According to an old story, the devil once held a yard sale, and offered all the tools of his trade to anyone who would pay the price. They were spread out on the table. Each item was clearly labeled: hatred, malice, envy, despair, sickness, as well as other names… all the weapons that everyone knows so well.

But off to one side, apart from the rest, lay a harmless-looking instrument marked "discouragement." It was old and worn-looking, but it was priced far above all the rest. When asked the reason why, the devil replied, "Because I know I can use this one so much more easily than the others. No one knows that it belongs to me, and with it, I can open doors that are tightly bolted. Once I get inside, I can use any tool that suits me."

No one knows how small the margin is between failure and success—faith and fear. All too often, discouragement is the deciding factor in the defeat of some person who was on his way to making good.

And though we might resist discouragement at times, it can often push us to the point of quitting when we are adversely attacked.

Trust me, I know how it feels to say, "Oh, what's the use? I might as well quit. There's just no point in trying anymore." I have faced that so many times in my life, and I watched my father face it as well.

WEEK 13: THURSDAY

All of us face it from time to time — but it's how we respond when we face it that can determine whether we fail or succeed in our lives.

I remember one night when I was a boy, I went with my father to the invalid tent at one of his crusades. He always went there first, before going to the main prayer line, to lay hands on people and pray for those who were too sick to stand in the prayer line.

One night, as we entered that small tent, we were faced with a man who was in the final stages of cancer. He had been brought by ambulance, and was lying on a hospital gurney with nurses attending him. He was very near death, and the smell of the cancer was so foul that I could hardly stand there.

My father walked over to this man to lay hands on him and pray, but as he drew close to the stricken man, my father threw up… right there on the sawdust floor next to the man. Then, he turned abruptly and walked out of the tent, leaving me standing there alone.

It was an awkward moment because I didn't know what to do. I had never seen my father do that before. About sixty seconds later, my father came back into the tent and walked over to where the man lay on the hospital gurney. He climbed up on it with him, took the man in his arms, and prayed for his healing.

Then he and I left that tent and went back into the main service. At the time, I didn't understand what had happened.

Many, many years later, when my mother went home to be with the Lord, my father and I were reminiscing one night in his home. As we talked about the great healings that we had seen and experienced around the world, what happened that night in the invalid tent came up. I said to him, "Dad, I never understood why you turned and walked out after you threw up. More than that, I didn't understand why you came back."

He smiled at me and said, "Son, at that time in my ministry, I was under such criticism and accusations. It seemed like they were coming from every direction. The national media was all over me, accusing me of things I hadn't done. It had hurt me so badly, and I was very discouraged."

"When I came into the room that night, and smelled that smell of cancer and threw up, it seemed like I had reached my load limit. I said to the Lord, 'I can't do this anymore. I quit.' And that's when I walked out of the tent.'"

I said, "Yes, Dad, you did. And you left me standing there alone."

He smiled and said, "Son, when I got outside the tent, the Lord spoke to me. He said, 'If you're not willing to pray for him, you're not worthy to be My child.'"

Wow! I can still hear my dad saying those words of the Lord today… If you're not willing to pray for him, you're not worthy to be My child.

Dad said, "That's when I came back into the tent, took the man in my arms, and prayed for him." Then he said, "I realized my calling was not to deal with criticism and accusations. My calling was to be an evangelist in the healing ministry, and to carry out that calling, no matter what was said or done against me."

That's the attitude that I have tried to maintain all my life. Many times, I have felt like quitting also. So many times, the odds seemed stacked against me. Every move I made was judged… so many things that I did were criticized. And the accusers seemed to be on all sides. It felt like I was being judged by people who did not know the real story, and possibly didn't even want to hear it, having already made up their minds.

Some people, even some Christians, can be very cruel. But I have kept my focus on God and my relationship with Him. I have obeyed the Lord and done what He has told me to do. I have not answered the criticism or accusations, and I have persevered. I believe I'm stronger for it.

So, I laid down discouragement just like my dad did, and I've kept my eyes on God. Now, I didn't say it was easy because it certainly wasn't. But it was the right thing to do.

WEEK 13: FRIDAY

I believe that God has a specific mission for you. Like anyone in life with a purpose and a future (Jeremiah 29:11), you may face difficult situations that tempt you to give up. But don't give up. Keep your mission and future in mind. Do not let discouragement, and what might seem like defeat, stop you. Keep your focus upon God.

I'm reminded of the words of an old gospel song titled, "Life Is Like a Mountain Railway." One verse says this, "Heed the curves and watch the tunnels. Never falter. Never fail. Keep your hands upon the throttle, and your eyes upon the rail."

YOUR GOD-GIVEN KEY FOR TODAY:

I will not let discouragement destroy me. I will not be defeated, because God is my Source.

[Friday]

KEY: *There Is Much Power in Prayer.*

Rule 7- Use the power of sincere prayer.

In dealing effectively with the effects of criticisms, accusations, and other stresses, you will discover there is one other principle that will help perhaps more than anything... and that is the power of prayer. Let me give you four ways to pray:

First, tell God everything about the problem.

Talk to Him without shame or fear or condemnation. Tell Him what has been said and done against you, and how the problem seems to be beyond your power to solve.

Second, freely acknowledge that you have been wounded and hurt.

Confide in God all your resentments, your bitterness, and your fears. Do not justify yourself or defend your own actions. Never let self-justification slip into your prayer; just let God be your judge.

Third, confess your own weaknesses and inabilities to overcome the problem.

If you've said or done anything that is wrong, repent, and ask God to forgive you.

Fourth, ask God to personally intervene on your behalf.

Ask Him to take charge and work things out for the good of all concerned. This is the unselfish way to handle difficult, hurtful situations. God will bless you for your seed of unselfishness. By praying this way, you are planting a seed that God can use to give you a harvest of good... out of a situation that seems all bad.

These four steps in prayer take the whole problem out of your hands, and place it squarely in the hands of the Lord, who never fails... for He is the Source of your total supply.

The final thing to do as you use the power of prayer is to put your faith to work to bring about the desired results you have asked for through prayer. With your faith, you form an image of God, your Source, doing the very thing you have asked Him to do. Begin to expect to see the answer! And keep expecting!

This is the guiding principle of believing-prayer given by Jesus when He said in Mark 11:24, *"Whatever things you ask when you pray, believe that you receive them, and you will have them."*

By this, Jesus meant that as you believe, you will begin to receive the things you have prayed for. By holding the image of these things before God and in your own thinking, your faith can begin to release them to you.

So, go to bed and sleep in peace, because you know God is awake all night working in your behalf. This is what Paul meant when he wrote in Romans 8:31, *"If God is for us, who can be against us?"*

There is an infallible secret of success for those who love the Lord—there is no one who can defeat us in the ultimate sense. So, don't allow yourself to become embittered or discouraged to the point of giving up. Defeat (and success) come from within, and it's not over until it's over. Once you decide to win this victory, the pattern of success becomes increasingly clearer.

Remember, life must be faced. You cannot run away from it. You either face it or it will face you. If you've been wrong, admit it, repent, and change. Lip service given to the seven rules in this week's worth of lessons will only end in frustration.

If you try to take matters into your own hands by resenting and striking back, God will then just let you fight your own battles. You will lose. Your energies will be wasted. You will be let down and find yourself in a bottomless pit of self-despair.

On the other hand, you can turn things over to God and be assured that He is on the job on your behalf. So, begin to smile again. *Let go and let God.* Relax. Your main job now is to go on with life and do your best through the seeds of faith that you sow… and that's the road to a Better Life.

YOUR GOD-GIVEN KEY FOR TODAY:

Say this out loud: *"If God be for me, who can be against me."*

[Saturday]

KEY: *Take the Seven-Way Test.*

Let's take this last chapter of the last week… the 13th week… the 91st day, and check ourselves with this seven-way test.

Rule 1: When you are criticized and accusations are made against you, ask yourself this question: Is it true? If it is, don't ignore it. Face yourself and make the needed changes. If you've done something wrong and you know it, then repent before the Lord. Thanks be to God that He is gracious and He will forgive us when our repentance is sincere (1 John 1:9).

Rule 2: If the criticism and accusations are not true, then form a faith image of the power of truth over error. Don't forget what God can do for you. Because you are in the right, you can afford to wait and be patient. Remember, the scripture says, *"Those who wait on the Lord shall renew their strength; they shall mount up with wings like eagles, they shall run and not be weary, they shall walk and not faint"* (Isaiah 40:31).

Rule 3: Practice forgiveness of those who have stood against you, and not resentment. By forgiving your critics and accusers, you will release yourself and begin to find peace.

Rule 4: Do not allow yourself to be drawn into the web of hatred. Hate will destroy you. You may have every reason, but you have no right to hate your fellow man. For he, too, is made in the image of God. Only love is stronger than hate.

Rule 5: Refuse to strike back. Meekness is power. This is because meekness is based on faith and not fear.

Rule 6: Do not allow yourself to become discouraged. Discouragement is one of the most dangerous feelings you can have. Remember, if you never give way to discouragement, you will never quit.

Rule 7: Use the power of sincere prayer, for prayer is simply the sincere desire of your heart. Prayer is the key that unlocks the throne of God's mercy. Prayer has cleansing and lifting power. It is turning to God in the ultimate sense. Once you have prayed, form a faith image of the fact that God will work things out for you. Believe it, in Jesus' name.

WEEK 13: SATURDAY

I strongly suggest that you go back to the beginning of this week and reread each chapter. Let these truths sink deep into your spirit.

Follow the seven rules above, focus on this powerful thought; and let it sustain you, as it does me:

YOUR GOD-GIVEN KEY FOR TODAY:

No weapon formed against me will prosper if I keep my spirit right.

WEEK 13 RECAP

- **Sunday:** No Weapon Formed Against Me Will Prosper…if I Keep My Spirit Right.
- **Monday:** Truth Will Always Outlast a Lie.
- **Tuesday:** I Will Walk in Forgiveness.
- **Wednesday:** Don't Let Hatred Get Hold of You, and Don't Strike Back.
- **Thursday:** Quitting Is Not an Answer.
- **Friday:** There Is Much Power in Prayer.
- **Saturday:** Take the Seven-Way Test.

FINAL WORD

Writing this book has been a great pleasure. It has taken me back to my childhood, and reminded me of those early days of my life, sitting under my father's great tent cathedral, hearing him preach those long, healing messages and watching him pray for the sick, hoping he would call me to stand by his side... which he did many times.

All through my life and ministry, I wanted a double portion of the anointing carried by my father, Oral Roberts. I would often talk to him about it.

He said to me, "Son, when I die, you will have the double portion anointing." He also told me that many people would claim his anointing, but that I should not worry because the anointing of God is generational. He told me that a double portion of his anointing was reserved for me.

I was in the room when my father passed away, and I remember what I felt when that double portion anointing came on my life. That anointing, which is designed to break the yoke of bondage off of people's lives, has reinvigorated my life in a way that I cannot describe.

My father laid his hands on me several weeks before he died and said, "Son, your calling is to preach, teach, and bring God's healing power to people in need wherever you go." I am endeavoring to follow that calling with every fiber of my being.

Now that you have completed reading this book the first time, let me suggest three things that can influence how you follow the calling and purpose God has placed on your life... whatever it may be.

1: You can choose to do nothing.

If you lay this book aside and don't let it get down into your spirit and follow the keys to miracles that I have set down here according to the Bible, then this book may have been a waste of your time.

2: You can choose to say, "That's really good stuff. It might work for some people, but not for me." If you do that, you will miss the miracles and abundance through Seed-Faith living that God intends for you to have. You'll also miss out on the road to a Better Life that I believe God has for you.

3: You can choose to take these words I've given you in this book and learn to live in it. I've staked my life on these keys. God will do just exactly what His Word says He will do.

Regardless of what you do for a living or if you're retired…Upon the authority of God's Word, if you will study this book, take each of these subjects one day at a time, at the end of thirteen weeks, I believe you will be a different person; you'll be surprised at yourself.

Your friends and family will notice the difference in you. Your business associates and others will too. I expect by the time you have repeated this thirteen weeks four times in a year, people around you will see the difference in you, both in your spiritual and material life. Best of all, you yourself will see and feel the difference, as you walk down the road to a Better Life.

In this book, I have given you the very heart of what I have learned from God; from my father, Oral Roberts; and through my own personal experience in ministry. This I have given you as the Spirit has led me. It's for you and your loved ones with all my love.

I pray that you have been helped by it. Now, I suggest that you start through it again. I am expecting you to get more and more and more out of it as you reread it and act on the principles in it.

Sincerely,

Richard Roberts

ABOUT THE AUTHOR

Richard Roberts, B.A., M.A., D.Min., has dedicated his life to ministering the saving, healing, delivering power of Jesus Christ around the world. God has put a dream in Richard's heart of reaching the nations of the earth for Jesus. Since 1980, he has ministered God's healing power in 39 nations spanning six continents.

In his miracle healing outreaches, Richard has ministered to crowds of over 200,000 people in a single service. Often as much as half the audience responds for prayer to receive Jesus Christ as their personal Lord and Savior. Hundreds and thousands more receive healings and miracles as Richard ministers God's Word and operates in the gifts of the Holy Spirit, especially the word of knowledge.

Richard is the Chairman and CEO of Oral Roberts Evangelistic Association. He and his wife, Lindsay, host *The Place for Miracles* — a half-hour interactive broadcast that reaches out to millions worldwide. On this unique healing program, Richard ministers in the power of the Holy Spirit, praying for those who are sick or hurting in some area of their lives, and often giving specific words of knowledge about how God is touching people with His healing power.

The Place for Miracles has received more than 148,000 phone calls to date from viewers who have reported miracles and answers to prayer.

Richard is a man on fire for God and consumed by the compassion of Jesus for sick and hurting people. His meetings across the United States and around the world are marked by a tremendous move of the Spirit, resulting in all types of physical, mental, emotional, financial, and spiritual healings. Richard says, "Jesus was born to step into a world of trouble and bring healing and deliverance, and that's the call of God upon my own life — to reach out to people in their troubles and heartaches, to pray and believe God, and to bring them His Word of hope and healing."

In addition to his responsibilities at the Oral Roberts Evangelistic Association, Richard also served as President of Oral Roberts University for 15 years. Since 2010, he has offered the Richard Roberts School of Miracles to help equip Christians with practical, hands-on experience in applying God's Word and His healing power in their own lives and in the lives of others, especially emphasizing how Christians can enjoy a life empowered by the Holy Spirit.

To date, more than 35,000 students in 100 nations have studied these online courses. Richard has also authored a number of books, booklets, and other inspirational material, including *Unstoppable Increase, He's A Healing Jesus, When All Hell Breaks Loose, Claim Your Inheritance,* and his autobiography, *He's the God of a Second Chance.*

Richard and his wife, Lindsay, have three daughters: Jordan, Olivia, and Chloe.

RICHARD ROBERTS
ORAL ROBERTS MINISTRIES®

Richard Roberts
P.O. Box 2187
Tulsa, OK 74102-2187

www.oralroberts.com

For prayer, call ***The Abundant Life Prayer Group***
at 918-495-7777, or contact us online at
www.oralroberts.com/prayer.